THE ART OF CLOSING ANY DEAL

HOW TO BE A "MASTER CLOSER" IN EVERYTHING YOU DO

JAMES W. PICKENS

WARNER

A Time Warner Company

Warner Books Edition
Copyright © 1989 by James W. Pickens
All rights reserved.

This Warner Books edition is published by arrangement with
Shapolsky Publishers, Inc., 136 West 22nd Street, New York, NY 10011.

Warner Books, Inc., 1271 Avenue of the Americas, New York, NY 10020

Visit our Web site at http://warnerbooks.com

W A Time Warner Company

Printed in the United States of America
First Warner Books Printing: January 1991
13   15   17   19   20   18   16   14   12

Library of Congress Cataloging in Publication Data

Pickens, James W.
  The art of closing any deal / James W. Pickens.
     p.   cm.
  Reprint. Originally published by author.
  Includes bibliographical references.
  ISBN 0-446-39098-4
  1. Selling.   I. Title.
[HF5438.25.P53   1991]
658.85—dc20   90-39063
                                                      CIP

Cover design by Richard Milano

AUTHOR'S NOTE

All of the information contained in this book is based on closing facts and strategies that produce superior sales performances when utilized.

All thoughts and situations included in this book are based on the author's own experiences.

This book was written to help the reader become a master closer — something every salesman should strive to be.

It is the sincere hope of the author that the lessons learned here are beneficial, not only in the reader's business future, but also in his or her personal life.

My Best Wishes and Blessings;

James W. Pickens

DEDICATION

I would like to sincerely salute all of the true master closers throughout the world.

I would also like to thank the very wonderful people whose love and whose belief in me made this book possible:

Dr. Jim & Evelyn Pickens
Lindsey Janell Pickens
David Rivera
Donna, Kim, Cameron, and Denise

Table of Contents

PREFACE

This book has three main purposes. First, it is a comprehensive reference book on closing sales. Second, it's a professional sales closer's guide to new closes in today's competitve market. Third, and most important, it introduces a closing formula (Sam's secret) whose proven success record exceeds all other sales strategies and techniques being used anywhere in the world.

This book is not a beginner's self-help manual; it is a "master closer's" Bible. It has not been written for the average, run-of-the-mill salesman or anyone who simply wants to gain a little knowledge about selling tips.

This book has been designed to help Master Sales Closers learn, brush up and study the best proven selling procedures ever devised.

There are no frills or superficial information here. Just bottom-line closing facts to get the reader's closing average up at least forty to fifty percent above what he or she is currently producing. That's why I wrote this book.

It is not the intention of the author to embarrass or upset anyone in the selling profession, although in places the book will take a close and very candid look at salesmen just like you. Hard-hitting, gut-penetrating, sales books—if they're worth anything at all—have to step on someone's toes, and this program is no exception. But this is a selling guide that actually tells you what all the other sales books *have not* and/or *will not*. In the past, authors of business books have maintained a certain level of respect and circumspection toward customers that salespeople generally agree with and accept. However, in this book no holds are barred. The customer is taken apart and completely dismantled, analyzed and thoroughly examined by the Master Sales Closer. After this dissection, the reader can understand any customer's position. Then the sales closer, after developing a sound strategy, goes in for the kill (the sale).

This book is a straightforward, honest discussion of proven techniques, tricks and traps that *do* produce sales. So, if you are really serious about your selling profession, no matter what field of sales you are in, then don't talk to another customer until you have read this book. Virtually every customer objection that you will ever encounter is covered. It gives you not only the answers but all the ammunition you will ever need to get the sale and keep it solid.

This book is in a league by itself and I can guarantee that you will not be disappointed in any way. The information is for you personally and should not be shared indiscriminately. It's a powerful aid to get the job done (the job of closing sales), and it does just that.

The Art of Closing Any Deal will turn you into a master closer in everything you do—the minute you say "Hello" to your customer. You will sell more than you ever have while learning hundreds of valuable tips that can also be applied to your personal life.

This is the only book you will ever need to masterfully close your customer one on one. So, let's get started.

You don't have to miss any more sales, beginning right now!

Introduction

THE ART OF CLOSING ANY DEAL

My name is Jim Pickens and I'm about to relate a remarkable experience that happened to me this past December. I've never written a book before, but facts and circumstances forced me to try. On December 21st, something happened to me that was so fantastic that I felt it had to be shared. The only way I could explain it to you was to take time off from my business and write it all down in my own words. I decided to just do that.

Before I start to tell you everything that happened, you should know something about me so you will realize that I am quite serious about this book.

First of all, I'm a family man with a wonderful wife, four lovely children, and, with the help of many people, a very successful real estate development company. The reason I'm telling you this is not to brag, but to let you know that an experience profound enough to make me drop nearly everything and take time off to write a book, had to be of extraordinary importance. And believe me, I feel it was just that. I've been through a lot in my life, but nothing compares to what you are about to read in this book.

The best way for you to understand the whole story is if I start right from the beginning — a June morning seventeen years ago in my home town of Pittsburgh, Pennsylvania. That particular summer I was looking for a job, something to do so I could earn a little spending money to see me through the summer, and for my sophomore year at college.

I just wanted to date good-looking girls and work outdoors, forgetting school and my future career. Oh yes, my dad — and this is just like him — had a great job lined up for me in a giant steel mill where he worked.

Now it's true there was good money to be made there, but I wanted to do something different, something uncomplicated; you know, just something simple. But at the same time I had to find a job that would meet my new sophomore status at the university, not just a freshman's job.

As it happened, I was looking through the want ads one Sunday when I saw a job description that looked pretty interesting: "Outdoor recreational company looking for young, energetic people for summer employment in public relations work. Good salary and many company benefits."

Now that hit the spot. The job was outdoors, with good pay, and I like the way that classy public relations stuff sounded. In addition, it was only fourteen miles away from my familiy's house. This way, I could work and feel independent while still having my good old room at home. I decided that was the answer; that was the job I wanted.

So on Monday morning I got all spruced up and in my three-year-old Volkswagen I set out to conquer my employment objective — *to get that public relations job.*

Driving out to the location given in the paper, I felt great. The weather was beautiful, and the foliage was in full bloom. It took me about forty minutes to get to my destination, and what a surprise! I was looking at a huge building that must have been a magnificent old hotel at one time. All around this building bustled carpenters, plumbers, painters, people with filing cabinets, people moving desks — just about everyone was trying to get this stately building into shape. It looked as if it had been abandoned for about twenty years, but at the rate everyone was working, this old hotel would see better days very soon.

I parked my car and went inside with my newspaper clipping in hand, not knowing where to go or whom to see about a job. I noticed an important looking man sitting in the middle of this great hotel lobby; he was reading a newspaper. With all the movement and activity going on around him he just sat there undisturbed. I went over and asked him where I should go to apply for summer employment. He looked up, then calmly stood. He was dressed in a golfing outfit and looked very distinguished. He stared at me with a puzzling look and finally asked what kind of job I wanted. Not having prepared a good, solid answer I replied, "Oh, just anything." Then he asked me about my family, my studies, my ambitions, and said, "Can you start working right now?" I said, "Yes!" and for the rest of that day and the next week I was relegated to help clean up around the old building, running errands, sweeping, moving, and being an all-purpose "go-fer," as they say.

It turned out that the man I had asked about the job application was the vice president of the company. He was in charge of all the renovation and development work being done. His name was Randell Billing, but everyone called him "Big Bill." My new job under "Big Bill" was working for an organization called the Duron Corporation. This was a land and recreational development firm with headquarters in New York City. The Duron Corporation had six developments in the Midwest and was starting a new one here in Pennsylvania. The name of this new project under development was "Green Vista Estates," comprising 15,000 acres of first class Pennsylvania hillside.

I soon learned that the Duron Corporation was a solid and well respected real estate firm that was more than twenty years old. So, all in all, I had lucked out. My new job amounted to doing anything and everything that would help out the total plan. That plan was simply this: The Duron Corporation was going to develop Green Vista Estates into a total recreational and retirement community. Facilities were to include private golf courses, tennis courts, lakes, swimming pools, town centers, and condominiums. The corporation was going to sell real estate (lots) and houses, along with building roads, country clubs, eventually developing a private, well-planned resort community. To accomplish this, they needed contractors, builders and the sales personnel to find the potential customers.

This is where you will see the story start to take shape, and this is where I really begin to fit in. I wasn't a salesman yet, but, as part of the Green Vista team, I did what I could to help meet the target opening date in July.

After being there a few weeks, armed with my positive attitude and aggressiveness, I felt I was ready to advance to a new and better job position. So I went to "Big Bill" and asked him for some of the public relations work the newspaper ad promised. After a long talk with "Big Bill" I got my new job assignment; parking cars for the duration of the summer. Oh well, at least it was outdoors, and there was some "public relations" work involved.

Opening the resort on time was a top priority. Throughout the hotel everyone hustled to meet the July 1st deadline for the grand opening. I wasn't too busy in my car parking job, since in the beginning there weren't too many cars to park (no customers yet).

Things were looking up and getting more businesslike every day. The old hotel looked fantastic, after four hard weeks of solid restoration. Even the huge parking lot behind the hotel — my territory — was nearly finished.

At the far end of the parking area the company had constructed a guard gate and a guard house. It looked good because it was designed in the same mode as the old hotel. The purpose of the guard house and gate was obvious: it added to the atmosphere of privacy at Green Vista Estates. This was going to be an exclusive resort, so the guard house would add to this overall concept. For a short time, I thought they wanted me to be a security guard, but no such luck. They wanted an older person for the job.

It was about one week before the grand opening, when I first met Sam Johnson, our new daytime security man. When we were introduced I was somewhat surprised because Mr. Johnson was a fairly old man. In fact, he was old enough to be my grandfather. But he seemed like a very pleasant old gentleman. That first day we didn't talk much because he was busy learning his new job and duties down at the guard house; I was doing my usual running around, conquering all the errands no one else wanted to do.

At this point, I want you to keep in mind that Sam Johnson and I had a common bond from the beginning. You see, we were the only people working in or around the parking lot area. Everyone else was either inside the old hotel, (the new sales office) or scattered throughout the development working on construction projects.

On his second day of work Sam and I got to talking. He told me a little about himself, and, in turn, I told him some things about me. We really had nothing better to do than sit around in his guard house and get to know each other through small talk. (Everyone else was gearing up for selling and promotion, or working with the builders and contractors who were developing roads and other needed amenities.) So there I was, sitting and talking to my new acquaintance, old Sam Johnson the security guard, just waiting for opening day when I could finally do my job — park cars. Well, it wasn't really so bad; parking cars could be a type of public relations work, sort of, and I was starting to get a pretty good tan. So things were looking up.

As I got to know Sam better, I realized that he was a peculiar and unique person. Over the next few days, working and talking together, we became pretty close friends. For example, if I was ever late for work — and I usually was — Sam would cover for me. With this kind of relationship, the parking lot was a pretty good place to work. We'd tell jokes and talk about anything and everything that happened during our working hours. So time passed quickly for both of us.

About two days before the big opening, Sam told me something quite curious. He told me that he used to be a master sales closer and that he had worked all around the country selling real estate for many years. He told me about the company that we worked for now (its good points and its bad ones), and all about its history. He talked about his old selling days, the productive ones and not-so-productive ones. About getting in and out of all kinds of situations. The strange part was that it seemed the more I listened to Sam, the more intense, sincere, and serious he became about this special subject of his — the subject of selling.

We would talk for hours about selling when we weren't doing other things. I found myself becoming more interested in this old man and his experiences. One day — and I'll never forget it — Sam told me that if he wanted to, he could out-sell any salesman Green Vista Estates could ever hire. Green Vista Estates was hiring the top real estate sales people in the country, and to hear Sam say something like that (and I sensed he really seemed to believe it) was kind of out in left field. I didn't say a word; I just sat there and listened. The next thing I knew, Sam showed me a ring, a simple gold one that he was wearing. The ring was old and quite worn. It looked like an old crest ring, nothing more. It certainly wasn't expensive. Sam told me that the ring had a secret inscription on the inside that would help make any person into a great master sales closer. The only thing a person had to do was read and understand the inscription and then practice what it said. Sam told me that this gold ring had made him a millionaire many times over, and when he practiced the ring's advice he never failed to get a sale.

Now I ask you, what would you do if some old man (and he certainly didn't look like a millionaire) just got through telling you a story like this? Well, what I then did was human. I asked him if I could read the ring's inscription. But Sam replied, "I'll make a deal with you. We're going to be working together all summer long, just the two of us, and we're going to see a lot of customers and salesmen come and go. I'm a little tired and I don't want to sell anymore. But if you listen to me, I'll point out things about sales and closing that will make you the best sales closer anywhere. I'll make you into a master closer. Not only that, if you practice what I tell you, you will become a complete and total success in any kind of sales field that exists."

Sam said that I could learn all this in a very short time. All I would have to do is listen and understand what he was telling me. Then, at the end of the summer, if he thought that I had been a good student, he'd let me read the ring's inscription. He said, at this point, I'd know the secret that every top salesman in the world could use to become even better. The secret that shows how to be among the greatest sales closers alive.

That was Sam's answer to me. So what could I say? I thought for a moment and decided that since I was going to be here for the rest of the summer anyway — and since Sam just might know what he was talking about — why not? I might really learn something. I couldn't lose, and besides, I wanted to know what that inscription said. I told Sam I would listen to him and try to learn what he would teach me. I knew if I played my cards right I would get to read the inscription eventually, and if it was a joke, a fake, or a real selling secret, I'd soon know what it said. If I could be a success in selling like Sam said he had been, then who really wanted to be a lawyer anyway? Certainly not me. Not with the potential of becoming a top Master Sales Closer dangled in front of my nose.

This is how it all started, seventeen years ago. Each day, Sam would talk to me and explain sales from top to bottom, and he didn't miss a thing.

The extra benefit was that we were in the middle of one of the largest developments in the East, with all the top salesmen in the country around us. We could study everything right before our eyes: the customers, the salesmen, and the powerful new techniques for closing any deal.

The Duron Corporation had hired the best real estate closers in the country. So, to my way of thinking, if our company had the best closers around (and Sam told me that he was better than all of them), then I had to learn something about sales, no matter what.

Well, I learned, I mean I really learned! In the following chapters you too will see and understand "The Art of Closing Any Deal". You will also discover the inscription on Sam's ring which changed me so much. Because of what I was taught that summer by one old man, I decided not to study law. Instead, I went on to become president of the Duron Corporation, one of the top real estate developers. I was a multi-millionaire at the age of 37.

This is just the beginning of an interesting story that can make your sales performance and closing percentage far better than any salesman you have ever known. This book is about what I learned from Sam. Not only what he knew concerning closing, but what Sam knew about human nature. It is all true, and it all really works. Read on and you'll find out for yourself.

Chapter One

THE ART OF CLOSING ANY DEAL:
Overview of Sales Closers

- A. Types of Salesmen

- B. Types of Closers

- C. Techniques Used by Closers

- D. Characteristics of Closers

- E. Why They Are Closers

THE ART OF CLOSING ANY DEAL:
Overview of Sales Closers

Sam gave me my first lesson in sales — or rather, closing — the same day our agreement began.

It didn't take me long to see old Sam didn't pull any punches when he spoke about sales and closers. He said exactly what he thought and always had closing a sale as the bottom line. Sam got so excited when he talked about closing and sales that it was contagious.

The salesmen had already begun arriving at Green Vista Estates — about ninety-five in all. Sam said the salesmen, some of who were "closers", would be my first subject of study. He told me that by using closers as a starting point, I could learn the basics and go right on from there.

The best way for me describe what I learned is to simply put it all down as if Sam himself were doing the talking. In this chapter, you will see exactly what I learned about closers. But keep in mind that for Sam, closing was a very, very serious business.

Types of Salesmen

Before we get into closers specifically, I want to explain the difference between salesmen and closers. But we have to understand salesmen before we can appreciate the skill of a master closer. This will bring everything into proper perspective.

Order Takers or Tour Guides

This person knows all about the product; he knows all about the company. In fact, he has all the right answers, and he appears to be tailored for the job of selling. (Note: To simplify things I refer to "he" or "him" throughout — but the examples are all equally applicable to women.) But there is one thing about him that's wrong: He cannot sell. Ever wonder why?

Well, there are a thousand reasons, but I'm not going to get into them now — you will understand once we analyze true sales closers. Order-takers shouldn't even call themselves salesmen. The reason is they don't have that one little thing called "magic." But don't worry; you will soon find out how to acquire that very special characteristic, if you don't have it already.

An order taker is like a book with a lot of knowledge just sitting on a shelf, waiting for someone to open up the pages and read. In comparison, a master closer is like a smash Broadway play; it jumps right out at you and hits you right between the eyes. It doesn't wait for anything; it's a full-scale production with all the trimmings.

The Salesman

He is better than the order taker; at least he can do some things on his own. He has some push, some drive, some determination. He makes a pretty good living, but that is where it ends. He requires help on too many deals. He doesn't study his profession to any great extent. The typical salesman has his limited client base, is satisfied with this minor accomplishment, and that's the extent of it.

Everyone calls him a salesman, but I guarantee that when he is alone, looking in the mirror, he knows he could be better. But he just doesn't go that extra step; he doesn't want it badly enough. So, he settles for his own mediocrity. He lacks that extra gut feeling of wanting to be the best. He does not want to upset his routine. He would rather be a good, average salesman than a master closer with true class.

The Closer

Now here is a man who can really deliver. He can sell, charm, and hold the customer in a deal. He can do all the things that are necessary to be a top-notch producer, and he is just that — always in front of the rest of the sales force. He thinks he is so good he will not study or listen to anybody. He believes he can live on his past record and all of his old war stories about those big past sales. He uses the same old pitches and closes and never changes except that he gets older.

Yes, he's a closer, and a good one, but not great, not a super-salesman, not a leader — just good. He thinks he is at the top, but in reality he isn't. He simply forgot to keep going forward and learning; that little oversight made him stop growing, and it shows.

The "Master Closer": The King of Selling

He's the person that everyone else calls for help on a deal. Why is he the one called and not you? Because he is the best, and everyone knows it. Something sets him apart from other salesmen. He not only acts like a master closer but thinks like one; he listens, he learns, understands, and uses a lot of charm and wit to solve problems simply and directly. He uses logic, and it is usually deadly.

Two things set a master closer apart from other salesmen; self- confidence and showmanship. A master closer knows he is good, and he shows it. He has manners, poise, and a super-positive attitude about himself. People want to be associated with and emulate him. He is good for everyone; he is a creative catalyst.

A master closer is special in many other ways. For example, he knows exactly how to act when he enters a room, a football stadium, or just a phone booth. He is always in control, and it shows. As you will soon learn, anyone can be that good if he knows how to act and direct himself — like a closer instead of a salesman. You can be a closer simply by understanding the power that accompanies this distinction and learning the importance of harnessing this very real power.

A closer (from here on I will use the term "closer" but I'll be referring to master closers) can chew up and spit out a salesman anytime he wants. I've seen it happen over and over again. The reason is that the salesman or customer can't out-think or out-maneuver the closer. The closer can out-mind-manipulate a customer every time. You will soon become aware of how this can actually be learned.

A closer can think faster and better on his feet than the customer and can change his approach to suit any environment he is in, any time. He simply blends into the surroundings as if he belonged there. He makes himself so comfortable that the customer has no choice but to also feel comfortable.

If we want to talk about showmanship, a closer uses all of the resources at his disposal to sell his product the way an actor uses props. The closer doesn't miss a trick. He is entertaining to the customers and makes them feel appreciated. The customer feels confident about the closer and thus feels confident about the product.

The closer is forever selling, convincing, driving, and always winning — because he is sold not only on his product but is also ultra-confident about himself. This doesn't mean that a closer is egotistical, but he does like himself and what he accomplishes. He likes people, and he wants them to like him. The closer is personal, personable, and in many ways, lovable. He is somewhat of a desperado and he can draw upon that tough quality as quickly as is necessary (desperado in the sense that he thinks for himself, is aggressive and is totally self-reliant). He is an independent self-motivator.

He is also hard to control to some degree, and that's good because any knowledgeable sales manager would not expect his best people to be totally controllable and obedient. The reason some sales people rise to the top and become the best is usually because they can think for themselves while having the freedom to maneuver "their way."

So you see, the master closer is many things, but all the elements in his character are aggressive, charming, and positive. He is the one who can carry the ball anytime and make the touchdown. He'll always win. He knows it, the other salesmen know it, and the customer soon learns it. The master closer is the king of sales.

Types of Closers

There are many different types of closers with their own styles and mannerisms, their own ways of doing things. But all closers have a common trait: they sell. Don't ever make the mistake of trying to be a certain kind of closer if it doesn't fit you. Keep reading — your sales style will show itself below.

The Jack Rabbit Closer

He's the one who talks a mile a minute; his enthusiasm is complete. His excitement is never-ending, and he is always happy. All this rubs off on the customers and gets them feeling happy too.

This kind of closer, like all closers, knows exactly what makes himself tick, and he uses it to his full advantage. This closer is a mover in every way; he is always on the go and always winding up in the same position: With a lot of sales under his belt.

The Turtle Closer

The "good old boy" attitude: Slow and down-home. He presents an air of honesty, integrity, and kindness. He has a believable manner and acts like an old friend of the customer's. He moves in slow, deliberate motions and lulls the customer into a relaxed, uninhibited state — and smoothly closes his sale.

The Positive Closer

He thinks and acts as if everything is great. He is crisp and sharp, always seeing the good in people and any predicament that develops. He thinks any problem is no problem at all. He simply overcomes them all. He builds the customers up in such a positive way, they feel that they can't lose if they buy from him — no matter what. This closer radiates good thoughts and attitudes; he makes everyone feel a lot better, no matter how they felt before meeting him.

The Negative Closer

He's the sleeper type. He has an "I don't care" manner as though he has other things on his mind, or is tired or lazy. He does a lot of listening to customers and presents them with a take-it-or-leave-it approach. He gets the customer in such a position that the customer wants the product (or service) because the closer seems to be holding back on some secret about the deal. The customer is manipulated into feeling the deal is so good that if he doesn't get it, someone else will. The closer discreetly encourages the customer to play mind games on himself. This closer is a country fox in every way. He is so good he can't lose.

The Jolly-Golly Closer

He is the clown of the closing bunch; he always has jokes handy and a happy-go-lucky air. He always gets laughs and is often playing games on the other closers. He fools around with the customers and gets them so relaxed and off-guard that they never know when he is going in for the close. All his customers love him. They don't realize that he is selling them all along. When the customer finally does realize what is happening, that good old Mr. Jolly wasn't just playing games and joking all the time they were with him, it is too late — the sale has already been made.

The Magic Man Closer

This is the closer who always keeps the customer off balance, always keeps him guessing and wondering what the closer is up to. With this closer, the customer never knows exactly what to expect next; he is always saying something interesting and amazing. He uses super-showmanship, keeping the customer entertained with his intelligence, product knowledge and antics. He keeps the customer spellbound and fascinated with his personality and friendliness. He's always pulling sayings or solutions out of his hat. He creates a magic, happy air about himself and his product (or service) that keeps those sales coming all the time.

The Razzle-Dazzle Closer

He is not like the magic man closer, so don't get the names confused. This closer is really different from the rest; he is the one who always has the special deals, the secret ones no one else knows about or can match. He can put together a package deal faster than anyone. He is always trying (and usually succeeding) to outwit the other salesmen; at least that is what he makes his own customers believe. He is always going and showing and telling and confusing and switching around ideas with everyone, until no one is really sure exactly where this closer stands on a subject. He's always jumbling up the issues and creating positive confusion, only to eventually come out the winner. The razzle-dazzle closer is a master of words, the whole double-talk vocabulary is part of his bag of tricks. He is good, intellectual, and proficient at his chosen closing technique.

The Psychological / Methodical Closer

He is the thinker, the solver of problems. He uses logic as his selling tool. He knows the customer's thought process, backward and forward, and can dissect the customer's personality in minutes. He knows how to play mind games on the customer's objections, and knows how to overrule any negative, non-buying thinking the customer may come up with. He analyzes the whole situation, then makes his move. He is versatile, smart, and serious. He closes the toughest of customers and gains their respect at the same time.

The High-Roller Closer

This closer shows his customers all he has done with his life and how he has made it to the top. He says if he can do it — anyone can. He flashes his diamond rings and drops hints about his cars, boats, and vacations. He is a master of intimidation and makes the customers feel slightly inferior because he has pitched himself so successfully. This closer knows his business, and he uses his props well. The high-roller closer has a purpose. He smoothly does his job, and people do end up buying from him because after putting his rap on the customers he then turns around and makes them feel equal to him as they are forming their buying decision. The customers usually end up buying because the act is so successful that they want him to feel they are indeed his equal.

The College Joe Closer

Here comes the student, (he could be your lost son or grandson); at least that is how he acts. He dresses, looks, and talks the part, but don't you believe it. He can close. He uses honesty, innocence, and sincerity to sell. He does a super job. He looks like he wouldn't try to sell something unless it was a truly great deal. He seems too clean shaven and inexperienced to be insincere. He is well-mannered, polite, and he has all the ingredients needed to put the customer at ease — that's when he does his number and closes the deals, one by one, day after day, and always with a courteous, innocent and deadly smile.

*   *   *   *   *   *   *

Every closer I have just described can out-sell any salesman in any field. They are all different in their own ways, and they all use their own special characteristics to the best advantage possible. Whether you call them fronts, disguises, or just their natural style, all these closers have that ever-present common factor between them — they can all sell, anything, anywhere, anytime.

Techniques Used By Closers

The Big Ticket Closer

He seems to want to sell only the high-priced items like real estate, boats, or cars. He won't sell something that is not top of the line with a big price tag attached to it. He feels that this is his specialty, and in many ways it is. He is a professional at dealing with the class of customers that can afford his product (or service). He plays the game well, smoothly pretending he can also appreciate the high ticket item he is pitching, even though he could never spend the kind of money his customer has.

The Small Ticket Closer

He's the bread-and-butter closer. He can sell more than anyone because his clients have a greater "affordability radius." He has a much larger field of customers than the big ticket closer. His sales volume might not be as large as the big ticket closer when the year is over, but his closing percentage will be right up there with the winners. A closer who can sell the lower priced products can and will sell the higher priced items — but his technique to get his customers to write the larger checks is special. He realizes that you can always pull a customer up from a small ticket to a larger one if the client can handle the finances. But try to bring a customer down from a high priced item he cannot afford to something that would fit into his budget, and it's tough. The small ticket is a sure way to get more deals and keep from trapping yourself by building up customer expectations that cannot be fulfilled because there isn't enough money to do the deal. The result is your customer gets too disappointed or embarrassed, and leaves. So just be a small-item closer and work your way up. If the customer wants more he will let you know.

The Older Closer

This closer usually has some years on the customer; he is no spring chicken. He can come across in so many ways it's uncanny. This closer can be a father or grandfather figure. He can give advice, offer solid suggestions, and plenty of food for thought. He has an aura of truth and wisdom about him and uses it constantly to his advantage. He is very good with younger customers who need guidance on his product (or service). Remember, all closers (and I'll say it a hundred times over) are actors. They have to be versatile and cunning while they are at it.

Closers Who Limp, Stutter, or Have Foreign Accents

Now we are getting to a tool that closers use all the time. If a closer has anything about himself that can be used to draw attention to himself, he should use it; it helps. In fact, a limp with a good story behind it gets sympathy from the customer. A closer who stutters gets interest and involvement from the customer. The closer who speaks with a Texas drawl, a Spanish accent, a French accent, a Brooklyn accent or anything else not only gets attention, but often becomes a subliminal and almost hypnotic fascination for the client. I knew one closer who took candies and told his customers they were heart pills. He couldn't get too upset, or he would have a heart attack. Well, the customers were all afraid to say no to him; they didn't want him to get upset. You must use everything you have in your bag of tricks (within reason) to gain the upper hand. You're the actor.

The Pressure Closers

All closers are pressure salesmen, some more so than others. There is high pressure and low pressure — hard sell and soft sell. It is all in the presentation to the customer: How you give it, and how the customer takes it. High-pressure or hard-sell closers are trappers and they do not give the customers any place to turn or save face. So in many instances the closer and the customer battle each other, and no sale is made. High pressure is good if it is used properly, but you have to control high-pressure sales just as you control a pressure cooker. If you don't, it will explode. You must know exactly how to handle that safety valve.

Low pressure, or rather low key, soft sell closers are more tactful and subtle. They play mind games using traps that leave the client an out but keep him thinking about buying. He can save face and still buy without feeling he was forced into anything. Low pressure is good, solid, steady selling, never letting up but ever so easily, minute by minute making the decision to buy for the customer plainer and plainer until, all at once, from nowhere a decision has to be made. This kind of pressure is very good for sneaking up on a customer and having that weight finally build so that a buying decision becomes inevitable.

Characteristics of Closers

1. The closer knows how to give glamour to his product; he can make even the dullest items look and sound great. He adds all the polish that is needed for a sale.

2. The closer is cunning and crafty; he knows the good and the bad points about his product, and he balances and arranges them to project the product in its most positive light.

3. He is an entrepreneur, a doer who wants to do things his own way. He likes to think of new ways to sell and then sets his personal unique plan of action. He is his own man, made up of all he has learned in the past and he continues to learn in the present.

4. He gives good service to his customers and stays with them, stroking them and taking care of their future needs.

5. A good closer is greedy; he has ambition and more motivation to obtain his goals than a customer has objections.

6. He has a great fascination with people; he learns from everyone and likes customers because he wants to know what makes them tick. A closer really cares.

7. He's a self-starter. He can get himself pumped up for a sale all on his own initiative. He does not need a sales meeting to do it for him. He is aggressive, he is positive, and he is a winner.

8. The closer is, in many respects, a loner. He will always assist a salesman or another closer when asked because he loves the chase. It is his life. Every time he is asked to help close a deal, it is just one more feather in his hat. As for religion, I have never known a closer who did not believe in God. Perhaps that is what makes him want to help others and that is why he also likes people so much.

9. He can make a stranger (customer) like him in ten minutes or less, by virtue of his powerful and smooth personality. But a true closer knows no strangers. Everyone is a potential friend or customer.

What Master Closers are Made Of

The basic breakdown of a closer's make-up are:

1.	Enthusiasm	**51%**
2.	Empathy and understanding	**25%**
3.	Manners and charm	**10%**
4.	Fun	**7%**
5.	Product knowledge	**7%**

You will see that the least important ingredient is product knowledge and the most important is a positive, *enthusiastic* attitude. You can always learn facts about a product from sales closers, books, manuals, movies, etc., but you cannot manufacture enthusiasm unless you really feel it in your heart.

Selling Tips For Closers

Whether you believe them or not, these selling tips are all proven winners, and they are quite valuable when it comes to maximizing your closing percentages.

1. In closing a customer, a black man can sell better to whites than he can to blacks. A black man will buy much faster from a white man than he will from another black man. The reason is that most blacks feel a white closer has more knowledge about his product because he has had some advantages that a black closer hasn't. The reasoning on this might not always be true, but believe me, this is how it is in the real world of selling.

2. There are two types of sales closers that focus on human feelings while selling:

(a) The Intellectual Type — He is the closer who is aiming at the mind, logic, and good common sense of his customers.

(b) The Emotional Type — He is the one who aims at the heart of his customers; he works on all emotions, both good and bad. This type of closer is a winner, above all others. He has the right stuff.

3. The closers who carry too much sales material or too big a pitch book around with them always scare their customers. They look more like IRS tax auditors than closers. When a closer is loaded down with sales materials he is weighted down physically as well as mentally. It's as though he were a racing boat dragging an anchor. So be light, calm and relaxed. All you need is your mind. If you have to give an in-home demonstration, you can always get your gear later, after you have said hello to your customers.

4. If you are a conservative closer, then forget the word "closer" because you are not one: you're a salesman. There is not a closer around who is conservative. A closer is a doer, a positive minded achiever, an aggressor; there is nothing conservative about him. In sales there is no such thing as a conservative closer.

5. A closer is a compulsively driven person with a desire to win, to succeed, to sell, to become the best — and nothing less. That's why he is a champion, and not just a winner. A champion knows there are going to be ups and downs in the game of sales so he keeps plugging away. He is always striving for the sale. The winner is fine when he is ahead but when he's not, he is down and can't get back up by himself. The winner just cannot play the serious game like the champion can — and with his attitude, he never will.

Why They Are Closers

A closer is a man who can and will do more than any salesmen even dream about doing. Why? Because he knows how to warm up to people and he knows how to get the customers feeling good about themselves. Customers like the closer because he shows interest in them. Closers have a way of building their clients up so much that they cannot possibly say no.

A closer is far more than a super-salesman; he is multi-talented in sales, psychology, management, humor, and in the art of strategic thinking. He's the one who can step into another salesman's troubled deal and solve the problem in minutes.

Don't think someone is a closer just because he says he is. There are so many phonies running around it is hazardous to the selling industry. Some salesmen who call themselves closers are all talk and no action. A closer sells volume and that is enough to take the place of any self-promoting, wishful thinking.

A closer is a special kind of salesman that people like, people get excited with, people believe in, and people feel special around. A closer is true and convincing — he is sincere. He wins.

A closer looks just like you on the outside, but always acts and thinks like a closer — and so can you with a little practice.

This is how I was introduced to the subject of sales closers by Sam. And this ended my first exciting lesson.

Chapter Two

CLOSERS' ATTITUDES:
How a Closer Thinks

- A. The Do's and Don'ts Concerning Attitude

- B. The Closer's Tidbit Check List

- C. The Closer's Personal Thoughts and Pressures

Chapter Two

CLOSERS' ATTITUDES:
How a Closer Thinks

My first lesson was completed, and I could now see the difference in the sales closers' styles. I understood their make-up and their actions. Sam explained that from this point on we would now study the closers' attitudes, how the closers think, and exactly how they maintain their optimism. Sam told me that a closer's attitude is his most precious or destructive weapon. Everything in sales closing depends on how the individual closer uses this very powerful force: attitude.

In my second lesson, I would also learn what really makes a sales closer operate, what makes him tick, and how he is psychologically motivated towards himself and others. Sam stated that with this information in hand I could actually start to act and think like a master closer. So, listening closely, my next lesson began.

The most important thing about a closer's attitude is his ever-present, overwhelming enthusiasm. Sam put it this way: Enthusiasm is the one ingredient that makes us special; it is what insures we are never mediocre and like all the other sales people, and it develops a power in us that is indestructible. Sam said enthusiasm radiates and lights up our faces no matter what the circumstances may be. It is the catalyst that makes us sing and dance and makes people all around sing with us. He said enthusiasm is the maker of friends and the producer of smiles from all strangers. It is the builder of confidence and explains to the world, "I've got what it takes to win and accomplish." Enthusiasm tells and shows people everywhere that you like your job, the company you work for, and all the folks you work with. Enthusiasm is the inspiration that makes you want to wake up every morning and be alive. It's the feeling that puts a spring in your step, a warmth and understanding in your heart, and a positive twinkle in your eyes. Sam said enthusiasm can turn a depressed salesman into a top closer, a pessimist into an optimist, and a loafer into a hustler — in just a heart-beat.

Enthusiasm is all these things and more; without it, you will never come close to being a closer. You have to have a great emotional attitude to be a closer. To demonstrate exactly what I mean, I am including a do's and don'ts check list compiled by master closers. These are the things a closer knows and is aware of all the time. These are the understandings and techniques that build and develop closers and keep them on top in the selling field. Without fully understanding this check list of facts, a closer would be just another salesman in a world of thousands — and there are thousands of mediocre salespeople out there.

Before studying the list, a note should be made at this point. Everyone is a salesman to some degree but most people don't realize it. A salesman knows about the items on this list, but he has only gone so far in the pursuit of excellence, and then has fallen short. The closer has perfected the art of selling and understands the power of enthusiasm which is a basic ingredient needed to win. The closer effectively utilizes enthusiasm as his secret power base.

Do's and Don'ts for Closers

1. Don't sell if you're not sold.

Do not sell anything you are not already sold on personally. If you would not buy the product yourself, then get away from it. Find a product you can be sold on — something you can believe in. I've heard old timers say if you buy what you are selling, you are dead in that particular sales field. That statement is incorrect. The customers can sense through a closer's motions, reactions and intentions, if he is sincere about his product or service. So don't fool yourself and sell an item just because it is the going thing at the time — unless you're genuinely sold on it. If you do sell just to sell, you'll be the loser no matter how hot the item is. You'll be selling phony, and no closer alive can be the best if his heart isn't in it; selling phony doesn't do anything positive for the heart. It'll just burn you out.

2. Don't sell just for commission.

I have seen many, many closers float from one product and service to another, just for a larger commission. For example, from land sales to aluminum siding just because the commission is bigger and there is more money to be made. All good, sound reasons to move around, right? Wrong. If a closer switches from selling one product or service to another, he should change because he is sold on that particular product, not because he can make easier commissions.

If a closer transfers for the commission only, he will not be as effective, as sharp, or as good as he thought he was. He will not be the same leading closer everyone had heard about because the "commission-only" attitude will show through to customers, just like the "product-only" attitude used to. The closer will not be as productive, he will not be closing the same percentages as in the past, and he'll wind up thinking to himself, "With this great commission to be made and my past performance record, I could get rich selling this product no matter what it is. If only I could sell these new items like I used to sell the other ones. I wonder why my sales are off and I'm not selling as I did in the past?"

This question will answer itself in the long run because the closer is slowly killing himself trying to get rich through "commission-only" and not through basic enthusiasm and product belief. If you believe in your product you shine in the eyes of your customer, if you believe in your commissions you can't fake it and it shows.

A football coach once told his team, "Take pride in your work, prove yourself on every play, have dedication, and have a good time, and the score will take care of itself." I have found this also applies in sales; the commissions will always be there if you honestly do your job.

3. Small talk is out.

Don't listen to a lot of small talk around the office. For example, don't waste time listening to old sales stories (unless you feel you can learn something positive), avoid negative talk about the other salesmen, the competition, things that need to be done or undone, etc. All this nasty chatter builds up to one big negative atmosphere. The best way to protect yourself is by sometimes being a loner.

Before you get into contact with your customer, always get away from the influence of the other salesmen — go anywhere by yourself (the bathroom, closet, outside) and think to yourself only good, solid, positive thoughts. Believe you are going to go out there and masterfully sell that customer, and nothing in this world can stop you — except you. Then, when you have yourself in the right frame of mind, with a positive, sincere smile on your face and your appearance looking neat, it is time to deal with your customer. He's yours alone; it's only the two of you involved, so be positive, alert and present yourself in the best manner possible.

Don't get close to any salesman who is feeling down or is feeling negative. Stay far away; he is poison. What can that kind of a loser salesman do for you anyway? He can do nothing except try to make you feel as down as he feels. He will destroy you as you listen to him or remain in his presence.

So become a loner before you meet with your customers — and then go in and close 'em.

4. Don't pre-qualify.

Of the many negative attitudes that can destroy you, this is a giant. Pre-qualifying may occur when you meet your customer and find out he is from a state, town, or area where your product or service has not had much success. Or, your customer looks poorly dressed; or, he has a depressing air about himself; or, his house looks like it is about to collapse from neglect and old age.

Please, for the sake of all sales closers everywhere, don't say to yourself, "I'm beat," or "I'm going to lose; there are too many strikes against me already." That is the very best way to defeat yourself before you even start. Remember, it's one on one, and every customer is different. Customers will always have similar objections and questions concerning the product being sold. But the customers themselves are different and separate individuals.

So, don't pre-qualify or pre-guess them. When you come upon a situation that you think looks tough or depressing, get by yourself, regroup your thoughts, and then go forward — knowing and believing in your heart that you will win and make the sale.

There is a secret to this regrouping action. It works like this: chances are that the customer was already pre-qualified by other salesmen and ignored because of his appearance. So, now here you are, treating the customer like a million dollars, showing him your best side, and putting him first; you are acting like he is going to buy and can afford it. Something happens at this point. The customer sees all this and feels the different approach he's receiving from you. He appreciates it, along with your showmanship — so he buys. He buys from you because you, the closer, made him feel special, made him feel wanted, and treated him like a millionaire no matter what he was driving or wearing or where he was living. You, the masterful closer, have won again.

5. Don't get down on yourself.

If you miss a few sales or are in a slump due to personal problems, outside pressures or all the things happening around the sales office, don't let yourself get down. The first thing to do is to look at your sales slump and try to see a reason for it. Here you have to be honest with yourself.

Now, before we get into the subject of you and self-criticism, let me tell you something about the sales that are missed. There is a good rule to know and remember: In sales there are usually only two reasons why a customer will not buy. Number one is an *objection,* and number two is a *condition.*

Why Customers May Not Buy

Objection — Closers can overcome
Condition — Can prevent a sale

An objection from a customer can and should be overcome by the closer. There should be no excuse for not overcoming a legitimate, honest objection from the customer. This is the closer's job: to provide answers, get an agreement, and conquer (close).

But there is another reason people don't buy — this is based on the circumstance known as a condition. This is a different animal altogether. A condition from a customer or a condition about a customer sometimes just cannot be overcome. For example: It is clear that the customer cannot afford your product. Obviously, the closer cannot produce money for the customer. This is a genuine reason for the customer not to buy. There are many different conditions that will stand in the way of a sale — conditions the closer has no control over and that cannot be avoided. If a closer misses a few customers, he should look back on his sales presentations and try to see what the reasons were for missing. If he feels that it was due to conditions involved, then forget about those customers and go after the new ones. There was nothing else you possibly could have done.

But if a closer is missing because of customers' objections, then the clients are selling the closer, and they are doing the winning — at your expense. This is when the closer had better take a good, serious look at his sales pitch — a hard corrective look. He should examine the total presentation to see if it needs any alteration or adjustment. If it does, then he should polish it up. The closer should start listening to other closers who are selling; he should see what they are doing that he is not, and then simply copy them until he is back on his selling feet.

Remember, you, as a closer, are in a numbers game, and you can make the numbers work for you if you hit every customer with a hundred percent effort — that total directed shot. But if you have missed some sales and are feeling sorry for yourself, if you are down and depressed, then you will probably stay that way; the numbers, the customers, and the whole closing business will get the better of you and you will remain mediocre — or worse. And if you're that weak, you deserve to stay where you are and you don't belong in the business of selling. You should go out and get a dull, salaried, 9 to 5 job and don't "dare to be great" through a career in sales.

A closer knows the way the game is played and always keeps on trying, hitting harder with more enthusiasm, and greater winnings. So, analyze the problem; see if it is you or the customer or both, and do something about it. Then, when you get to your next customer you can give him or her your revised best. Be a professional closer at all times and don't get down on yourself. It's not worth it.

6. You can get angry.

I just told you not to get down on yourself. That statement is correct. But you can and should get angry or annoyed with yourself if you miss a sale and know that it was your fault. That's good for you; take some pressure off — get out in a field and yell at the top of your voice — anything you want. I've seen top-notch closers throw chairs, hit walls and doors, yell at the trees, and be so mad at themselves for their stupid mistakes that the secretaries all run for a corner. I'm sure these men can control their fits of anger if they want to, but that's not my point. The point is this: a closer who knows he has lost a sale through his mistake and consequently gets mad at himself is better than a salesman who misses a deal and says, "It's the customer's fault; you can't win 'em all." If you're going to be a closer, act like one, take some blame and do something about it for the next time.

If you lose a sale through your own fault, then admit it to yourself; don't allow it to happen again. Don't put up excuses or alibis or push your loss off on the customer. Remember, the sales percentages tell all in the long run. The company you're working for didn't hire the customer to win the selling game, they hired you. If you mess up and get angry at yourself, that is your right. But make sure you focus that anger on self-improvement for those next sales.

Don't dwell on the customers that you miss, just learn from them. Remember your mistakes so you don't make the same ones again. Go from there. The rule is: Don't look backward for very long; that is not the way to progress.

7. You can't learn enough.

I'm talking here about learning for closing reasons and that wanting-sales attitude. You will always have new things to learn about closing and yourself. You learn about new ways to work, how to improve your closing habits, distinguish your style, and polish your manners. You learn every day, and you learn from everybody, no matter who they are or where you are. Every single customer you deal with, whether you win or lose, makes you that much stronger. You learn with every objection, problem, situation, or maneuver you encounter; these make you a much better master closer. Always keep your eyes and ears open. You cannot learn a thing with them closed and your mouth open. Acknowledge all that goes on around you. Be aware and alert. Watch and observe what the top closers are doing, and follow their patterns.

To improve your closing percentages you must become an awake closer. You have to study and learn a little bit about everything so that you will know something about most subjects — current events, vacation areas, or anything your customer might bring up. The new knowledge that you pick up will open additional horizons for you with your customers. If you have a little extra knowledge you will make them feel at home and relaxed with you. This common ground is your springboard for more successfully selling that customer — the common bond you have established because you learned and studied about something you both could talk about. It's easy. The more you know, the taller you grow; and, a master closer grows pretty tall, mentally and financially.

8. You're the giant

I'm not talking about physical size in people. Different heights, weights, looks, long hair or short, thin or fat, old or young — in closers it does not matter. All you need to be a master closer is your mind. You do not have to be a 6' 7" football star to be a good closer; you don't have to look like a movie star to sell. You don't even have to be a university graduate to be a top closer. All you need is your mind — and that wonderful thing called heart.

I'll put it this way: You need love for people and a fighting spirit. With these two assets, plus wanting to be the best, you've got it made. That's all it really takes, plus a little know-how.

For example, I've seen closers sell who couldn't even talk because of laryngitis. I've seen men sell who couldn't walk, write or understand English, and sell more than ten so-called salesmen put together. They believed in themselves, and they wanted that sale badly enough to go and get it. If you want to be a master closer, if you give it your best shot and believe that you will win, then you will win. No matter what size you are or what you look like, it's all that is inside you that counts. Basic desire and spirit is your key.

9. Feel comfortable.

Keep your mind and thoughts geared and cleared so you never feel uncomfortable around your customers. You are in charge and in control. At least you should be. If you feel awkward or out of place around clients, they will feel this. Before you know it, the situation will be out of hand, creating an atmosphere that is not conducive to any kind of sales, much less closing. By feeling out of place, you create another obstacle that does not have to be there. If you feel at home around your customers, they, in turn, feel comfortable around you.

Your customers might be completely opposite from you racially, financially, and geographically. You may be in their home, and it could be a shack or a mansion. Just analyze the situation and comprehend it; relax, be courteous, and become chameleon-like — blend in. Belong. This way, you will actually be the calming factor that the situation demands. Use charm, manners, and class as your keys to closing the sale.

10. You're hot; stay that way.

How many times have you heard it said, "You are what you think you are"? It is true. The saying, "When you're hot, you're hot, and when you're not, you're not," is wrong. So don't believe it. If you are a closer, the saying goes like this: "When you're hot, you're hot, and when you're not hot, you get hot."

As a closer you have to know deep down that you are top drawer material. A power inside you drives you to be the best. If you know you're hot, then who in this world is going to say you are not? Do you think any other salesman or manager is going to try to get in your way when they see that you believe in yourself? When you really do, and you're out there talking to customers and trying, you always know that you have what it takes. You never give up, which is a closer's most important attribute.

There is not a closer in the world who wouldn't respect, appreciate and relate to that kind of effort. That kind of commitment and tenacity creates sales. One cannot help but to close deals. See for yourself who is out-selling everyone around. It will be those who have faith in themselves — all because they believed in something pretty special; their own ability to do the job. They make themselves hot and they keep themselves that way.

11. Be confident.

This is a super-must. You have to show confidence in yourself. It's like believing in yourself, but to a more intense degree.

This is how confidence will work to your benefit:

1. If you show confidence in yourself when you walk into a room, your customer begins to feel confidence in you.

2. This makes the customer feel secure in believing the things you say and secure in the feeling he can safely give his money to you.

3. Through confidence, you build up trust and credibility in yourself — something the client has to have before you can sell him anything.

Confidence is always positive; it is power. Confidence is the leadership quality that a closer needs to have. To acquire confidence one should: dress well, smile, stand tall, be polite, be courteous to everyone, and show your best manners when closing. If you do these things confidence will radiate from you. You will not be able to hold it back.

Another thing you should know about confidence and how to maintain it: Don't get frustrated or uptight when things don't happen as you expect them to. Stay calm and tackle one problem at a time. All this time your customer is watching you and saying nothing; he is thinking and forming his opinion about you. So be sure to show that confidence in yourself, and the customer will be on your side. He really wants a strong leader selling him, not a salesman who is unsure of himself or shows weakness. This is showmanship at its best. Confidence can make or break a sale, so be aware of it at all times. The confidence in you will show through if you let it.

12. You can be replaced.

No matter how good you are, or think you are, there is someone else out there in this world who is standing by to take your place on the sales line. That person probably has more energy, enthusiasm and go than you do. You had better remember this, because if you let up, slide, or coast on your past sales history, it is back on the interstate for you. If you keep this fact in front of you, you'll be motivated to stay ahead of the game.

A good lesson for closers who think they're indispensable is this: Go and put your finger in a bowl of water, then quickly pull it out. Watch how long the hole lasts. Get the point? In sales you have to keep on top of everything to be the best and to stay there. Otherwise you become expendable.

13. Burn your bridges.

I like this way of thinking — Go for it; don't forgo it. In other words, to get a sale, go all out and give it everything you've got. Burn your bridges behind you if that's what it takes, so even if you feel like backing out of something or retreating, you can't do it. You have to go forward and win.

The customer is your challenge. Your job is to sell. How can you sell your best going into a presentation if you always know you can back out of a corner if you have to? I'll tell you exactly what happens. If your pitch is half-hearted, just fifty percent — then so will be your closing average. Burn your bridges and force yourself to charge toward the sale. Don't worry; you'll get it. Again, a positive, aggressive attitude wins.

14. Leave your work.

A good rule to remember: Don't take your work home with you. When the day is over and all has been done, relax, hang it up until the next day; take a break. Get your mind off the hook for awhile. This will do a very important thing for you and that is it will keep your head and your entire personality sharper. Give yourself a break and you'll be more productive when you start work again. That's one of the reasons all sports have halftimes and breaks.

The same holds true in the closing field. You have to learn to relax, regroup, and calm down so you can be at maximum strength the following day. You're recharging. It's normal and makes closing a lot easier and more fun. When closing and sales become work for you, and you are starting to fight it, then your sales will go right down the drain — faster than the blink of an eye. So keep things in perspective; you work hard at closing, so play hard with your free time.

To go along with this philosophy, plan your days off. When you're working, concentrate and devote total energy to closing; when you have a day off, enjoy it. Forget closing, customers and the office. Get them all out of your system. By planning your days off and knowing when they are, you give full attention to your closings and to your selling time. You should have nothing else on your mind while closing. Work is work, and days off are just that. You've got to understand the difference; and make the difference work effectively for you. You are a professional, so treat yourself like one.

*   *   *   *   *   *   *

We have been talking about the do's and don'ts of attitudes for closers. Now we are going to touch on some tactful things to know — all of the little notes and phrases that keep the closer alive. Everything you see and learn concerning attitudes are a culmination of tidbits that fit together; they bond to form a sound working pattern for the closer. To have an attitude that is positive, you have to be aware of everything that makes you think better and clearer. So, following is a closer's "tidbit checklist" showing the little things you just have to know.

The Closer's Tidbit Checklist

1. Treat them with respect.

Every man or woman, no matter what his or her character or behavioral pattern, wants to be a winner and wants to be accepted and appreciated by others. Use this approach with your customers to build them up for favorable sales decisions. This build-up manifests itself through your attitude toward your customers, how you treat them and think of them. You've got to sincerely convey to customers you are interested in them — and make them believe it.

2. Compete with yourself first.

The less you concern yourself about out-selling the other salesmen the better your closing percentage will be. You should be competitive but you will not sell anything by watching the other closers sell while you're standing there in awe. Remember, it is you and your customer that make the sale, not the other salesmen who are looking on. If you want to compete in sales, be competitive with yourself first. Then, at the end of your selling season, you won't have to worry about the other salesmen because you'll be the winner. They will be the ones worried about you.

3. The closer, then the product.

The main thing in sales is not really the product but the closer himself. He represents the item being sold, and he is the company's personal representative. The closer is the one who knows the product's positive points and plays down the negative ones, and is familiar with everything else that goes with the final sale. It all has to be filtered and shown through the closer, no one else. He is the flag and front door for the whole company, and the closer is the first impression presented to the customer.

4. Your impression on the customer.

The customer will develop and form an impression of you when you first meet; whether that impression is good or bad depends only on you. Your attitude and appearance are the initial keys. It is easier to sell when that very first impression, even without a word being said, is positive.

So, act like you want a sale, and give that image. It will show in your manners and actions. You have to act positive and be in total control when you meet your customer.

5. Customers are people.

If you forget that the customer is a warm human being, with feelings and a family, with emotions and needs just like yours, if you look at him as a dollar sign, a way to get your commission, then you had better hang it up. You're not a closer but a wimp. You will show about as much class and professionalism as a genuine loser or a salesman who thinks he is a winner and is really only as close to being a closer as a hobo is to becoming president of a Fortune 500 company. Keep your customers first; treat them with love and understanding, then the sale will develop — producing your hard-earned commission.

6. Build up the customer.

Get the customer sold on himself; set him on a shining pedestal. Always let the customer see himself in the best light possible; make him want to be with you for the sincere respect and admiration you show him. Make your customer feel special, a cut above other prospective buyers. When you have him feeling high on himself, he will glow with the added self-confidence you have instilled in him. Then, when you ask for the sale, you'll be more likely to get it because the customer has built himself up so much that he would be a little intimidated and embarrassed to say no.

7. Be organized.

Keep yourself and your business organized. Keep records of all your sales; keep names, addresses, phone numbers — everything — not only for tax purposes but also for referrals and future business. Know your own good and bad points; and your own habits. Work on your worst ones so you can get control of future sales situations you are involved in.

By keeping yourself and your business records organized, your mind will be free to concentrate on sales and closing. This eliminates all the nit-picking items that a good closer should not be bothered with in the first place. Your personal organization is the foundation of your professionalism.

8. Contribute to teamwork.

To work in a sales office with others, you must have teamwork — if the company you are selling for is to prosper and have an effective sales atmosphere for its closers to close in. If the company you work for doesn't prosper — you don't prosper. Be constructive. Help other closers when asked, and be happy for them when they sell; you'll have your turn many, many times over.

If things get petty around the sales office, such as little differences of opinion, tacky gossip, and jealousy, put yourself above and beyond it. Just go out and sell your customers; they are not involved in your office politics. Remember, your customers are the ones you make your living from — not those involved in the office wars. In a sales office, whether it has an atmosphere of teamwork or the aforementioned problems, always keep things in the right perspective — sales first.

9. Don't procrastinate.

Don't delay a customer who calls you after the sale has been made. Call them right back. It could be good news, a product pay-off or a new referral. Or the customer might want his hand held; he might need reassurance from the closer that everything is fine. If your customer has bad news, at least you can deal with the problem immediately — nip it in the bud. Whatever you do, don't procrastinate; the problem involved only gets bigger.

If you have a new customer when an old customer calls, wait until you've sold the one you're with before you call back. If you don't, and the old customer gives you bad news — for example, a cancellation or, worse yet, a lawsuit — your negative thoughts and bad feelings could ruin the deal with your present customer. You could end up losing two customers instead of one. Use your head. Keep your priorities straight.

Another thing concerning calls and recent customers: when you do call them back and you solve the situation, don't just solve it temporarily. Get it over with so the same problem doesn't keep coming back to mess up your mind, distracting you from more productive uses of your time.

10. A few ways to kick the sales slump.

There are three good ways to get yourself out of a sales slump. First, instead of giving your presentation in your usual way, reverse it and give your pitch backward, from last points to first points. This gives you back the enthusiasm and momentum you usually save for the end of your sales talk, that is possibly now lacking. When you pitch backwards, that is explain your product in reverse, you don't really know what you are going to say next to the customer. You are extra alert and on your toes to keep the presentation and your thought process organized. This automatically creates a spark in you, the missing enthusiasm, and that will translate into sales. After selling this customer, go back to your original sales presentation format; if you keep using the reverse pitch it will lose its unique quality and purpose. Remember, the objective is to get you out of your slump.

The second way to re-group and start selling again is simple. Instead of trying harder to sell, go completely negative. When you are with your customer, act like you don't care if you sell or not. Tell him you've already been quite busy today, and you're tired. Tell him the product is better than you can even try to explain right now, and if the customer really wants a good deal then he should buy the product while they are still available. Assume a take-it-or-leave-it attitude, and watch some customers turn around. The customer is capable of building up his own presentation for the product, thinking it's too good to pass up. Because of your attitude he psyches himself up and buys. Try it — it works.

The third method is a fun way to get out of a sales slump. Just go out and buy something — a sports coat, a shirt, a new pen, a book, anything. But, you have to spend some money on yourself and no one else. Then go back to the office or project and get your next customer. You'll be in an improved mood to sell him. This present to yourself gets the excitement back in you that you may have lost from being in your sales slump.

    *   *   *   *   *   *   *

When thinking about attitudes keep in mind that enthusiasm is always your power base. To think like a closer you must be aware of all the factors that affect the closer's total outlook. You have to understand how a closer views each new situation and solves it. All the pointers in this chapter are designed to produce a positive attitude. Every statement and tidbit contributes and you shouldn't underestimate any of them.

    *   *   *   *   *   *   *

The Closer's Personal Thoughts and Pressures

We are now going to look at some short "closer's anecdotes" that add to the development of a closer's winning attitude.

1. There is only one you, and you are unique. No one else can do what you can in the same way you do it. Always show your personal style, and don't try to be anyone else. Exhibit your own brave, successful, generous spirit.

2. "If you got money, you're a honey; if you're broke, you're a joke." Sound silly? Think about it.

3. In selling a customer, some rules of thumb:
Your heart equals his heart.
Your mind equals his mind.
Your understanding equals his understanding.
Your reasons equal his reasons.
Your sales presentation equals his acceptance.

4. Some salesmen say, "Good morning, Lord." Some say, "Good Lord, it's morning!" Guess which ones are the producers.

5. When you have used all the mental tricks you know to get psyched up for a sales presentation and you're *still* not ready to face the customer, tell him your problem, and start a polite conversation. Your customer will usually help you out, believe it or not — and then they'll buy.

6. Every person you talk to is a potential customer — a person who makes your living for you. Always treat people in that manner.

7. With the combined ingredients of enthusiasm, control and product knowledge, you can sell anybody.

8. To be a top quality closer you have to have self-confidence, self-control, and self-respect; these produce self-satisfaction.

9. A good point to remember: "A man is stagnant if his dreams equal his present existence."

10. Talk about having a good attitude, once a closer went broke on his own business venture and some salesman asked him, "How are you doing, 'Has Been'?" The closer was calm. He smiled and answered back, "Pretty good, 'Never Was'." Closers must always have a strong, believe-in-themselves attitude.

11. There is not a customer anywhere who wants to do business with a semi-pro when they could be doing business with a professional. Act like what you're supposed to be — a professional master closer.

12. If you don't sell the customer than somebody else down the line will. Ask yourself: Are the other salesmen better than you?

13. Some salesmen think it is a big joke when they sell a customer something that he doesn't need or if they sell the customer more of the same product. Well, it is a joke all right, but only on the salesman. It all comes back to haunt him and disrupt future sales. That's the way a salesman creates future problems for himself.

14. A salesman who is forever telling old sales stories (war tales) about himself and elaborating on all he's sold is bragging only to build up his own ego. Chances are he has an inferiority complex and has never done very much in the world of closing; he probably never will.

15. Know how to expound on a particular subject; know how to use the correct words and phrases to express yourself.

16. A good thing to keep in mind: When most of a closer's bad dreams and fears disappear it is a sign his subconscious mind is finally clearing.

17. Be a closer to your customer, not just a good conversationalist; anyone can talk or be a nice guy.

18. If you take the letter "C" out of the word closer, you have the word "loser." The "C" stands for confidence, control, compassion, and courage.

In studying the sales closer's attitudes, we must first look at his personal thoughts and pressures to fully understand the main dimension of his complicated world.

For a closer it is a great feeling to know that he is the best in his selling field because not only he knows it, but all the other salesmen around him know it as well. The main goal is staying a winner, to always be the master closer you want to be. But every closer, no matter what he may say, has a hidden fear of being known as a loser; it's a feeling any kind of world-class competitor has occasionally. It's built-in, and it is normal. It is all part of being a closer. The fears stem from the pressures. Being a closer involves coping with many personal pressures, as the illustration on the following page demonstrates. This is why the closer's attitude is so important. A closer cannot do his job, he cannot function, if he is not 100% prepared mentally.

Closer Pressure

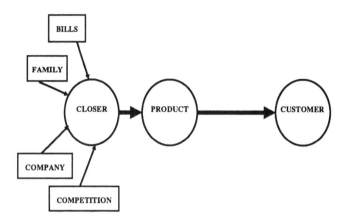

A closer also has to think about his goals in life. (See illustration on next page). A closer knows about the ups and downs of life and he also knows you have to stay on a well-defined game-plan — in order to succeed. If you don't have a long-range goal, you could be in real trouble. You'll drift and never gain anything in life. One day you will look back and say, "What happened? Where did it all go?" Then it will be too late.

To have a closer's attitude, you have to be bold enough, gutsy enough, humble enough, classy enough, and most of all, human enough to go out and work hard to become number one at the art of selling. It all happens with an understanding and love for people and that ever-present enthusiasm that will enable you to become, anytime you decide, a master closer.

The Closer's Personal Pressure

Closers have the same problems everyone else has except for one thing: A closer can't afford to be down. If he does, his closing percentage is shot. This is why a positive attitude is so important. Being a closer is the only profession in which you must be mentally up all the time.

The customer can be down, feel bad, and act depressed, but it's the closer who has to be up mentally so he can get the customer feeling good, and make the sale. In addition to being up mentally for the customer, the closer has to be a big brother, a father, a minister, a friend, an advisor, a baby sitter, and a good listener — just to get a word in.

Closer's Goals

Every closer has to consider the future at one point or another and see what direction he is going. If he doesn't, any goal he had hoped for will vanish. It's like driving a car: If you take your eyes off the road, you'll run into a ditch. You'll be off the track for good and miss your original objective. Just think for a second how many closers you have seen that have all the talent in the world but are still down and broke. The diagram below illustrates this point. It didn't have to be that way. Keep your eyes on your goal, and go for it.

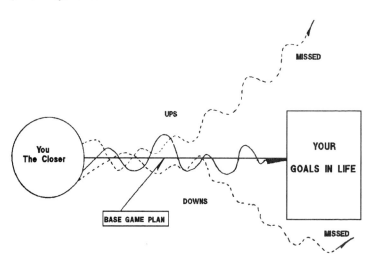

A good note for yourself:

Write down on a piece of paper your ultimate goal in life. Then look at it every day — this is a simple way to constantly check and remind yourself. See if you are maintaining your original course toward your objective. Above all, be honest with yourself because you are the person who is either going to make it or fail.

THE CUSTOMER:
The Opponent

This chapter describes the characteristics of customers and shows how the Master Closer handles each one in preparation for the close.

- A. Categories and Types of Customers

- B. The Age Factor

- C. The Ethnic Make Up of Customers

- D. Professions, Businesses and Trades of Customers

- E. Facts You Should Know About Customers

Chapter Three

THE CUSTOMER:
The Opponent

July the first had finally arrived at Green Vista Estates, and our grand opening was in full swing. The customers were arriving from all across the country thanks to our company's outstanding marketing department. Everywhere there was activity and excitement. As for me, I was parking cars like there was no tomorrow — and enjoying every minute of it.

Sam wasn't just sitting around, either; he was at the guard gate giving directions and information to everyone. In fact, Sam was so busy he looked like a swamped-under travel agent. Whenever we got, or took, a work break, we'd sit down together and continue our discussions about sales and closers. Sam had explained sales closers to me over the past weeks in a way I could understand and I came to appreciate the job they actually do.

But the time had come to start studying, observing, and learning about the closer's number one opponent: the customer himself. Sam told me that no matter what label you put on a customer — an up, an out, a unit, a bimbo, a peep, a dog, a shlepper — the customer is the fascinating element of sales work. Before we start, two facts have to be stated. First, the customer is the name of the selling game, and the closer has to know everything he can about his customer. If the closer wants to make a sale, he must know his customer as well as a surgeon knows his patient. If you think people involved in a sales situation are different in Boston than they are in Kansas City or Los Angeles, you're kidding yourself. People are customers, and customers are just that — customers. Period.

People may have different accents and mannerisms and they act and react differently because of their environments. But when it comes down to bottom-line sales — the close — all customers are basically the same. They will have the same basic thought patterns, the same objections and questions, and the same hesitations. It's as though they all read the same cue cards and scripts.

It is important not to confuse sales presentations with closing. True, customers are individuals. They have to be treated and approached in many different ways in a progressive sales presentation, but we are not talking about that now. We are talking about closing a sale on a product or service, whatever it may be. The customers are the same in that they are the opponents — with all the aforementioned common basics. They are either going to tell the closer yes or no. As stated previously, the customer is the name of the selling game. With this understanding we can start to study the many fascinating types of customers.

A closer knows that the first thing to learn about a customer is the kind of customer he is dealing with. Then the closer uses that information to develop a sales presentation suited for that particular customer.

Categories and Types of Customers

(Using a one-to-ten scale for measuring the customer's degree of closing difficulty, with ten as the most troublesome customer.)

The Yes Man

(Description) This is the customer who will agree with you on everything; he will nod his head in the affirmative and say, "yes" to every statement that is made. The closer could give any kind of ridiculous sales presentation, and this customer would still agree.

(In Reality) The customer has already made up his mind that no matter what the closer says he isn't going to buy today (if ever). This customer keeps agreeing just to get the sales presentation over. He thinks the affirmative nod of the head, or an occasional "yes" will pacify the closer into letting up on the sales pitch. This customer is basically scared that if he does let his guard down, the closer will indeed sell him. This customer is pretty easy to close, and on a scale of one-to-ten (with ten being the most difficult) the yes man is rated a solid four.

(Solution) To snap this customer out of the annoying "yes" habit, the closer should turn to the customer and ask directly, "Why aren't you going to buy today?" This kind of shock question will catch the customer off guard, and he will most likely give you a legitimate answer, not having anything else planned to say. With this, the closer can then work toward really selling the customer and the final close.

The Know-It-All

(Description) The title speaks for itself. This customer already has all the answers and thinks he knows more about the product than you do. He will tell you that he personally knows the president of your company or that at one time or the other he was in your particular business. This customer will say just about anything to make you feel off balance or uncomfortable. He continually acts as a smart-aleck, and tries to take control of the sales presentation. His favorite statements are, "I know," or "I understand."

(In Reality) This customer does not want to be out-classed, out-shown or intimidated by the closer, especially if he is trying to impress the person he's with. He knows that he is weak around a good closer, so he puts up that strong "I know" guard to protect himself. He feels he has to show-off in front of everyone around when he is with a closer so the sales closer will not make him look like the uneducated idiot he truly is, while discussing the product. This customer is fun to work with because you can program him easily. On a scale of one to ten, this customer rates a four.

(Solution) Let the customer trap himself; go along with him and allow him to explain the product to himself or the people he's with. All you, the closer, have to do is be polite and agree with him, acting like you are learning something yourself. This customer will keep talking and eventually talk himself into a corner. This is when you ask him, "Well, since you know all the advantages of this product, how many do you want?" Then you take his answer and run with it. The customer will feel all the pressure because he explained the product himself and now has to answer the closer in front of other people. He won't know what to say and will most likely start backing down. That is when the closer moves in smoothly for the sale.

The High Roller

(Description) This customer has to tell you all about how much he is worth, how much he owns, and all the things he has been into and accomplished. He will tell you about all the important people he associates with, and he'll explain that if he likes your product enough he will tell all of his friends to come back and deal with you and he may even buy a dozen or so — money is no problem. He'll flash the diamonds, the gold watches, the gold chains, and make sure you know he is a man of means. And, if you're lucky, you may be able to even visit his country club sometime as his personal guest.

(In Reality) This high-rolling customer is most likely up to his eyeballs in debt. He lives a pretty good life, or so it would seem, but nothing is really paid for. He probably spends more nights awake worrying about bills to be paid than about where he will invest his money. The customer sees himself as something he is not and tries to get that facade across to the closer. This client is polite and shows manners, but he is hurting for cash and he will not admit it to the closer. He just practices his act and plays his little game (in his own world) in front of the closer. On a scale of one to ten, he rates about a four.

(Solution) Go along with the customer, be impressed with him and all he has acquired. Show admiration, and ask him for his secrets of success. Become his friend by idolizing him to a degree. Then, when it comes time to close, ask him how much time he would need to transfer some of his investment monies so he can purchase your product. This gives him time to accumulate some money and save face and embarrassment by not being asked if he has money now. Do not confront him by telling him you know that he may not have the ready cash; just act as if he soon will and don't let on that you know differently. This customer will trap himself almost every time, so the closer should just give him some room. This pompous ass will high roll himself into his own sale. Needless to say, it's advisable to cash this guy's check immediately.

The Thinker; The Quiet One

(Description) This is the customer who just sits back and doesn't say a word. He could be smoking his pipe or looking out of the window, but he simply will not talk. He'll look at you with skepticism in his eyes and act bored. He will have a firm handshake and be quite courteous when he meets you, but that's when it all stops. He makes you feel like an actor on a stage, and he's the audience just waiting for the performance to begin. This customer instills the feeling of pressure on the closer because of his unnerving silence.

(In Reality) The silent customer is really a thinker; he wants to listen to what you have to say, and he wants to see if you're honest and sincere. He is analyzing you and sizing you up. This customer is most likely pretty intelligent and probably somewhat knowledgeable about your product and your company. He is more like a country fox than a city tiger. He is cautious, slow moving and protective of his statements and answers. He's like a slick lawyer. On a scale of one to ten, this customer is an eight.

(Solution) First of all, be on your toes and keep alert to everything this customer has to say. Pick up on any little hint or slip he might make so that you can figure out this client's thinking. Be courteous, sincere, and give a somewhat negative pitch; go soft sell and low key. Don't get over-excited. Instead, present basic logic about your product and company. Also, explain something about yourself, your family, and your job. You just do the talking and relax. This will let the customer get to know you better first; he, in turn, then relaxes his own guard and cautiously lets you know something about himself. This opens up a conversation so the closer can accumulate some extra ammunition to use for the sale. Treat this type of customer as an equal. You must convey with confidence that you are a professional and know your product completely. Note: This is the kind of customer that will send you more business than any other!

The Scared-to-Death Customer

(Description) If you should sneak up behind this customer and yell, he would have a heart attack. This customer is so nervous it sometimes even scares the closer. This person is always looking around and never staying in one place; it seems he is fidgeting with a pencil or something on the sales desk continuously. This customer is afraid of the closer, and it shows. He is wound up tight and talks sharply to his family and friends, even in the presence of the closer.

(In Reality) He is scared because he thinks he will be put in an embarrassing position and have to answer personal questions or make a buying decision that he doesn't know how to say no to. For example: The closer may ask something about which the customer is ashamed. The customer doesn't want an outsider, the closer, to find out something that he would rather not have known. He feels out of place and totally uncomfortable around sales closers because he also knows he can be persuaded to buy anything. He knows his weaknesses and doesn't want them to show, but he knows they do. On a scale of one to ten, this customer is a three.

(Solution) Treat this customer with kid gloves. Be slow, low-keyed, and compliment him on something positive that you have observed about him; this will allow you to build up his confidence. Make him relax by talking about yourself and not about him. Touch on his job lightly in conversation, and don't dig deeply into his personal life. Make a friend out of him. Find a similarity in your life and his own. This will help ease the tension. Put this nervous buyer up on a pedestal, and show him respect and convey that you think he's special. This will be an experience that this customer has never had before. He will now become easy to control and close. All he needs is confidence in himself and the leadership and friendship of a Master Sales Closer.

The I-Don't-Care Customer

(Description) He fits the name. He acts like it is no big deal if he buys or not. This customer has a take-it-or-leave-it attitude with the closer. He seems as if he couldn't care less if the product is great or if it will just barely do the job. This client is nonchalant and acts like the closer is boring him. He could be rude and discourteous with his manners and hard to get to know.

(In Reality) This client does not want to be pressured or sold by a closer. He wants to examine the product for himself and not be bothered with a sales presentation. This customer could be the silent type or the boisterous kind. He wants to do things on his own and in his own time. But don't let him trick you. This customer acts as though he doesn't care, but he is wide awake and alert. He is taking in all the information he can find, and he is thinking about all that is being said. On a scale of one to ten, this customer is a seven.

(Solution) Don't try to sell him with the usual presentation or you will be fighting a losing battle. This customer has to be turned around and injected with excitement about the product. The closer has to be sophisticated and create a sudden interest in the product for the customer and spark his curiosity. This curiosity will cause the customer to show more interest and get more involved in the closer's presentation. This will then develop into a more normal closer-customer relationship and the closer can overcome the initial negative feelings and progress toward the final close.

The "We Don't Buy Today" Customer or "The Looker"

(Description) This customer says to the closer the minute he meets him, "I'm not going to buy anything today, it's my policy." Or, "I'm just looking; I wouldn't buy today no matter what the deal." This customer will not let the closer even say one word until that fact is out in the open. This is the customer who sounds like he memorized his questions and answers before he entered the sales office. He believes he is ready for the closer. He thinks he is fully prepared.

(In Reality) This customer is easy to sell — probably one of the easiest. He puts up a negative front because he knows when that is destroyed, he is finished. He will buy anything. This client is likable once you penetrate the facade and get to know him, and his sales resistance is very weak. All this customer can do is give the closer that one big "no" at the front end of the sales presentation, and from then on it's easy sailing for the closer. On a scale of one to ten, this client is a three.

(Solution) Don't listen to his first statement; let it go in one ear and out the other, because he doesn't mean it anyway. Give him your regular sales pitch with a lot of enthusiasm and kindness. Then give him a special sales price that's good for this particular customer only — and you have a sale. This customer cannot resist a good deal. In essence, that's what he is saying to you when you first meet. He is telling you that he is a pushover and to please not present a good deal on a product or he will be forced to buy. These customers are fun.

The Curious Customer

(Description) He really doesn't have any buying questions, he just wants to know what is going on. This customer wants information to take home so he can read about the product. He is willing to listen to a complete sales presentation if time allows, and he is nearly always polite and courteous. This customer can get involved in your sales pitch easily and start to participate by asking questions — and some good, positive questions at that. This customer is a bright spot on a slow day.

(In Reality) This customer is a buyer all the way. He first has to like what he sees and then develop a desire for the product. This person is a shopper but also an impulse buyer who can make a decision at any time if he is motivated. He has a good personality to go along with his curiosity and is a good person to get to know. This customer wants to buy — and will, if he feels good about the closer, the sales office, the environment, and the product itself. On a scale of one to ten, this customer is a solid three.

(Solution) Give a dynamic sales presentation with a lot of showmanship; get the customer excited and involved. Get him thinking about how he would feel owning this product. Work on his ego and his pride. Tell the customer that there is an overstock situation involved and the customer can really take advantage of the price. This customer just needs to feel that he has stumbled onto something great and special. With that planted in his mind, he will buy almost anything you show him.

The Good-Natured Customer

(Description) This customer is polite, courteous, and shows class. He is open-minded and respectful to the closer. He will sometimes even tell you (in a light manner) that he is hard to sell. This client is a pleasure, and thank heavens for him.

(In Reality) To be short and sweet, this customer is genuine and for real. He does have an open mind and is willing to listen to what the closer has to say. He usually has the money to buy but will turn away from a high-pressure salesman. He wants to be treated the same way he treats other people. This customer is a breath of fresh air to any closer. He makes the sales business that much more enjoyable. On a scale of one to ten, he would be rated four.

(Solution) Treat him very courteously, with a lot of charm. Show your professionalism with gentlemanly manners. Give this customer a solid, logical sales presentation without going overboard in any one area. Assume he is going to buy from the beginning; then treat the close as something quite natural. This kind of customer is especially good for your referral business. Do *not* high pressure or push this customer. It won't work.

The Rude, Skeptical Customer

(Description) This customer comes into the sales office with a chip on his shoulder. He is far from being the nicest customer that you ever had. He acts as if you are the cause of all his problems, and it would be easy for a tense situation to develop between you and this customer. He doesn't believe anything you say and has great doubts about the product. In actuality, this customer is a problem, not only to the closer but to anyone in the general area.

(In Reality) This customer has personal problems; it could be in his home life, job, finances, or anything. He will try to take it out on someone else — and it could very well be the closer. Remember, this customer is not in his usual frame of mind. But if he is always like that, he could very well have a serious problem. He is just looking for any excuse to start an argument. On a scale of one to ten, he rates about a seven.

(Solution) Destroy him with kindness. Do not get into an argument. Stay away from any pressure subjects that might irritate him. Play your sales presentation down, be low-key. Be polite, and show concern for his predicament. Ask him if there is anything you can do for him. Become his friend, and he will calm down because he doesn't have anyone to spar with. He will start to talk to you, and then you can present your product in a calm and orderly manner. It would be easy to forget this customer and let him go without making a sales pitch. To stay with him — to turn him around — is the difference between a professional closer and a salesman. Be nice to this customer; he needs that friendship first — the sale will follow right in line.

*   *   *   *   *   *   * .

The Age Factor

We are now going to take a look at various customer types according to age. This area of study has more to do with couples and families. It shows the different kinds of situations the closer is regularly confronted with. We will also see the procedure you should use to channel customers of different ages toward the final sale.

The Elderly Customer

(How They Think) The label "elderly customer" also pertains to couples, widows and widowers. Older people have a common characteristic: loneliness. They might have a large family and friends or a small family and not know many people, but they still have a great deal of time on their hands. The older customer wants to contribute and do something with his life; he wants to be involved in activities and surrounded with creative projects. This customer does not want to feel left-out or useless, which is a problem he is facing in many ways everyday. The elderly customer has an understanding personality and simply wants to fit in somewhere — to belong. Having the peace of mind that comes with knowing he is sincerely wanted, the elderly customer is slow to act and react. To him, decision-making is not urgent. When this customer is unsure about any sales or buying situation, he will most likely want to seek advice from a friend or family member. This customer wants to believe in the closer, but he knows elderly people are always being taken advantage of and is therefore cautious.

(How To Treat Him) The closer has to do one thing right off the bat which is imperative for this kind of customer: he must slow down his sales presentation. The closer has to be deliberate with his words and demonstrate understanding with a sincere attitude toward the customer. The closer cannot push or pressure the customer at the end of the presentation. Instead, he has to build up to a decision-making point. This process is accomplished by a slow, steady, positive and gentlemanly sales presentation. The closer has to show warmth and charm toward the elderly customer and must always take the time to listen to his stories. This customer needs patience from the closer, combined with ever-present empathy. The closer has to make this customer feel wanted, appreciated, and needed. The closer has to show the customer not only the benefits of buying the product, but how the product will help meet the needs of the elderly person. This can be illustrated in many ways. The key is to get the customer involved so he can trust the closer. When this is done, the closer not only has made himself a good friend but has also gotten himself a sale.

The Young Couple or Young Single Customer

(How They Think) These two types of customers can be approached and treated in the same manner. They both have a common factor to focus on when it comes to any sales dealings — excitement. Both of these types also prefer a financial program that will help them to become secure and advance themselves in today's world. These couples may have just gotten married, or they may have just gotten a divorce; they may have children or only be dating; in sales it doesn't matter. Younger couples want something that will put them ahead of people in their own age bracket. They are aggressive when it comes to self-advancement.

The younger customers will probably have financial problems and won't be willing to admit them to the closer. But they have something that will, in most cases, counterbalance that negative problem. That is their optimistic outlook and their willingness to do something to change things. The closer simply has to show friendship, authority, and leadership, and the sale will be made.

(How To Treat Them) The closer has to demonstrate a lot of enthusiasm and showmanship. The sales presentation can be made a little faster than with the average customer, and the presentation should have a great deal of excitement. The closer can turn the younger customer into an impulse-buyer by using examples involving family, future, and self-pride.

The closer will have to work out finances with this customer in most cases, but he should always act as though it were a normal part of the sales procedure. This keeps the younger customer in a more comfortable frame of mind.

The pressure sale works better on younger customers than older ones because the young ones don't have the sophistication of the oldsters. They can easily be intimidated into a sale, but in most cases that will not be necessary.

The closer should draw a parallel between his life and the young customer's, showing how making the right decision about the product (or service) will pay off in the long run. The closer has to be confident in himself and the product (or service), and sympathetic about any problem the customer may bring up. The younger customer will buy if he is excited and can be persuaded to believe in the product. These elements can be inspired by the closer for the sale, if he keeps the younger customer fascinated and involved with the product.

The Middle-aged Customer

(How They Think) This is the customer who usually has a family and a good job. He might own his company or be working his way up in one. This customer generally has a good education and is at that special age where he is not a youngster anymore but neither is he ready to retire. This customer wants more from life than he has and is concerned about his future. This customer is aggressive and tries to think and act younger than he is.

The middle-aged customer is a person who believes, deep-down, that everything is going to change for the better, either through a sudden lucky break, or a run of good fortune.

The middle-aged customer wants top rated products (or services) for his family and he is willing to pay what is necessary for them. This customer can make his own decisions and can take care of any problem or situation that develops during the close. Once this customer is sold on a product, he will buy it from you. He is a closer's bread and butter.

(How To Treat Him) The closer has to become a friend to this customer. The closer should show respect and admiration for the customer and his family. Treat this customer as though he is younger than he really is, and be sure to flatter him about something. Build the customer up, work on his ego, and create a positive feeling while he is in your presence. Show this client how your product (or service) will contribute to his future success. Put this customer first in everything you do and make him feel very special. Use emotions involving his family's future and compliment him on the progress he has made so far. This customer will buy if you put a spark of spirit in him — something that is commonly lacking in middle-aged customers. Then proceed to the close. This customer will get more excited and motivated about your product if you speak to him as if he is superior and show him constant respect. The closer can compliment this customer into a sale almost every time.

A word of caution: The technique of complimenting can back-fire on the closer if it is not handled properly. When the closer compliments a client on anything, he had better sound honest and sincere. If the closer thinks that he can easily fake compliments he is in for a big surprise; the customer will know exactly what is happening and simply walk out — and I don't blame him. The closer has to use his head before he can use his mouth.

*   *   *   *   *   *   *

The Ethnic Makeup of Customers

This is an area of sales study that has to be touched upon if a closer wants an honest guideline to follow relating to the ethnic mannerisms of his potential customers. The statements and analysis below are based on tens of thousands of sales presentations that I have personally participated in. I do not wish to imply that every customer has these characteristics. But rather, I am generalizing about observations that should hold true for you more times than not.

The Black Customer

This customer is unique in many respects because of his background. Black people have not always enjoyed total freedom of buying. Because of that past history, I have been able to characterize black people as two distinct types of customers.

The first type is the older customer who remembers the years of limited sales freedom. This customer is still, to some degree, reluctant to purchase and cautious when buying. This type of customer also tends to have total trust in most people and has to be treated with understanding and confidence by the closer. The black client is often willing to buy if finances can be handled in an uncomplicated manner. The older black customer is a wonderful referral generator, and is usually a good, solid buyer if he believes in the closer's sincerity and integrity. This customer will generally buy if he is treated respectfully.

The second type of black customer is the younger and middle-aged client. We can treat both of these customers similarly because their thinking is closely related. This customer is an aggressive buyer and takes every opportunity to advance his other acquisition dreams. He or she is willing and eager to listen to a good sales presentation. Younger black customers have to see how the product will contribute to their future dreams. These customers can and will get excited about a product if the closer uses good showmanship and enthusiasm. Here you are often dealing with impulse-buyers, so the closer should use an emotional sales presentation relating to the customer's needs or family. Given these circumstances, the closer can usually go in successfully for the sale.

These clients are the types who buy from the closer because of his or her personality, not from the large company the closer represents. These customers buy because of the trust inspired by the sales closer and they will continue to be good customers if the closer does not misuse that trust.

The Hispanic Customer

This customer is totally family-oriented. The closer must involve the entire household when giving a sales presentation. The Hispanic customer is a delight to work with and he or she will buy easily if they feel the closer is being honest and understanding toward their personal situation. This customer generally will make payments on time, even if the whole family or distant relatives have to help out. This customer has a very religious background, and friendship means a great deal; he is also good with referrals, which is an asset for any closer.

Always treat this customer with respect for him and for his family, and try to create a desire to buy the product through total family participation. The Hispanic customer will go out of his way to buy if he feels the closer is working with him to get the best deal possible. The closer has to become part of the customer's family, and the customer will invite this relationship if the closer demonstrates personal concern and sincerity.

The Jewish Customer

Any sales pitch to this customer usually has to be brief. The Jewish customer generally wants a good bottom-line deal on the product (or service). This customer is generally easy to deal with if the closer shows a good price up front and refrains from a long sales presentation. This customer often shops around and probably knows something about what you are selling and therefore wants only the pertinent information. This customer is not easy to sell or control and should not be confronted with any arguments or he will probably walk out and do business elsewhere. This customer can be good for much referral business if they like you, and when he or she buys it is a good, solid sale. The closer should show professionalism and apply only low-key pressure.

The Oriental Customer

This customer should receive a slow and deliberate sales presentation. The closer should use logic and documented facts. This customer is intelligent and a careful buyer. He or she is not the easiest person to get excited over a product. This customer is business-oriented in most respects. The more extroverted closer will find it hard to establish an immediate close relationship with this client. The Oriental customer thinks in hard line basic realities. The closer must show sincerity, honesty, and good common sense to relate well to this customer. The Oriental customer will buy — and buy big — if and when they are convinced about the value of a product.

The Professions And Businesses of Customers

This analysis of customers will show the general thinking patterns and habits unique to each one's business life. The general advice given below will help the closer make a more effective sales presentation when dealing with customers in these categories.

Accountants

They are naturally skeptical and conservative in their thinking. They have to study all the financial aspects about a product (or service) before buying. They have to display their accounting and financial background even if they do not understand the subject being discussed.

Accountants can often be closed using a negative presentation, with steady intimidating pressure applied. The closer should always let the accountant think he is in control. This customer will more times than not trap himself.

*   *   *   *   *   *   *

Airline Pilots

They fall into the categories of conservative and aggressive. Pilots are decision makers and individual-minded with a high degree of professional pride. They are good-natured, personable and open-minded, as well as logical and optimistic.

They tend to be happy-go-lucky in outlook. They are big buyers all the way. They can be closed by building up their egos and showing respect for their profession. An enthusiastic sales presentation is a must to get them properly motivated.

*   *   *   *   *   *   *

Artists

They are often unfocused and have to be brought down to reality. They tend to see things in a different light than the average customer. They can be both optimistic and pessimistic in their outlooks, depending on their moods. They tend to drift in their trains of thought, viewing your product (or service) in a casual manner.

They can be closed by demonstrating the advantages of owning the product (or service). Steady, clear, hard-hitting pressure is often needed in your presentation to insure that they really understand your pitch.

*   *   *   *   *   *   *

Bankers

They are conservative and generally skeptical. They are thinkers and analyzers, not excitable buyers. They will study and pick a product apart with a pompous air of supremacy. They don't like pressure and want everything in a presentation to be organized.

They can be closed by a negative sales presentation if it is given with a confident air of professionalism. Low-key pressure can be successfully used with a casual and well thought-out close.

* * * * * * *

Barbers-Stylists

They are independent and know how to make a decision; they generally see things with some optimism and a creative mind. They are artists to a degree and will have similar characteristics, except that they are more logical in their thinking.

They can be closed with a solid, logical, positive sales presentation. The keys are enthusiasm and ownership advantage. The closer needs to work on the stylists' egos.

* * * * * * *

Bartenders and Club Owners

They are independent thinkers who know how to make a decision. They are good buyers and will often make quick buying decisions. Because of their independent streak they know what they want and go after it. They are personable, understanding, and self-motivated. They are good for referrals.

They can be closed by using a positive, enthusiastic sales presentation showing plenty of excitement.

* * * * * * *

Coaches

They can make a buying decision, but they have to be led. They tend to sometimes be out of place when not around the team, where they are leaders. They are not as self-motivated as you might expect. They want a good deal and don't worry too much about details.

They can best be closed by working on their ego and pride. A positive pressure presentation should be used. The closer should attempt to get involved in discussing the coaches' sports field. You should try to get friendly and comfortable with this customer before putting on the close.

* * * * * * *

Computer Industry

They are not excitable and must be guided into a buying decision. They are number crunching customers and tend to look into too many unimportant details. Have all your facts and figures handy and you can dazzle them with information most other customers couldn't care less about. They are generally not self-motivators nor are they great conversationalists. Don't try to be too personable or you may make them feel inadequate and hurt your close.

They can usually be sold with a pressure close using steady intimidation. They often have to be pushed into the sale. To accomplish this, the closer should always first build their confidence up and try to make them feel special, prior to closing.

*   *   *   *   *   *   *

Construction Industry

They are money-oriented and will buy after being shown the advantages of the product. They are a positive and quick decision-making group. They will not go into great detail over a product, but want to be sure it is sound. They are personable and will take a chance. Construction industry employees are serious buyers all the way.

They can be closed by showing logical financial advantage and excitement concerning the product. A positive aggressive sales presentation should be used. The closer should allow this customer to have some control. They respond especially well when you focus on the ownership benefits of your product (or service).

*   *   *   *   *   *   *

Dentists

They do not have the same self-centered air of importance that most physicians have, but they are still thinkers and analyzers, not impulse buyers. They want logic and facts concerning the presentation and the product. They are independent and will make a decision if sold in a professional manner.

They can be closed with facts and a very personable sales presentation. They are also in a people business and can relate well to the closer if the closer can open him up. Enthusiasm and manners are a must to close this type of a professional client.

*   *   *   *   *   *   *

Electricians, Carpenters, Plumbers, etc.

They are buyers, and they will react on impulse if excited about a product. They work hard, make good money and want to spend it. They are very open-minded and will ask only basic buying questions. They are not usually detail people; they just want the satisfaction of knowing they got a good deal. They will buy if shown basic logic. They are good referral customers.

They can be closed with a positive, enthusiastic sales presentation. Use friendship and some leadership when selling them. Showmanship will also contribute to closing this sale.

*   *   *   *   *   *   *

Engineers

They are obviously numbers people. They want to examine and analyze everything. They are careful thinkers and to some degree procrastinators. They are not impulse buyers and are difficult to motivate. They think logically and reason with little emotion.

They can be closed by a negative presentation using logic and facts. They have to think they are in control and like to direct the conversation, especially into areas where they have expertise. They will often trap themselves, if given enough time and maneuvered properly by the closer.

*   *   *   *   *   *   *

Entertainers

They can be sold if you can separate them from their egos. They are optimistic and aggressive. They can be very independent and stubborn in their decision-making, but are easily persuaded to buy if motivated. They are extremely moody and need some leadership. Work gently on their egos.

They can best be closed with a sales presentation that is full of excitement and enthusiasm. The closer should go out of his way to make this customer feel important and respected, something the customer is very used to and, in most cases, comes to expect.

*   *   *   *   *   *   *

Entrepreneurs

They can lead the closer through the sales presentation if you aren't careful. They are self-motivated, aggressive and optimistic. They are open-minded and very quick in their thinking. They can and will make a buying decision on the spot. These people know how to handle themselves and know what they like, so a soft-sell is a must.

They can be closed by showing admiration and respect for their successes. The closer should give a positive, enthusiastic sales presentation while all the time working on their egos. Don't start boring these customers or you will quickly be history, as they'll move on to another source for your product (or service). Remember that they are also great at sales or they wouldn't be successful entrepreneurs — so don't ever underestimate them.

*   *   *   *   *   *   *

Executives

Believe it or not, these people often need leadership when buying for themselves. They are self-motivated and optimistic but need some gentle guidance. They want a good deal and like to think they made the decision themselves concerning a product they are buying. They can be sold all the way if their egos are properly massaged.

The closer should show professionalism and logic, treating the executive as if he were the owner of his company instead of just a pencil-pushing manager. Work on this customer's ego and ability to make a decision — and he will make one concerning your product (or service).

*   *   *   *   *   *   *

Factory Workers

They want security for themselves and their families. They are money-conscious and skeptical. They think everyone is out to get their hard-earned money. They are generally thinking about price so appeal to them on this level. They need to see proof of any claims about the product.

The closer must not be too pushy because this customer is quite suspicious of salespeople. Focus on affordability, guarantees, and financing terms. No matter how they are dressed or sound, maintain respect for this customer and never let him perceive you are talking down to him or you'll lose the sale. They are very used to having this happen and obviously don't like it. Treat them right and they'll buy.

*   *   *   *   *   *   *

Farmers

They are conservative in their thinking and are obviously fiercely independent. They can make a decision when they want to or are motivated to. They are good listeners and usually open-minded. They are personable, trusting and understanding, and will give anyone the benefit of the doubt.

Farmers can be closed by using logic, friendliness and a positive, enthusiastic sales presentation. They will use common sense more than emotion. They will often buy big if they believe in the closer.

*　　*　　*　　*　　*　　*　　*

Firemen

They are personable and understanding. They have open minds but are cautious and security-oriented. They are independent in their thinking and can make quick buying decisions. They generally want a good deal and are excellent on referrals. They are buyers all the way.

They can best be closed by showing respect for their job. The closer should also present the product with enthusiasm, emphasizing the advantages of ownership.

The closer should eagerly listen to any fire stories that the customer can be persuaded to talk about.

*　　*　　*　　*　　*　　*　　*

Government Workers

They need leadership and are not self-motivated. They can get excited and enthused if shown the advantages of the product (or service). They are security-minded, but can be turned into impulse buyers. They are obviously bureaucratic in thinking and have to be pushed into buying.

They can often be closed by using pressure in a low-key presentation. They can also be successfully intimidated into buying. The closer can use enthusiasm to a great extent, but should always be pushing toward a final, quick close — before they have a chance to change their indecisive minds.

*　　*　　*　　*　　*　　*　　*

Judges

They are conservative and slow in their decision-making. They are, needless to say, careful buyers. They have an optimistic attitude and a gentlemanly air about themselves which you should play up to. They work with logic and reason and cannot be pressured. They are independent in their ways and open-minded.

They can be closed by showing a great deal of respect for their profession. They should be given a positive, enthusiastic, honest sales presentation. The closer should show professionalism and courtesy at all times. Judges have seen it all in their careers and are good at spotting phonies. Don't try to oversell this razor sharp consumer.

Lawyers

They tend to have a know-it-all attitude about every subject under discussion. They are aggressive and open-minded. They are independent and think with optimism. They will make a decision when necessary but have to be enthused, motivated and led.

They can be closed by working on their egos and carefully building them up. The closer can use positive pressure and should show professionalism so the buyer doesn't think he is simply another fast-talking "salesman".

Be careful with your presentation as the slick lawyer will often try to catch you in a white lie or exaggeration.

*   *   *   *   *   *   *

Managers, Administrators

Believe it or not, they often have to be led into a decision. They are personable but feel out-of-place when not in their own environment. They are not very open-minded but can be gently pressured into a sale. They are not overly optimistic, but can be motivated to buy sooner than they wish if you carefully work on their egos.

They can be closed by showing respect for their job and the high responsibility they hold. Massage their egos and show parallels between your job and theirs, but always acknowledge that their job must be much more complex. Use pressure and bring up the fact that decision-making must be a major part of their responsibility, so it must be more easy for them to make buying decisions than for the average customer.

*   *   *   *   *   *   *

Mechanics

They are hard workers who also play hard. They want improvements to their lifestyles and security for their families. They are open-minded when it comes to a good deal. They will buy if convinced of the product's (or service's) quality. They are personable and trusting to some degree.

They can be closed by giving an enthusiastic and exciting sales presentation. They need to be shown emotion more than logic in most cases. They will buy all the way if they are motivated and believe in the advantages you have presented. They can be pressured in a positive, low- key manner.

*   *   *   *   *   *   *

Military Personnel, Officers

They always have to think they are in control and making the decision. They are open-minded when they think they are respected and that they're the center of attention. They can make a quick decision, and often will. They can be motivated easily when the ego is played upon because they are sold on themselves and their own leadership abilities.

They can be closed by making them feel they have elicited more information from you than other people have. Let them feel they are on the inside concerning the sale. Let them trap themselves and convince themselves to buy because of their own knowledge about the product.

*   *   *   *   *   *   *

Military Personnel, Enlisted

They are buyers all the way. They can become interested and excited about your product with little effort. They are completely optimistic and have a lot of faith in their future. They are looking for a good deal and will show you a lot of trust. They can be effectively pressured, and do require a bit of leadership and manipulation.

Enlisted men can be closed if you give them an enthusiastic sales presentation. Use a great deal of positive excitement. Show this customer respect and friendliness in your presentation. The closer should always try to build this customer up in front of his family.

*   *   *   *   *   *   *

Ministers, Preachers, Priests, Rabbis, etc.

They all seem to want a super-discount or to be treated specially because of their obvious contribution to society. They can be pressured into buying, but have a tendency to cancel. They can be led and motivated easily. They think optimistically and are usually personable because of their vocation and experience with people.

They can be closed with gentle pressure and a little intimidation. They can be trapped easily with a positive sales presentation. With this customer the closer can be aggressive, as long as you are also respectful of their honorable profession.

These customers expect they will not be lied to and they are sophisticated when it comes to judging people. Be straight with these influential customers and they will come back to you many times over.

*   *   *   *   *   *   *

Nurses

These people are proud of their profession and will make a decision if they are even slightly motivated. They are aggressive and more likely to think about most products (or services) with optimism than with pessimism. They are open-minded and personable and react best to a friendly sales presentation.

They can be closed by using a positive, upbeat approach. The closer has to use enthusiasm and show respect for this profession. The closer can use logic, but emotions work far better.

*   *   *   *   *   *   *

Physicians

They truly imagine themselves to be prima donnas, standing on their golden pedestals. They behave with a conservative air and are obviously highly intelligent, though they demonstrate it quietly. They are thinkers, and will buy eventually — if shown logic and the financial advantages of the product (or service).

The closer can sell almost every doctor if he shows he is a professional and handles himself in a respectable manner. The closer should work on ego, calling this customer "Doctor" and not "Doc." He also must show control and not be overly impressed by people's titles.

Doctors have the well-deserved reputation of being terrible businessmen. It is true. They make their money too easily and therefore often don't know how to hold onto it. They've been taken many times before and you must be sure to be above board in your dealings and in your presentation, or else they will equate you in the same category as the many dishonest sales people they've had problems with in the past.

*   *   *   *   *   *   *

Policemen, Detectives

They think in a skeptical manner and try to find fault in most sales presentations and products. They are personable if there is a common factor to talk about. They are proud of their profession and will show it.

Policemen can be good customers if some kind of common bond or friendship is established. They like to do business with people that have a high respect for their profession, so show it.

They can best be closed by working on their egos. The closer should listen to police stories and show tremendous respect. An enthusiastic, exciting sales presentation should be used. Friendliness works well with this type of customer, as he can not be too friendly on his job.

*   *   *   *   *   *   *

Professors

These are usually very conservative customers. Professors are most definitely thinkers. They are "mull-it-over" customers. They are not excitable, and are very low-keyed. They will often ask questions about the product (or service) that no one else would ever think about.

They can be closed by showing respect, and by building up their egos. They should be complimented on their questions about your product (or service), no matter how far-out they may be. The closer should try to learn something from these customers (or at least make the customers think they are). Professors should always be shown a positive, enthusiastic sales presentation.

*   *   *   *   *   *   *

Retired

They are worried and concerned about their futures. They are usually on a limited income, and will be ultra-conservative buyers. They are slow in their acquisition habits and in their decision making policies. They will not jump into anything. They will be fairly passive to most enthusiastic, aggressive sales presentations.

Surprisingly, they can be closed by giving an exciting and enthusiastic sales presentation at first, just to get their full attention, then by showing logic and the soft sell, the closer can develop the emotions and spirit in this customer. The closer should attempt to inspire trust, sincerity and understanding with his retired potential buyers. These customers are excellent for referrals because they often live in communities with many other retired people who will especially rely on recommendations of their friends.

Salesmen

Believe it or not, they can be sold just about anything. They are generally aggressive and independent people. They are positive thinkers and will make an impulse decision when buying. They are motivated and optimistic — always looking for a good deal and thinking that they will find one.

They can best be closed by making them feel they know the inside story concerning the product. The closer needs to carefully build up their egos and show enthusiasm and respect for their sales knowledge and the fact that they are also in the business of selling. The closer should first gently build up the salesman and then let him trap himself. Intimidation and pressure will usually not work because they use the same bag of tricks and will know exactly what you are up to.

*   *   *   *   *   *   *

School Teachers

They are used to talking and will show that in their conversation with you. They generally think in a conservative manner and will not jump into something until they really understand it. They are low-keyed and not highly self-motivated. They are not overly optimistic in their thinking.

They can be closed by showing respect for their profession, and it helps to get them talking about their favorite student stories. They can often be pressured into a buying situation. The closer should work on ego while giving a positive, low-key, highly credible presentation.

*   *   *   *   *   *   *

Small Business Men

They will make a quick decision and stand by it. They are aggressive, self-motivated, optimistic thinkers.

When it come to referrals, they are so-so. This customer understands your problem. He is often running his own company and doing much of the sales as well.

To close these customers all you need is a very positive, logical sales presentation. The closer should show plenty of enthusiasm and excitement. Be professional, work on this customer's ego and show respect for his accomplishments. Use a little showmanship, but keep in mind that this customer is usually razor sharp and often sales-oriented himself.

*   *   *   *   *   *   *

There are many professions not mentioned here, but the ideas are basic. Customers are individuals and must be approached as such. The master closer has to deal with each of his customers on an individual level. He must alter the presentation according to his observations about their needs. The more he understands what their needs are, the better he will be able to close them. The best closers customize each pitch to the identifiable preferences of his clients. The secret is to properly analyze them before saying too much. There are no short cuts in successful selling, so don't expect to cut corners if you want to be the best.

Facts You Should Know About Customers

This list contains important insights and observations concerning customers. It will enable closers to better understand all buyers, even if they aren't sure what category the customer falls into.

1. If a closer asks a customer directly if he can afford the product (or service), the customer will automatically say yes. Even if the client is completely broke, he will lie to the closer because no man will admit to a perfect stranger that his finances are in such bad shape. Always remember: Customer are generally notorious liars.

2. When working with couples, no matter how strong a family leader the man appears to be, the wife is usually the most important one to convince:
a) The wife, in many families, handles the finances.
b) The wife will often have an extra job, along with being the homemaker and mother.
c) The wife will be the one who worries most about the sale.
d) The wife can become more enthusiastic about the product, helping the closer make the sale.
e) The wife can suggest shopping around first, thus losing the sale for the closer.
f) The wife can handle the children, keeping them quiet during your sales presentation.
g) The wife can, and does, handle the husband.

3. People are followers, in most cases. Customers are like sheep: they want to be led and have someone else do the thinking for them.

4. The customer always wants something for nothing. He is, in most cases, a good, healthy mooch. He is looking for the best price on the product, and has a grain of the free-loader in him. This is a fact that every closer must be aware of and appeal to.

5. People like to spend money. They really want to buy new things for themselves or their families. This is true of all customers because buying something new makes them feel good. We are truly a consumer society.

6. Most people like to feel that they make the buying decision themselves, without being pressured by the salesman. This is why closers do so well: they can lead a customer into a sale without the customer ever knowing it was the closer's idea in the first place.

7. Don't dare underestimate the customer for one second. He has a brain, and he can use it. The old saying, "Simple men believe everything they hear; and smart men want proof," is not an accurate rule of thumb. All customers are thinkers; they know more than you believe they do.

8. If the closer goes out of his way to make the customer feel important and appreciated, that customer will usually buy something. The customer wants someone to show genuine interest in him.

9. Customers want a good deal on a product, they don't want to be taken for a ride. Customers generally will buy with optimism, but don't try to hoodwink them, you can only get away with fooling them once.

10. The customers who are thinkers (and likely buyers) can sometimes be easily spotted. This list highlights some general give-aways to customer attitudes:

a) A pipe-smoker often equals a thinker and buyer.
b) White socks, not worn as sportswear, often equals a thinker and buyer.
c) Crew-cut hair sometimes equals a thinker and buyer.
d) A camera carrier often equals buyer.
e) Loud or flashy clothes usually equals buyer.
f) Cigar smokers generally equal buyer.
g) Cowboy boots often equal buyer.

11. The master closer has to believe in his own heart that people are more likely than not — good. There is good in everyone and it is the closer's job to find it. He must bring it out, and use it toward getting the sale. Everybody — no matter who they are — loves something. The closer should try to find the love in his customer and develop it into a positive selling tool.

*   *   *   *   *   *   *

In summing up customers, this one thought will suffice: People are distinctly themselves; they have their individual likes and dislikes, good points and bad. To really get to know a person, the closer has to get him away from others, away from all outside influences. When the closer is alone with a customer, that person's true self appears. This is when the closer can get to know and best relate to that individual. When someone is alone with the closer, there is less pretense and faking. Most sales defenses are relaxed and the parties are able to converse as equals. If the closer is doing his job correctly, both he and the client should come to a fair consensus and conclude a deal.

A sales presentation is only as good as the closer's attitude about himself, his product, and most important — his customer. This all relates to knowing and understanding people.

Sam enjoyed telling me about customers, and one thing I knew for sure: He did know people and how to analyze them. This lesson was complete, and I was certainly impressed and eager to learn more.

THE CUSTOMERS' ATTITUDES:
Both Serious and Foolish

Chapter Four

THE CUSTOMERS' ATTITUDES:
Both Serious and Foolish

After describing the customers' characteristics Sam said it was time to learn exactly how customers think and reason. He said no one can really know what a customer is thinking every moment, but a master closer would know about 95 percent of the time and the other 5 percent of the time he could guess correctly.

With this statement as my guide, Sam began to explain customers' attitudes. The key fact is that a customer is human, with normal human needs — food, shelter and clothing. Security, love, understanding and recognition are also needs we all have.

In addition, most customers are frightened, awkward, skeptical individuals. They generally know very little about the product being presented and are afraid of being intimidated, embarrassed and pressured into buying. They've all been taken advantage of at one time or another.

They are equally afraid of missing an opportunity or overlooking a bargain. This creates a customer who has a love-hate relationship with a master closer. A master closer has to understand the customer's thoughts and motives and develop them into active, positive movement — movement that produces a sale.

Information about your customer's attitudes is vitally important, because without understanding the customer's reasoning and logic the closer cannot understand the problems and objections that arise during his sales presentation. The customer's attitudes make up the customer's personality and if those attitudes are understood, half the battle of closing the sale is won.

To understand customer attitudes we will take a look at how the customer views himself and the closer.

Customers' Personal and Secret Thoughts
About Themselves and Closers

1. Scared and Uncomfortable. The customer is basically nervous and feels out of place when he enters the buying and selling situation, especially when he is in the closer's sales office. This applies not only to the customer who is financially well off but also to the customer on a limited budget. The reason is simple: the customer doesn't know the closer so there is no initial basis for trust.

Furthermore, the customer is in the closer's territory — his sales office — which makes the customer feel even more out of place and awkward. This puts the customer in a guest position, with limited privileges and many doubts, ranging from: where the bathroom is located and whether or not he can smoke — to: is this company reputable and can I believe this "closer." The customer isn't totally himself because he isn't in familiar surroundings where he feels relaxed and more in control.

Just think back for a minute and remember all the customers who said they had to go home first before making a buying decision. This does not include the customer who just plain wasn't sold, but the customer who sincerely feels he can make a better buying decision in his own home surrounded by a familiar environment. The master closer must acknowledge this basic fact and do everything in his power to make the customer feel totally comfortable while in his sales office.

This can be accomplished through charm, personality, understanding and a sincere interest in the customer's needs. If the closer can relax the customer and make him feel comfortable this objection about going home first will never materialize.

2. The unknown presentation (pitch). The customer is always unprepared for the closer's sales presentation. Although the customer knows he's going to hear a sales pitch he doesn't know how the closer is going to present it. This unknown element makes the customer more suspicious and guarded about what he does and says. It's a great advantage for the closer to know and recognize this uneasiness and to do everything possible to make the customer comfortable and at ease. If the closer does not understand this fact he will think the customer is stand-offish, or make some other misjudgment. The closer can accomplish a great deal if he will only see himself through the customer's eyes, understanding their viewpoint during the sales presentation.

3. The lead shield. The closer *must* keep in mind that the customer does not want to ever feel like he was pressured or tricked into buying a product (or service).

The customer wants to believe that he is in control of the buying decision, if there is to be one, and also wants to have the last word, keeping his self-respect and integrity intact. The closer must remember that the customer has been telling himself and his family he will not make a buying decision the same day the product (or service) is presented to him. This attitude makes the customer feel he has control and won't be trapped into buying. To maintain this attitude the customer builds up a lead shield around himself to resist all sales temptations presented by the closer. The customer has been telling his family and himself all the way to the sales office the many reasons a decision should not be made that day. And I assure you the customer has every intention of keeping that commitment. The customer and his family can come up with some fantastic stories and excuses for not buying, and I mean some real academy award material.

The master closer who understands that lead shield can destroy any excuse with logic and charm, sprinkled with a little enthusiasm.

4. The white hat. The customer sees himself as the good guy *all the way. He* is the one who is going to make a decision to buy or not to buy, and *he* has the money to execute that decision. *He* is the one who can make the closer his commission — or deny it to him. This type of customer thinks he is in complete control, wearing his white hat and pulling all the strings. (He's still scared and uncomfortable, but we are not talking about reality yet.) This type of customer thinks he knows where he stands against the bad guy (closer) and expects the closer to pull some sneaky sales trick or hide the truth.

He is playing up his good guy role, determined, ready and waiting. The customer feels if he himself stretches the truth or misleads the closer in some way it's all fine and fair. The customer's reasoning is "Let the buyer beware." The customer wears the white hat and the closer wears the black hat, as far as this buyer is concerned.

This is something every sales closer in the world should know and accept. If a closer doesn't realize that some customers see themselves in this manner he will never have a chance to "break the ice" with buyers of this mentality, eventually convincing them that closers can sometimes wear the white hat. This is accomplished through a closer's personality, understanding and charm.

5. His creed is greed — the customer is greedy. By "greedy" I don't mean the customer is rude or dishonest, but that he wants to use his buying power to its fullest advantage in any sales situation. He wants the best deal possible and will use every trick he knows to reach that objective. The customer will try to outmaneuver a closer through a hard luck story or a line like "I can get a better deal at some other place. Why should I spend more with your company?".

That is wonderful for the master closer — the more greed in a customer the harder he will bite. A customer will trap himself every time if greed is his creed. A master closer can always come up with a convincing bottom line close when faced with this attitude. All he has to do is play around with his numbers.

Now we're going to examine how customers scheme and connive against their perceived opponents — the closers. This is a truism if there ever was one. Customers have that basic feeling of "I'm going to be taken," so they prepare for it and set a game plan. There are even shopping classes that teach customers how not to be intimidated or trapped by sales closers.

How Customers Scheme Against the Closer

1. The customer game plan. The customers — husband and wife with family — will all have their speeches and parts down pat before meeting a closer. They often will have all their excuses outlined and perfected well before any objection is needed in the sales presentation. (The closer must realize this and relax shoppers' defensive feelings so they will be attentive and open-minded. Otherwise they will never pay close attention to your sales presentation.)

The customers will say, "We don't have that much money" or "Our kids have to look at it before we decide," batting it back and forth between each other, just like the good guy, bad guy approach many sales people use in selling. The husband and wife will play off each other until the closer finally hears one of them say, "We might buy if you would do this or that," making the customers feel that they will get a better deal by working on the closer together and wearing him down.

The closer should go along with this slick, customer game plan because any sale is usually better than no sale at all, and the master closer can easily recognize this strategy and respond appropriately. Let them have a small break in price so they believe their little game worked and they will be eating out of your hand.

2. Customers won't tell. The customer will never tell the closer the truth about how much money he has or doesn't have. He will not volunteer any information to the closer that will make the sale easier, and the customer will lie to the closer in a second if he feels the closer is about to set up a trap or intimidate him into buying. The customer will also lie about most other things they tell you, so be careful. Remember, the customer has a game plan and is suspicious of his enemy, the closer. This suspicion will continue until you manage to break-the-ice.

3. Customer and friends (customers feel safer with friends). The customer will arrive at the sales office with a friend or another couple and try to use this third party as the "bad guy" who won't let him make a buying decision that day. The customer will rely on this third party to speak negatively and give the customer his way out. The customer may also use the telephone to call his father, brother or lawyer, or whoever, as a typical, transparent, third party excuse.

But don't worry, it's all been planned and as we will see later it's really no big problem. The customer, with all due respect, is just trying to assert himself, and the master closer knows this.

4. Comparison customers. The customer will be simply shopping around, but won't tell the closer he just wants to see what the closer's product (or service) is and compare it with a similar product he has pretty much made his mind up to buy. This type of customer usually wants the full sales presentation from the closer and nothing less will do. So take a deep breath and give him your rap.

5. Discount customer. The customer will tell you he wants a discount for paying cash or no deal. The customer knows you have spent valuable time with him and to get a sale you just might go for a take-it-or-leave-it cash deal. So what; let the customer play his game, the closer is the one who wins in the end by getting the sale.

In looking at some of the schemes customers use it's an indisputable fact that they usually have a made-up story arranged to protect themselves and their money. The closer has to be aware of this because every customer has their own individual approach to this type of chiseling negotiation.

At this point we are going to examine the customer's attitudes about himself, which he unknowingly communicates to the closer. We will see how a master closer can detect attitude give-aways by simply observing the customer and his environment. This is not to be misunderstood as pre-qualifying the customer, but is merely a study of the customer through "telltale" signs that he himself lets slip.

Recognizing Customer Attitude Give-Aways

The master closer knows there are two basic ways to observe the customer: The first is for the closer to be selling a product (or service) in the customer's home or office (in-home sales); the second way of observing is for the customer to be in the closer's territory (on-site sales). From these two vantage points we will study the customer, paying attention to his many give-away attitudes.

1. In-home observation. If a closer is selling books, vacuum cleaners, home improvements or similar products, he will often be in the home of the customer. In that situation the closer will have an open book on the customer's life. Simply by looking around the closer can know the life style of the customer, his attitudes about himself and his family, and nearly anything one would like to know about this buyer. So how in the world can a closer miss a sale?

In a home the closer can observe if the customer is religious or if he is poor or rich. The closer can see the customer's neighborhood, if the drapes in his home are clean or dirty, his furniture, the floors, wall pictures, cars — everything. The closer can tell if the customer has pride in his home or not. The closer can write a book about the customer without having heard a word! With that kind of information at hand the closer will be able to target his presentation of the product or service he is selling.

I've seen many sales missed because the salesman didn't look around and make mental notes of the customer's environment. Such information gives the closer a complete picture of the customer's attitudes. There is no excuse for a lost sale with such a wealth of information at one's disposal.

2. On-site observation. This is much more complicated and requires the closer to use every little bit of information the customer brings with him. It is not like the in-home attitude observation, where everything is spelled out for the closer. The best way to begin on-site observation and connect it with a customer's attitude is to analyze those easy to spot external details about your potential buyer.

(a) Car observation. Always try to see what kind of car the customer drove up in. This is the fastest and best way to get a quick hint about the customer's attitude. You will be surprised at how much you can tell about someone by their car. If it's an old model that looks run down don't pre-qualify; examine the tires and see if they are new or safe. If they are new there is a good chance the customer simply likes that old car or uses it on errands and his other car is at home. But if you look at an old car whose tires are bald and falling apart, there is a good possibility this customer is hurting financially. Think, what kind of customer would risk his family's lives on unsafe tires if he had the money to replace them? With that information the closer knows what approaches not to use with the customer and he hasn't even talked to him yet. This guy is obviously broke, a bad credit risk, looking for the best price, and not worth spending too much time with, especially if there is a room full of other "live" customers waiting for you. (Note: if you didn't see the customer's car, you can politely ask where he parked; he'll tell you. Then you can excuse yourself for a moment and examine it before beginning your presentation.)

(b) Financial appearance. If the customer drives up in a new car, notice the model, size of his family, the age of the customer and how he is dressed. Then the closer can evaluate what his car payments are and get a pretty good picture of the customer's financial situation before even knowing what kind of business the customer is in. (Now everything will fall into place when the closer talks to the customer and finds out more information, but at least the closer has a fairly sound idea of the customer's attitude through this quick and easy observation.)

(c) Clothes and appearance. When the customer first meets you, notice his fingernails, hair, his general appearance and his wife's and children's clothes, as well. Every little thing that the closer observes tells him something important about the customer, and I mean everything. Shoes, rings, watches and jewelry are always good give-aways. The closer shouldn't miss one item because without all this information how in the world can he know how to best begin a sales presentation geared to this particular customer? If a closer has the wrong presentation for the customer, the sale is lost and so is his time.

(d) Wise guy laugh. If a customer laughs a lot and does silly things, or acts like a smart aleck, the closer shouldn't think that he has a problem customer. It simply means the potential buyer is frightened. He is nervous, and nothing more. I've seen many sales lost because the closer sees his customer laughing and acting like everything was a big joke, when in reality the customer just needs some warmth and friendliness from the closer, so he can relax a little and calm down. (The customer needs to know that the closer is a friend and not someone who is going to try to manipulate and intimidate him.) No closer should misjudge this scenario and believe the customer is a wise guy; the customer, in nearly all cases, is not.

(e) Customer poise. Always notice the customer's manners, his etiquette, how he controls his children and how his wife behaves. By observing these things the closer can see who runs the family, who gives the orders, and who controls the money. The closer can tell a great many things by how a man controls himself and his family. The closer should observe the customer's vocabulary, which will indicate his educational background. All this can be noticed without really getting into any detail with the customer. At this point the closer can tell the customer what he wants to about himself and his product (or service), but the customer (if observed properly) is an open book. And yet sales are still lost. It's unbelievable.

(f) **Home location and where he comes from.** Be observant about where the customer comes from, where he now lives, whether it is a big city, farm country, north, south, the west coast. Everything will tell the closer something about the customer's financial status and attitude. Always keep in mind that the closer shouldn't generalize and believe that every customer from one area thinks the same way, but there are common attitudes that do go with different geographic areas. The closer should prepare and direct his sales presentation with those attitudes in mind.

(g) **Wait, watch and learn.** If a closer watches the customer for a short while, the customer will tell all. The closer can see if the customer has a limp or has something physically wrong with him. He can tell whether the customer is nervous, by noticing if he goes to the restroom too often. He can see if the customer has an outgoing personality, and makes friends easily, or if the customer is introverted. The closer should be patient and just observe, use logic, and be alert. By noticing details the closer can know his customer before a word is spoken.

Even with the wealth of information that is available, the closer should never pre-judge or pre-qualify any customer. But a closer can make logical and basic assumptions about the customer before ever being introduced by waiting, watching and learning. This is a professional process the master closer must use because the attitude of the customer *is* the customer.

"Hot Tips" To Remember About Customers

1. The customer will generally not buy a product (or service) if his legs are tightly crossed or if he's sitting and fidgeting nervously in a chair or is in some other uncomfortable or unrelaxed position. The customer usually has to have both feet on the floor when sitting in the closer's office, and has to have an alert posture to make a buying decision. Body language tells a lot about attitude, and a closer must be aware of this kind of non-verbal communication.

2. A closer can usually tell if a customer is lying from some of the following tell-tale signs:

(a) Dryness of the mouth.

(b) Sudden perspiration on the brow, sweating hands.

(c) Nervous movements, shuffling of the feet, twitching of an eye.

(d) The inability to look the closer straight in the eye for very long, looking down when talking, looking ashamed and uncomfortable.

(e) The customer will stumble on his words and use too many "uhs" or ums," because he's not sure of himself.

(f) The customer will start licking his lips more often.

(g) The customer's voice will change to a more deliberate and practiced soft tone.

(h) The customer's voice will embarrassingly crack in the middle of words.

3. A customer wants to be proud of his purchase, he wants to feel good about it so he can brag to friends and feel comfortable with it.

4. All customers have been burned on products before and they expect to be burned again so their guard is always up at the first meeting.

5. Customers want to be treated as if they're special. It's up to the closer to make them feel as if they are being treated with special respect so they can relax and get in the mood to buy.

6. The customer has a weakness somewhere and he knows it, so in this area the customer will be over-protective. The closer has got to search for and find this weak point.

7. The closer should observe a customer and all his actions and then try to be a friend to the buyer before closing him. If you convince your customer you really like him, you're halfway there.

8. Take mental notes and listen to everything the customer says. *Don't pre- qualify,* but *do analyze.*

9. If a customer can develop a positive attitude toward the closer, it really doesn't matter what product is being sold; the customer will usually buy with enthusiasm.

10. The customer's actions can be influenced by the closer's actions, but the customer's attitude can only be effectively shaped by the closer's persuasiveness and likeability.

This completed my lesson on customer attitudes. While smiling, Sam told me to always keep in mind that when a closer goes to buy something, *he* becomes the customer. That gave me something to think about.

Sam then said, "A closer should always remember: Customers are people with their families' interests at heart. The closer should accept and respect this fact. While the customer may be the closer's opponent, he is also the closer's way of life."

Chapter Five

PSYCHOLOGICAL MANIPULATION:
Mind Game Warfare

- Closing By Psychological Manipulation:
  The Basic Foundation For All Sales Closing

- A. How the Closer Manipulates the Customer To
  Think As He Wants

- B. Customers' Different Listening Levels

- C. Why A Customer Won't Buy

- D. The Master Closer and His Rules

- E. The Weapon Called Reverse Psychology

- F. Customers and Money

- G. Thirty-Five Tactics For Psychological Manipulation
  (The Master Closer's Mind Game List)

Chapter Five

PSYCHOLOGICAL MANIPULATION:
Mind Game Warfare

By the later part of July sales at Green Vista Estates were going out of this world. Every single goal the Duron Corporation had set for the start of the selling season was being surpassed by the master closers.

Green Vista Estates was developing into one of the most exclusive private resorts in the country, and I was more than proud to be a small part of it.

Every once in a while "Big Bill" would come out to the parking area and ask me what I thought about the real estate development and selling industry. I would always tell him that I thought it was unbelievable and I liked everything about it. That seemed to make "Big Bill" happy because he would tell me that I wouldn't be parking cars forever and that I could go a long way in the company. This made me feel pretty good, especially coming from "Big Bill." (He was never known for his compliments.)

Anyway, all I really wanted to do was get back with Sam Johnson and learn more about sales closing and master closers. Sam was still at the guard house, directing traffic and giving out customer information.

By this time Sam and I had become very good friends, and he knew that now, more than ever, I wanted to see what the inscription on the inside of his ring said. Sam had asked me many times in our conversations if I could guess what was written inside the gold ring, but despite all the information I had learned so far about closing I really didn't have any idea. He said I would just have to wait a little while longer, until my sales closing lessons were over before he would let me read the ring's message — the secret inscription that would make anyone who practiced it a top master closer.

Sam said my next lesson would be on the psychological warfare used in actual closing situations to get the sale.

So far we had studied the closer and the customer separately. Now it was time to get the two opponents together and analyze typical sales scenarios. Sam said "closing psychology" was the most important weapon a master closer had in his sales arsenal. He said that to understand the "mind game phenomena" the closer had to know certain closing rules and also must know how to manipulate the customer. Sam stressed that from this point on, we would be getting into the more advanced techniques of the fine art of closing the sale.

Closing By Psychological Manipulation:
The Basic Foundation for All Sales Closings

Here we will be getting into the hardcore subject of "mind game warfare," or "psychological manipulation," and how it is used by the master closer. This is the foundation for all sales closings and involves the techniques the closer uses to sell his customer one on one, eyeball to eyeball.

The master closer has to know everything that goes on around him and his customer that could interfere with or help a sale. The closer should be aware of and avoid any distracting factors that might catch the attention of the customer: another sales presentation going on in the same area, loud noises such as traffic, music, or other customers talking. *The closer and his customer should be the only important interaction that takes place in the closing area!* The customer has to concentrate on the closer's voice and actions, and the closer must pay strict attention to every word the customer says. One missed word or sentence could lose a sale. (The closer has to have maximum control of the customer in every situation.)

Psychological manipulation is simply a head game the closer plays with his customer. But the closer has to have control before this process is effective. By using psychological manipulation the closer can examine and analyze a customer and determine exactly what tactics are necessary to get a sale. The closer can also guide the customer's thinking so he will be more open-minded and receptive to any sales presentation.

In short, the master closer can actually lead the customer to think as he wants. This can be accomplished by mastering the following techniques. These will assist in setting up the customer so he is attentive while observing the closer's sales presentation.

Before we start there is one rule a closer should keep in mind: A customer can't be properly conditioned unless he wants to be and the only way he will want to be is if he first believes in the master closer.

How the Closer Manipulates the Customer
to Think as He Wants

1. Tell about you. Tell the customer about yourself. Explain to him that you are a family man, or just engaged, etc., where you are from originally, and something about your life. This makes the customer more relaxed, and he will feel some obligation to tell you about himself.

The customer won't listen to you if he thinks you're a mystery man or just another salesman with a commission in mind. A customer wants to be appreciated and liked. He wants to feel like he is part of an inner circle of your friends. The customer has to trust you from the start, and that can be accomplished by sharing a little of your life story with him. But don't bore him with details. The customer will feel this sharing is something special, and that you think enough of him to reveal your personal side.

2. Ask the customer about himself. The closer should ask the customer questions: what type of business he's in, about his family, about his home — if he has any pets, everything. (Note: The closer should do this sincerely, without sounding nosey.) The closer will get all the answers he wants if he shows genuine concern, understanding, and appreciation for the customer. But if the closer shows the slightest hint of an "I don't really care" attitude, all of the conversation will be wasted. The customer can spot insincerity in less than one-thousandth of a second, and this is something the closer should never forget.

When the closer is asking the customer questions, he had better involve the whole family. Don't leave anyone in the customer's party out, because the person who was left out of the conversation will be the one who tries to kill the sale, every time.

3. Common bond subject. When the closer first meets a customer, he should find some kind of common bond, such as kids, business news, educational or religious background, sports, an illness in the family, etc. Just about any subject will do. But the closer has to set this common bond early in the sales presentation. It not only relaxes the customer, but puts the product (or service) being sold in a less prominent position. This allows the customer to lower his guard somewhat because he isn't as defensive talking about a subject that doesn't relate to making a buying decision. This common bond will be a springboard for the closer later in the sales presentation, and a good ice-breaking technique between the customer and the closer since both parties can relate to the subject in common. The closer should always use this technique to the fullest extent.

4. Don't ignore the wife. In talking to a customer team (husband and wife) if you say five thousand words to the husband, you'd better say five thousand and one words to the wife. The wife is the most important part of a husband and wife team. What man wouldn't buy something if his wife seriously wanted it?

The closer can even go as far as talking *only* to the wife, not saying a word to the husband. This sounds ridiculous, but it's true. No man would let a stranger talk to his wife and not listen closely to every word being said. Even if the husband looks uninterested, believe me, he's listening to the closer — closely. So when the closer talks to a husband and wife team, let the conversation go 49 percent to the husband and 51 percent to the wife.

5. The secret rules. Here are four fundamental rules which, if used properly, will usually never fail to get a sale:

Like, Listen, Believe, and Buy.

(Rule A.) For the customer to like the closer, the closer must first **like** the customer.

(Rule B.) If the customer likes the closer, he will **listen** to what the closer has to say.

(Rule C.) If the customer listens to the closer, he will generally **believe** the closer.

(Rule D.) If the customer believes the closer, he will **buy**.

To illustrate how the rules work, I have provided the following examples:

(Rule A.) Like: The closer has to look hard and deep into the customer and find something he really likes about him. It could be his children or something the customer has accomplished — whatever. But it has to be sincere on the closer's part. If it is faked the customer will feel it and all will be lost. The closer can and will find something to like about the customer; it might take a few seconds or it might take thirty minutes. But the customer *does* possess some likable qualities and the closer must find them. When this is accomplished the closer should comment to the customer on some of those qualities. This makes the customer feel great because he believes the closer sincerely means the compliments. (Note: The customer knows what his likable qualities are and he was proud of them before he ever met the master closer, so the customer can tell if the closer is being sincere or not.) This does one basic thing: It makes the customer immediately like the closer. If you are believable, there is no way this approach can hurt you.

Let's say you know someone who is a truly miserable human being. He's rotten through and through. All right, let's say this bad guy comes up to you and tell you he really admires you and your accomplishments, and means it. No matter what everyone else says about how bad he was, there is no way you, personally, could thoroughly dislike him. Think back, and see if you've ever disliked anyone who genuinely liked you. You just can't do it. The customer will automatically like the closer if the closer sincerely likes the customer first.

(Rule B.) **Listen:** This step is easy because the customer now likes the closer, so he will listen more attentively to the closer and be open- minded about what he hears.

(Rule C.) **Believe:** This is where the customer starts to believe the closer, simply because the customer is listening and because of the closer's enthusiastic presentation.

(Rule D.) **Buy:** This is the final phase, when the customer buys because he believes in the closer and what he is saying.

The whole secret to selling is encompassed in these four words, **Like, Listen, Believe,** and **Buy.** This rule is so true it can't be stated enough. If it is followed correctly it won't fail.

6. Kill the "I have to think about it," line before it is said. This is a sure way of never having a customer say at the end of a sales presentation, "I have to think about it." The following statement will put the customer at ease and eliminate nearly all the defenses the customer has developed before the beginning of the sales conversation. This opening statement will work every time, if it is executed properly. The best way to illustrate this opening remark is to show it as if it were being given by a closer:

"Mr. and Mrs. Smith, my name is Sam Johnson. May I call you Bob and Mary? Just call me Sam, the mister scares me. You know I'm a salesman and I'm going to try to sell you something, right? Well, I'll tell you what I'm going to do. I'm going to make an agreement with you, and I think you're going to like it. I'm not going to try to sell you a thing. I promise. All I'm going to do is tell you why other people bought. If it makes sense to you and you like it, or you think it's advantageous to yourselves and your family, and it fits into your budget, then try it, buy it, get your foot in the door. But if you don't like it, or you don't think it's a good product for your family, or it doesn't fit into your budget at this time, then don't buy it. Now is that fair enough?"

The customer will answer this question with a "Yes, that's fair enough," every time. But the customer is really saying that he will give you either a yes or a no at the end of your sales presentation. This opening statement also relaxes the customer, because then he isn't being sold something, he is merely listening to the reasons other people have bought. To the customer's way of thinking this lets him off the hook, so he relaxes his defenses.

When you say, "Then try it, buy it, get your foot in the door. But if you don't like it etc..." you should emphasize the word *but,* and keep on talking. Don't pause at this critical point or the customer will put a word in and that ruins the whole statement. Don't allow this train of thought to be broken.

This kind of front-end pitch is a great way to lead the customer and get him off guard. The customer never expects a statement like, "I'm going to try to sell you something, right?" This knocks the customer off balance every time.

7. Degrees of Friendship. There are different degrees of friendship and a closer has to establish a friendly relationship with the customer in a limited time period.

To understand this time element better, we'll look at three different degrees of friendship, and see how each one can help the closer get a sale. The first degree of friendship is a light one, but it works. The higher we go in degrees the more solid the relationship must be.

First degree friendship: This friendship can be developed early. People love to talk about themselves, so talk about them and the many accomplishments they've made; flatter their egos, but always with as much genuine sincerity as you can muster. (This is a shallow way to get someone to like you, but it works.)

Second degree friendship: This type of friendship can be cultivated if the customer has known the closer for a period of time, and both parties have been through a variety of experiences together. This kind of friendship is based on mutual trust and respect, and it has to have time to develop.

Third degree friendship: This degree of friendship exists when two parties have known each other for a very long time or all their lives. This relationship shares a common ground, in that both parties know each other completely, all the good and bad habits. And still the parties remain close friends. This friendship will endure many, many hardships because it is based on a past history of friendship. This degree of friendship is of the highest quality and is the most lasting.

The closer needs time to establish a friendship with the customer, and time is not usually on the closer's side.

To get as close as possible to the customer in a limited time period, the closer can do something rather simple: He can identify with the customer, share a common experience and relate to a common belief, such as religion or politics. This will develop into a friendship that is deeper than the "First Degree Friendship Level" and will expand into the "Second Degree Friendship Level" in a short period of time.

8. The mirror technique. This is a way for closers to control and manipulate the customer. It's a difficult process, because it takes total concentration on the closer's part. If the closer uses this method with every customer he talks to (let's say he sees three or four customers a day), the closer will be completely exhausted by the end of the day. This mirror technique usually works every time, but it isn't easy to perfect.

This is how it is used: When a closer looks into a mirror he sees his reflection; if the closer smiles so does the mirror reflection. This kind of reflection can also work with customers. The closer should imagine the customer's face as a mirror, reflecting the closer's face. If the customer is smiling, it's because the closer is smiling or saying something funny; if the customer is sad or unhappy, it's because the closer is reflecting that same image. The closer can look the customer straight in the eye and lead him into producing any expression he wants. This really works, but it takes a lot of concentration on the closer's part. This method is a completely manipulative mind game and it works. It requires great intensity and total control of the presentation and conversation. The closer leads the customer and influences him throughout this complex and intense mind game. Of course, this method has to be practiced many times with different customers, experimenting with one emotion at a time, but when the closer feels comfortable with the technique, it becomes a powerful closing weapon.

9. Pace your sales presentation. When a closer talks to a customer, he has to pace his pitch at a sharp, clear, crisp level. If a closer talks lethargically and draws his words and sentences out, the customer has to slow down his listening pace to the speaking rate of the closer. So if the sales presentation is mellow and relaxed, the customer is going to be listening in a slow and relaxed manner. Then, when the closer asks the customer for a buying decision, the customer will automatically say, "I have to think about it." This happens because the closer has geared the customer for a slow and relaxed decision. It is all the closer's fault and he winds up wondering, "What happened? Where did I go wrong?" (Note: with older customers, a slow, deliberate presentation is needed. But we're not talking about that now, we're talking about the average young to middle-aged customer.)

The customer has to be attentive, or he won't understand what's being said. So, just like the "mirror technique," the closer must control the customer through his voice and speech patterns. If the closer uses a sharp, crisp, snappy presentation, the customer has to be attentive so he won't get lost or left behind in the conversation. Don't use a fast and furious sales presentation either; use a pace that moves right along in an understandable fashion, with enthusiasm and freshness. The closer can keep a customer alert, awake and excited with this type of speech control.

A closer can lull a customer into indifference or just plain boredom if he uses a slow, drawn-out pitch. The closer has to be aware of the fact that he is pacing the customer's mind through his own speech and voice patterns. If a closer wants an attentive, alert and listening customer, then he'd better have that same attentive and alert attitude himself. This way the customer will be more likely to make a buying decision when the closer asks for one, because he was paced properly from the beginning of the sales presentation.

10. Build on emotion. To keep control of a customer from the start of a sales pitch until it is closed, the closer can depend on one powerful word, *emotion*. If a closer uses this correctly and builds on it, he will always have a captive audience in the customer. Emotion will produce some type of action in a customer every time. Emotion will make a buying decision, emotion will cause a reaction to what is being said; emotion can produce friendly or hostile results.

The closer can relate to a customer's problems and develop a rapport with the customer by using emotion. To illustrate the effect of emotion: The closer can show sad emotions by thinking of something unfortunate or disheartening from his own past. Then, working on these emotional impulses, the closer can tell the customer his story and instantly he will have a believing, captive audience. Customers love to think they know the real salesperson, and a sad emotional story will often do the trick. When a customer hears an intense and personal story he will relate much better to the closer, and will further let his guard down.

The closer can also evoke emotions from the customer's children, his love for his family, and concern for their future. Every customer wants the best for his family and a good closer should draw upon that great source of emotions to get action out of the customer. Believe me it will.

Many sales books stay away from the use of emotions as leverage. This is because emotions are the most powerful motivators of man and consequently, closers must be careful when using this tool on a customer. But the closer can and should use emotions intelligently. The closer should always keep in mind that a customer won't buy if he is hurt or upset by emotions, but he will buy if he sees a sound reason, shown through emotion. (Note: emotion can be shown by the closer through his voice control: soft and deliberate, or excited; his eye contact: with tears for sadness or happiness; and his facial expressions that reflect the emotional feelings needed at a particular time, whether happiness, sadness or concern.)

One more thing the closer should remember about emotions: Love, fear and self-pity are the most powerful factors that make up a customer's emotional force field.

Sam said that since we have seen different ways to control customers in sales situations through mind manipulation, we were ready to study how the customers listen to sales presentations.

Customers' Different Listening Levels

The closer must fully understand the three different levels of customer listening. This understanding is basic and it can't be stressed enough.

The three distinct levels of understanding and thinking that customers will exhibit during a sales presentation are:

1. First Level: The customer hears only bits and pieces of the closer's presentation. The reason is because the customer is not concentrating too hard on the conversation — he simply lets the words go in one ear and out of the other.

2. Second Level: The customer hears the closer's words and sentences and will understand what is being said, but that's it. The conversation with the closer just does not register in any meaningful way with the customer.

3. Third Level: The customer hears what the closer is saying, understands what is being said and then — most importantly — *thinks* about what is being said. This is the level of listening a closer must inspire in his customer because if the customer is on any other level, there won't be a sale. If a sale is miraculously made with the customer on the first or second level, it will most likely be cancelled when the customer gets home, because he bought the product without fully understanding it.

Why a Customer Won't Buy

(A) He doesn't like the product.
(B) He doesn't believe the closer.
(C) He has some unseen personal reason or problem.
(D) He can't afford the product.

Objection: (A) Not liking the product. A closer should solve this problem with showmanship, persuasion, ownership advantage and/or some reverse psychology. The sharp closer can overcome this objection. If a sale is not made because of this objection, it's the closer's fault.

Objection: (B) Not believing the closer. The closer can overcome this problem by using printed material, customer testimonials, consumer reports and actual test results for the product. The closer has to be sincere, have an interest in the customer's needs, and genuinely believe in his product. If the sale is not made because of this objection, it's also the closer's fault.

Objection: (C) A personal reason or problem with the closer. The closer can conquer this objection by uncovering the customer's problem through friendship, interest, understanding and empathy. The closer should help overcome the problem and find a solution for the customer. The closer should read between the lines to understand what the customer is really saying. When the problem is out in the open and a solution is found, the sale can be made, and not before. If a sale is not made because of this objection, it's again the closer's fault.

Objection: (D) Not being able to afford the product. The closer should do one thing when he feels he has exhausted all avenues to close a customer. The closer should just acknowledge that the customer cannot afford the product. The closer must accept this as a fact and believe he has done his very best. The closer should never get angry at the customer for this condition. Instead, the closer should wish the customer well and tell him that when he is in better financial shape to please come back and see him. This will make the customer feel more comfortable and allow the closer to demonstrate a little compassion. The closer can't make the customer's money for him, so if a sale is lost because of this objection it is not the closer's fault.

Concerning the four customer objections, only one — the last objection — is beyond a closer's power to overcome. The other three objections could have been overcome by the closer. So a master closer should be able to resolve 75 percent of the objections raised.

Now, that is how black and white it is. The master closer can out-sell anyone, anywhere, anytime through head games, psychological manipulation, and knowledge. He just has to think.

The Master Closer and His Rules

Sam taught me an ironclad rule associated with psychological warfare and customer control. Few closers think about it or acknowledge it, but it is of vital importance: *The master closer should know beforehand all the questions the customer is going to ask about the product and have all the answers*. The master closer should also know more about the product's good and bad points than the customer can ever imagine.

The customer is on unfamiliar ground with the closer, because he does not know the closer's methods of presentation. The closer knows the rules and runs the whole affair; the customer is at a great disadvantage.

At this point the contest begins between the closer and the customer. If the customer wins and there is no sale, it means the closer lost control.

With all the advantages the closer has over the customer, shouldn't the closer win? Of course he should. The closer has the upper hand from the beginning; it only stands to reason that the closer should prevail.

The Weapon Called Reverse Psychology

When we talk about psychological manipulation, warfare tactics and head games in selling, there is a very powerful approach the closer can and should use. This method of selling is a phenomenon in itself — one of the strongest closing weapons the master closer possesses; reverse psychology.

The closer can sell significantly more by using reverse psychology. But the closer has to know how it works and how to prepare the customer before using it. To use reverse psychology the closer has to know every other method of closing backwards and forwards. The average salesperson cannot use the reverse psychology method correctly if he doesn't have a solid background in overall closing techniques. (Note: A closer could use reverse psychology once in a while and get away with it. But that same closer couldn't use this method day in and day out because he would start missing too many sales by becoming too negative.)

Reverse psychology works in this manner: Customers are aware that in any sales situation, the closer will give a positive, aggressive sales presentation. The customer is alert and geared for this. By doing the exact opposite, the closer can completely disarm and destroy the customer's finely tuned resistance.

For example: The closer should meet the customer with a positive greeting and assume a nonchalant attitude from that point on. The closer shouldn't be rude or take an "I don't care" attitude, but should act as if it's no big deal if the customer buys or not. The closer should let the customer know that sales are going great, and should act as if he has had a very good day in sales. The closer should explain his product in a simple, relaxed fashion, with an air of satisfaction and contentment. This impression has to be conveyed to the customer, or the reverse psychology method won't work. (The customer has to believe the closer and think he is not really worried about getting a sale.)

The closer should answer the customer's questions calmly, and not seem too eager. The closer should simply be polite, cool and reserved.

What this does to the customer is unbelievable. The customer can't understand this approach and will let his guard down every time, because he is not prepared for such an indifferent attitude from the closer. The customer can't spar with an opponent because the closer is not acting like an opponent. He's not trying to push his product, he's just cool, calm, and content to lose a sale.

So the customer is completely off balance. This makes the customer even more alert and attentive to the presentation because he is trying to find out what is really going on in the closer's mind. The buyer will be far more attentive than if the closer had used any other kind of sales approach.

The customer will start to think that the product is far more special than the closer is letting on, and he will start selling *himself* on the product. The customer will let his imagination go to work and that's one of the best selling tools ever.

All this goes back to the customer's greed and ego. Customers don't want to miss something good, or something secret that will benefit them. So when the closer acts like it's not the end of the world if the customer doesn't buy, the customer will then become more inquisitive, attentive and aggressive in his attitude.

The reason a closer who does not have a thorough sales closing background can't use reverse psychology every day is this: A closer will see many different types of customers, and if he acts negatively toward everyone, trying to use reverse psychology all the time, he will become negative himself, and genuinely turn-off customers' interest rather than excite them about his product (or service). He will shortcut the customer (not giving the complete sales presentation) or act so reversed in his pitch that the customer thinks the closer truly doesn't care and that the product is really nothing special, and will leave.

To use reverse psychology the master closer has to know when to be positive and aggressive with the customer to get a sale. If a closer doesn't have a well-rounded closing background he won't know when to stop going in reverse or when to accelerate into a close. Reverse psychology is a great weapon, but the closer has to have a solid knowledge of the basics before he can use this special sales closing method.

Customers and Money

Sam made an observation about money and customers to me, which explained a way of thinking that made sense. Sam said the only reason for a customer not to buy a product from a closer, if he is completely sold on it, would be the objection of money. In other words, whether the customer wants to spend his money or not.

To illustrate this let's say we are giving away old used Volkswagens on a street corner, and the only thing people have to do is tow the cars away. No strings attached, no money needed, just take the car and receive the title free. I don't care how many Volkswagens we had on that street corner, in one hour there wouldn't be a single car left. Every one would be gone, even if people had to push them away. If something is given away, it will always be taken.

That is true of sales too, with only one difference — money. If a closer gave his product away, he wouldn't have a product left at the end of the day. Since money is the only obstacle, the closer must convincingly justify the cost of the product (or service) to make his sale. Sales closing is that simple when you analyze the true reasons behind people's behavior. But to get to the point of closing the sale, the master closer must effectively use his knowledge and techniques of psychological manipulation.

In this section, we're going to look at some notes and reminders you must use when you are with a customer. These notes are closing tactics that keep you in control. The following information should be viewed as a closer's mind game list:

35 Tactics For Psychological Manipulation:
The Master Closer's Mind Game List

1. Touch people. Use your hands to touch their hands or arms or some other part of their body. This personal contact makes people more attentive and draws them closer to you. Use your hands and fingers for explaining and pointing; this has a hypnotic effect on the customer. (Use this approach with discretion and in short doses.) Touching is the most basic form of communication — talking is the second degree of communication. If done properly, this is an ice-breaker every time.

2. Don't ever use a red pen or pencil to sell a customer. This makes the customer subconsciously think, *stop!* (Red is usually associated with danger and can bring back bad school day memories.) Don't wear any red clothing or have red markings on your sales material. Always, when possible, use blues, greens and tans — they are more relaxing for both you and the customer.

3. Remember: "If you confuse them, you lose them." The closer should always keep his sales presentation simple.

4. Don't ever complain about your customers — no matter how many times you've been burned by them, or else you'll be defeated before you start. Always think positively about customers and go in knowing you will get that sale.

5. You might have a million problems, but nothing makes you feel better than a sale! A closer can cure himself of all his ailments by getting one little sale; that one sale creates the additional enthusiasm you need to get others and it goes on from there.

6. When you are giving a sales presentation, always nod your head in the affirmative. Give a positive "yes attitude" to your customer. The customer will react subconsciously by also nodding yes. This is like the mirror technique. It works to the closer's advantage every time. (Note: be subtle when you use this positive nodding movement with the customer; don't over-act. If the customer is aware of what you are doing or even if he's not, he will think you are a nut.)

7. If it's raining, snowing or if it's just a dreary day, you will usually sell more. Most people think you have to have beautiful weather, blue skies, birds singing, etc. to get a customer in a good frame of mind. But on a bad day the customer will most likely have nothing else to do, so he is willing to spend more time with the closer. The customer will not have as many distractions on a cold, rainy day as he would on a sunny day, so he'll be more attentive. This gives you more control and time with the customer, making the sale a little easier.

8. If you create or make the customer feel nervous tension during or after the sales presentation, a sale will be lost every time.

9. You have to get to the same level the customer is on. You should attempt to do or say something the customer can relate to. For example, if the customer drives a truck so does your father; if the customer is a welder, so is your father, etc. The customer needs some common ground to feel comfortable with you. (Note: do not make things up as you will sound like a crook if you get caught in a lie. Someone you know or are related to has something in common with your customer! Just think hard and come up with something!)

10. You should always tell the customer a secret, some information that he believes is special. Customers love to think they know something that no one else knows, so you ought to let the customer in on something special, whatever it may be. Tell the customer the secret is not to be made public. Believe me, the customer will appreciate your confidence in him.

11. No customer, no matter how little money he has or does not have, is poor. Every customer you talk to is rich in some way. It could be the customer's children, his health, his past or his dreams, but every customer has something worth more than money, and you should appreciate and be aware of this fact. Try to connect with the customer and discover his pride and joy.

12. You should be alert to the moods of the customer. You should be able to read between the lines and know if the customer is under-reacting or over-reacting to a normal situation. (The customer may have had a fight with his wife or tough words with his kids just prior to his meeting with you.) You must decipher the customer's moods and make an appropriate adjustment in your sales presentation. This adjustment will encourage your customer to become more comfortable and therefore, more receptive to your sales presentation.

13. You should never let the customer team (husband and wife) get mad at each other. You must make them feel the buying decision is a fifty-fifty agreement between both of them. You should always be a referee and keep both parties happy and involved in the sale. If you lose control of one of the parties the sale will be lost, in most cases.

14. You are selling to a customer team (husband and wife); it's you against both of them, one against two. But during the sales presentation, when you start to win over one of the customers, it creates additional buying pressure on the one remaining customer, and the sale is that much closer to being consummated. (Note: If you have more than one couple to deal with, it is obviously going to make it more difficult for you to control the situation. You should use the very same procedure as you do with the husband and wife. All you have to do is win over one customer at a time, until the odds are in your favor.)

15. Customers are very suspicious people. If they don't understand something, there is a good chance they won't mention it to you. The customer will spend a lot of time thinking about what's not clear and he will build upon this in his mind creating negative feelings about your product (or service). These negative ideas will stay locked in his mind and become an unseen obstacle for you. Many sales are lost because of the unasked and unanswered questions. The solution is to answer everything you feel might be a question in the customer's mind, up front and voluntarily. For example:

explain why you have out of state license plates, if you're selling away from home; or why you are giving such a large discount on a product (or service), even if they don't ask. You should explain your position in your company, and anything else that might become a hidden objection in the customer's generally suspicious mind.

16. This is a good thought for every closer to remember: The customer who is hard to close — I mean *really* **difficult, had to have been sold by someone, sometime.** The customer has clothes, a house and a car. So there *is* someone out there who can close him. Is that someone better at sales than you? You should think about this anytime you come up against a real tough cookie. It will give you added strength to keep on selling.

17. You should never wear dark sunglasses, either inside a building or outside, when talking to a customer. The customer has to see your eyes to gauge your sincerity. If the customer can't constantly see your true facial expressions, he will think you are hiding something or there is something shady about the product. The same is true for the customer. You must see the customer's eyes also. If the customer is wearing sunglasses, you can get them off by simply saying, "I have a pair of glasses just like yours, may I see them?" or "I really like your glasses, may I see them?" Then, when you get hold of the glasses, look at them and give some kind of a compliment, and set them down. Don't give them right back to the customer. (This can be done courteously and subtly without anyone becoming offended.)

18. You should never say, "I'm sorry" about anything. Instead say, "I apologize" or "Excuse me." When you say, "I'm sorry," your subconscious mind will be influenced by that expression and it will affect your performance. It's a negative thought. You should remember you are a closer and not a sorry person.

19. It's a good idea to tell your customer he is the most important part of your company, and that your company would be nothing without him. You should say aloud that the customer comes first and will always be first in the eyes of your company. The statement, "We are only as successful as our customers allow us to be" will work wonders on the customer. You should always work on uplifting the customer's ego.

20. You have to build a dream for the customer, a dream that fits into his own personal goals. When you have established this vision for him, you can proceed to close, using emotion to relate your product (or service) to the customer's future and his family's welfare.

21. When you are giving a sales presentation, and the customer answers with "Ummmmmmmm" (meaning yes) or a silent nod of the head, stop right there and take action. The customer is not really listening to you. You have to make the customer say the word "Yes" or "No" aloud. You have to get the customer to participate with you in the close. The customer can then actually hear himself respond and his subconscious mind will be more aware and alert to what is going on in the sales pitch. This can be accomplished by politely saying, "I didn't hear you," or, "Pardon me, what did you say?"

22. It's all right to tell the customer you are one of the best Master Closers around. You must convey an authoritative air and use charm when you make this statement. Don't say it with a snobby attitude. If this message is handled correctly, the customer will be impressed. Remember, potential buyers would much rather be with one of the best closers around than someone who is a loser.

23. Don't ever argue with the customer. You might be right, but it won't help get a sale. Instead, use a tactful approach and let the customer correct himself. You might win an argument but you'll lose the sale in the long run. Besides, if you lose an argument and get the sale with its commission, who really is the winner?

24. Recognize that in the course of the whole sales presentation, from the front end until closing, the customer will open up to you more and more, telling everything about himself. In other words, if you listen you will get more ammunition to use against the customer. All you have to do is be polite, understanding, and — most importantly — remember what they say. Sooner or later the customer will let his weakness be known.

25. You should allow the customer to think he is in control to some degree. Let the customer believe he is in the driver's seat some of the time. If the customer sees you as having complete control, he will feel resentful and may resist buying, if for no other reason than to get back some of his self-esteem.

26. Should something bad happen while you are with a customer (example: someone says something rude to someone else and you and your customer overhear it) do *not* ignore it. Comment to the customer about it, and apologize for that rudeness. This action will bring the customer closer to you, making you and the customer feel a tighter common bond.

27. If potential customers ask you, "How are things going?" or, "How's business?" tell them everything is great. Be positive. This attitude will rub off on others and will produce a better atmosphere for sales. It doesn't matter if you are sick as a dog, or if you haven't sold anything for weeks, you should still project that winning attitude. Believe it or not, the good feelings you spark in others will rub off on you and then you will start feeling better too. (Note: You have to work harder at being positive than being negative. To illustrate this point: a negative sign only takes one mark to make (-), but a positive sign takes two marks (+). Being positive will always take more effort than being negative, but the effort will be well worth it. Something to remember.)

28. You should be aware of the weapon of intimidation, in every sales presentation. For example, a customer goes into a clothing store looking for a dress shirt. The customer finds one and asks how much it will cost. The closer tells the customer it's a very expensive shirt, and the less expensive ones are on the other counter. Well, the customer gets mad because he thinks the closer believes he can't afford the nicer shirt. Just to show up the closer, the customer buys five expensive shirts, instead of one. This is a good demonstration of selling the customer by intimidation. There are many, many ways to use intimidation in sales closing, and they will be studied later in this book.

29. You should use third party stories with a customer. This is an excellent way to put tough-to-resist pressure on the customer indirectly.

To get your customer to relate to the third party story, use a fictional or factual customer who is similar to your customer. Also, the third party customer has to have had a common problem or objection. Then show how this person's problem was solved, through your story. This approach is a wonderful closing tool, if handled properly. But you must show sincerity and true emotion when telling the story. The third party story can have either a good or bad ending, depending on what is needed. (This method of closing does work, but the story had better sound convincing or it will sound like a big joke.)

30. You should maneuver yourself into a psychologically advantageous physical position when talking to a customer, especially when closing. One technique is for you to be above the customer, looking down at him. This can be arranged by using chairs of different heights, or by sitting on the edge of your desk while the customer is sitting in a chair. The main factor is for your eyes to be higher than the customer's eyes. This makes the customer look up at you. Subconsciously the customer will feel less defensive, more believing, and more attentive to your words. In movie theatres, the screen is elevated above the audience and the patrons sit in quiet concentration, watching the movie. You can use a related approach and inspire greater concentration from your customers.

31. You should realize that you can sometimes over-sell. You can be too enthusiastic, too excited, too pushy, and too talkative. You can actually scare the customer off. You should use reason and control, not only with the customer, but with yourself while preparing to close.

You can also lose a sale by over-selling the product. You can show too many facts, relate too many testimonials and demonstrate the product too many times. All this makes the customer think you may be trying to cover something up or over-compensate for a flaw in the product. A buyer objection can often develop because of your over-presentation and the sale is lost. You should know the product and yourself well enough to deliver a sales presentation that is well-balanced, comfortable, controlled, and easily understandable.

32. If you are shorter, taller, thinner, or fatter than your customer, mention it with humor. For example: If you are short and the customer is tall, say, "Where did you play pro-ball?" or anything else that will flatter the customer's ego.

You should build the customer up a few steps above where he actually is, making him feel special and proud of himself. You should make fun of yourself a little to get the customer to the comfort level you want. When this is accomplished, you can go ahead and give your sales pitch. Now the customer will be open-minded and attentive, because he will actually feel that he is somewhat superior to you.. He will feel the least he can do is show you some courtesy and listen to what you have to say. (The customer won't realize it was your intention to make him feel that way in the first place.) This is where everything falls into place and the fun begins. When you ask the customer to buy, he can't say "No" without getting down off that pedestal you put him on. He won't want to lower himself because he's been acting like a big shot in front of you and if he takes a step or two down he'll be on your level where he knows you could tear him apart. So the customer will stay on his comfortable high level and usually buy the product. The customer lets himself get trapped by his own ego. It often works.

33. If you don't understand the product, how can your customer? This is a little reminder you had better address. If you don't believe in your product, how can your customer? If you are not happy or excited about your product, then how in the world is your customer going to be?

34. You can't sell anyone anything, if you don't understand the customer. You have to take the time to think about what makes customers tick. You have to examine them and develop a sound approach for each one. What this all breaks down to is the following: "You can't close if you can't open." You have to open up the mind of the customer and know his thinking, before you can get a sale closed.

35. The customer does not depend on you; *you* depend on the customer. Truer words were never written. If sales professionals don't please the customers they won't close the deals. Always please your customer. Always.

Sam said that this ended my lesson on psychological manipulation. He told me the head game war was actually much more complex, but I now had enough basic information about it to be able to continue my studies on master closers.

Sam summed up all the material I had learned in this lesson, with one statement that stuck in my mind: "A master closer is the person who finds a positive solution for a customer's problems through sophisticated and well planned mind manipulation."

Chapter Six

CLOSER VS. CUSTOMER:
The First Meeting

- A. The Master Closer's Strategy:
  The Attack Plan

- B. The Closer's Initial Approach To the Customer:
  Five Essential Steps

- C. Twenty Tips and Tactics That Work:
  Candid Information to Use and Remember

Chapter Six

CLOSER VS. CUSTOMER:
The First Meeting

August the second started out poorly. On my way to work at Green Vista Estates my car tire went flat. The delay made me late, and "Big Bill" did not like to have any of his people running behind schedule.

When I finally got to my job, Sam was waiting for me. He seemed particularly happy and excited — quite the opposite of how I felt. "Big Bill" had just given me his late-to-work lecture and it didn't do much for my morale.

Sam called me over and told me that today was going to be special. Not only would we be starting an important sales lesson, but for the first time we were going to study the master closer's initial approach to customers and the techniques that are used. Sam said it was finally time to put the two opponents together, closer and customer. Now I would see how the closer actually manipulates and controls his customer, from the first eye contact to the beginning of the basic sales presentation, to the final close. This was the point where all of my earlier sales lessons started to fit together and really make sense.

This was the hardcore sales training I had been waiting for: How the closer must handle the first meeting with the customer, one-on-one.

The Master Closer's Strategy:
The Attack Plan

Sam told me the first thing a sales closer must do — even before he meets his customer — is establish a game plan. The closer must have some kind of strategy outlined in his mind if he wants to get a sale. If a closer does not have a game plan, he might as well give his customer to some rookie salesman and hope for the best.

Game plan strategy simply means that the closer has pre-developed an attack plan for selling his customer. The closer not only knows how he will approach his customer, but also knows his inventory, his product, and himself, backwards and forwards, one hundred percent. The closer must know where he is going with his customer, and how to get there with confidence. In fact, the master closer has already envisioned a closed sale.

The following pointers will provide a foundation from which to build a game plan and demonstrate the techniques a closer uses to prepare himself for a customer, both physically and mentally.

Note: There is no certain time or set place in the sales presentation to actually close the customer. The master closer is continually (from the first second he says "Hello" to his customer, until the sale is made) going after that sale with every question and statement he can think of. The master closer knows that every single "Yes" or positive response he gets from his customer brings him a step closer to getting the sale consummated.

The Attack Plan

Fifty percent positive

When the closer is with his customer, it's one-on-one. No one else is involved. The closer represents fifty percent of a selling situation, and the customer is the other fifty percent. With this in mind the closer should go somewhere in the office to be alone, before he meets his customer.

The reason for this is simple: By being alone and thinking nothing but aggressive thoughts, the closer will create a positive selling attitude for himself that will spill over to the customer, pushing him a little closer toward following your advice. When the closer feels positive, strong, and comfortable enough, he is ready to meet the customer for the first time. This is a mental attitude the closer should attempt to induce if he wants to win a greater percentage of sales.

Product Knowledge

The closer must know his inventory, his price list, his product, the monthly payments, the pay schedules and company facts before he ever meets a customer. When a closer has all this information down pat, he will feel more confident and relaxed. This self-confidence will show when he encounters his customer for the first time. A closer cannot be completely confident in himself and feel prepared and poised if he does not know precisely what he is talking about. The customer can spot this weakness in a closer in no time, and the sale will usually be lost.

Without detailed knowledge of his product, the closer will be vulnerable to any kind of detail question or trick question the customer might come up with, and this too can easily kill a sale. Customers like to play the game of stumping the salesman by asking petty, difficult questions to see if the seller can answer them. The closer should never allow himself to get into a position where he can be caught off guard.

Look in the Mirror

The closer should take the time to stand for a few seconds in front of a mirror before he meets his customer. The closer should check his clothes, shoes, fingernails, hair and overall appearance; he should make sure he doesn't have bad breath, dandruff or body odor. The closer has to look neat, well groomed and sharp if he wants to make a sale. Customers do not want to deal with unkempt, malodorous, sloppy salespersons. Your appearance will subconsciously affect their impressions of your product (or service).

Something else that is important about looking in the mirror: The closer should look at himself and tell himself he's the best closer around and that he *is* going to get that sale, no matter what. Sound silly? It isn't. A closer can actually psyche himself up and build his confidence by looking in the mirror for a few minutes and giving himself a pep talk. (It's a form of self-hypnosis and it works.) There is only one you, so you'd better make it the best you possible. No one else is going to help you succeed.

The closer should remember he is an actor getting ready to go on stage for his customer, so he should give the best performance he can.

The closer should loosen up before meeting his customer by shaking his arms for a minute at his sides. This will make the closer more relaxed and get his blood flowing.

The closer should present himself to the customer with a good appearance, and an air of confidence. The mirror can help you pump yourself up, if it is used properly.

Self-Made Enthusiasm

The closer has to have enthusiasm before he meets any customer. Here are two ways to build enthusiasm and excitement: The closer can simply start tapping a pencil or pen on a table, slowly, then faster and faster until he feels himself changing moods. The same results can be achieved if the closer claps his hands together, slowly at first, but building the tempo. All this movement and noise builds excitement in the closer and excitement is enthusiasm's first cousin. (If you have access to music that inspires you, play it before your important meeting and this will also create enthusiasm.)

The closer has to be alert and expecting to win before meeting his customer for the first time. To achieve that frame of mind, he has to use enthusiasm, excitement and positive thinking. These qualities are always available to the closer and are always on his side. But it's up to him to strategically unleash them during his sales presentations!

Pre-Game Strategy

To establish any type of effective pre-game strategy, the closer must first know his product inside out. When he feels confident of that knowledge, he can move on to develop his attack plan.

Pre-game strategy is illustrated in this example: The closer already knows where he wants his customer to sit, or what room he wants to use for his sales presentation. The sophisticated closer will determine in advance what product, model, piece of real estate, insurance policy, etc. he is going to show the customer. He also knows what price range he wants to work with. The closer must have all this information prepared and pre-planned so he will know exactly what he is going to do when putting his closing moves on the unsuspecting customer. He has total control and confidence in himself, and it shows. With a solidly prepared game plan the closer will have a strong foundation to work from and build upon. The closer can then give the customer an organized and understandable sales presentation, leading the customer in any direction he wants. He can show a more expensive product, or a smaller product, a different model or other real estate locations. It doesn't matter because the closer's strong foundation strategy will always act as his focal point, allowing him to appear knowledgeable in front of the buyer at all times.

Another benefit to having a strategically prepared game plan is that the customer too will have a basic starting point (which you have determined) to compare with other models and prices that you show him. This way the customer can listen to the entire sales presentation in the proper perspective (which you have determined). A game plan keeps the customer from getting confused, and gives him a basic knowledge of the product.

The closer's game plan or pre-game strategy is really the closer's ability to develop a controlled sales situation before he meets the customer. The closer knows what steps he is going to take with his customer and he has enough product knowledge to have back-up plans ready, if needed. He understands the need for a solid sales presentation with a pre-developed foundation that can be built on and expanded in any direction necessary to close the sale.

Game Plan Notes and Ideas

1. The closer should remember that he is the leader. He is the person who must take control and lead his customer toward the sale. The closer has to get himself into this frame of mind and demonstrate these qualities when he meets the customer. The closer should not cross over the line and become pushy or arrogant while attempting to convey these qualities.

2. The closer should think of nothing but victory when he meets his customer. He should go into the first meeting knowing he will like the customer, and he will get the sale. (You can inspire yourself to like almost all of your customers if you psyche yourself properly before meeting them.)

3. The closer has to know what direction he is going with his customer, and how to maintain control. The closer shouldn't allow himself to be distracted with irrelevant conversations and petty questions, allowing the customer to knock him off balance.

4. The closer should never have a canned sales pitch. It sounds phony and stupid. His basic sales presentation should have a good foundation, it must be spontaneous, and the closer has to be flexible.

5. When psyching up for a customer the closer should tell himself, "You are going to use everything you've got to make this sale and nothing less; *nothing less.*"

Sam summed it all up by telling me that the closer is programming and controlling his customer from the very first eye contact until the sale is made. He is literally closing the customer throughout the entire sales presentation, not just during the closing part of his pitch.

This made a lot of sense to me and I never forgot it.

The Closer's Initial Approach To The Customer:
Five Essential Steps

1. Approach and handshake

When a closer first sees his customer he should walk directly to him in a controlled, poised and confident manner. (Note: Never carry anything in hand when first approaching a customer, such as a pen, brochure, or any other type of sales material. This will only put the customer on the defensive.) When the closer says his first greeting, he should give a quick look at every person in the customer's party, out of courtesy and respect.

The closer should shake hands firmly and pleasantly with the customer, and look him straight in the eye. Do not use any old handshake tricks. When one salesman friend of mine shakes hands he gives a slight pull toward himself, throwing the customer a little off balance. He feels this maneuver gives him some edge of control over the customer from the beginning. It's a cute trick that works *sometimes,* but in most cases his customers are offended and suspect that he is tricky and not to be fully trusted.

After the handshake the most important thing to do is get the customer relaxed so he can feel comfortable and at ease around the closer. This *has* to be accomplished if the closer wants the customer to be attentive during his sales presentation.

2. Getting immediate control of the customer

There is a vitally important moment after the first handshake when the closer can take direct and instant control of the customer, without the customer even realizing what is happening. That moment is crucially important to the success of the sale.

Right after the first handshake and general exchange of greetings, the closer must move his customer to another location — a different closing room, or even another desk. If a closer walks up to a customer, shakes hands and proceeds to give his initial sales pitch, he will lose control of the sales situation almost every time because the customer has picked his own battleground; he has decided where to stand or sit, either in his own home or in a sales office or on a sales lot. The customer has established his position, and is ready and waiting for the closer (at least he thinks he is).

If this sounds silly then you haven't sold much, because this is the way a customer actually feels. The customer is in strange territory when dealing with the closer in the closer's office, store or lot. Once a conversation starts the customer begins to feel he is in control. When the closer moves the customer to a new location, the customer's game plan is thrown off balance. (He simply does not expect anyone to ask him to move after he begins talking in a perfectly good spot.) This relocation will confuse and disorient the customer for a minute — enough time for the closer to take charge.

This moving trick has to be done politely, smoothly and courteously to work. The closer can relocate his customer by saying, "Let's find a better place to talk than this, it's too noisy in here," or "This office is not private enough." Any excuse that shows concern for the customer will work.

Diagram A:

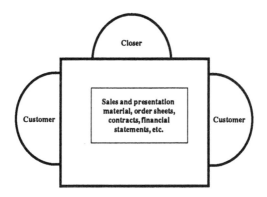

Once the move is made the closer should make the customer feel comfortable and relaxed again, or he will be right back where he started, with a defensive and uncontrolled customer. Many closers have overlooked this controlling tactic and for that reason many sales have been lost. The closer must gain control of the customer from the beginning, and this maneuver will do it.

3. Seating the Customer In a Sales Office Environment

The closer should keep this rule in mind when seating his customer: Sit close. The greater the distance between customer and closer the less control the closer will have.

(Note: I'm not talking about a desk where the seating arrangement is obvious, but a closing table where the seating is flexible. It should be pointed out that all desks are barriers between the closer and the customer. The closer should try to eliminate that barrier by sitting at the side of the desk during parts of the sales presentation. This way the closer can get nearer to the customer, and make everyone feel more comfortable.)

Diagram B:

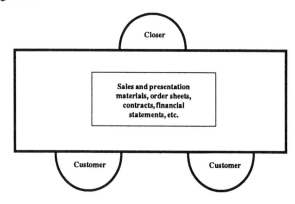

There are two ways of seating customers and each way has its good and bad points. These two seating options are explained below:

SEATING ILLUSTRATION A

I. In this seating plan the closer has a big advantage: The closer has placed himself in a central position where he automatically becomes a part of the customer's party — he has joined their family. This seating arrangement also breaks up the bond between customers (that feeling of strength from closeness) and weakens any pre-planned sales defense the customers may have prepared.

II. Another advantage is that the closer can equally share his sales presentation, both verbally and on paper, with both customers at the same time. The customers can read and examine sales materials from their positions and the closer can have physical contact with each customer for emphasis without looking awkward. (For example: Touching the arm or hand of the customers, to keep them attentive and alert during the entire sales presentation.)

III. With this seating arrangement the closer can prevent the customers from communicating through discreet contact with one another (whispering, nudging). Without such gestures or signals between the customers, the closer will have much more control over the sales presentation, and will be able to keep the customers off balance (because now the customers' pre-arranged signals are useless). These advantages will work best for the closer if he sits in the middle of the opponents' camp.

SEATING ILLUSTRATION B

I. The main advantage of this seating arrangement is that the closer can maintain eye contact with everyone in the customer's party, at just about the same time. This is the only legitimate excuse for sitting in this manner.

II. There are several disadvantages to this seating arrangement. For example: The customers can see what is going on behind the closer and that activity could hurt a sale and the closer would never know why. The unseen distraction could not interfere with a group seated in Illustration A because the closer will always have controlled eye contact, and can see everything the customers see.

III. In this seating plan the customers can nudge each other and make unseen contact, exchanging pre-planned signals that the closer may be totally unaware of.

IV. In Arrangement B the closer is not a part of the customer's family as he is in Arrangement A. In addition, the closing table becomes a barrier, putting more distance between the closer and the customers and creating a two-against-one environment. In other words, the closer is on one side of the table talking *to* the customers, not in between the customers talking *with* them. There is a big difference, and the closer had better realize it.

The sharp closer plans his seating arrangement to allow him to have maximum visual and physical contact with the customers. The key rule is: "Distance is a barrier."

4. Three-step introduction

This is a great approach every closer should know. The technique will make customers feel like old friends just minutes after the first greeting. Not many closers use this approach because it is not well known, but believe me, it's fantastic and really does work. This is how it is done:

Step 1. When you (the closer) meet your customers, after the handshake greeting and relocation maneuver, tell them you have to go check on something (a phone call, your inventory, etc.) and ask them to relax and help themselves to some coffee. Then leave them for a few minutes.

(Note: Let the customers get their own coffee, try to avoid getting the coffee for them unless they are elderly. If you get coffee for them you may strike some suspicious types as a "smoothey" trying to get their guard down, making them even more difficult to close. You are also putting yourself in a subservient position and the customers may begin to feel they are in complete control.)

Step 2. After you have been away from the customers for a few minutes, go back to them and sit down for a minute. Ask the buyers a couple of easy, relaxed questions such as: "Where are you from?" "What kind of business are you in?" "Is this your whole family?" Listen to the answers with interest and excuse yourself again for some believable reason (you're going to get yourself some coffee, etc.) and leave. This ends your second meeting with the customer.

Step 3. After you have been away a minute or two (or even longer, if you think the customers need more time to relax or more time to get accustomed to the environment) go back to your customers and start the sales presentation. This will be your third meeting with the customers and they will actually feel as though they know you by this time. This ends your third meeting with the customer.

Now I'll explain what took place during the three-step introduction. Initially customers are on guard and have built a defense shield around themselves to skeptically view all sales presentations (especially those from strangers). When the closer first excuses himself, letting the customers get some coffee and relax a little, that defensive shield starts to weaken because the expected sales pressure is not present.

In Step 2, the closer comes back to the customers and asks some general questions, and then leaves again. The customers' defensive shield is weakened even more because the customers get to know the closer from these brief conversations and have some breathing room in between.

By Step 3, when the closer approaches for the third time the customers have had time to observe the closer, nearby and from a distance so they feel they now know him much better. (That protective defensive shield really starts to come down at this point.) The customers have also had time to begin to like the closer, feeling that he is their representative, responsible and caring for them.

Now the closer can make his sales presentation in a relaxed and comfortable manner, with an atmosphere that is pleasant both for himself, and for the customers.

The three-step introduction works if it is used properly. I have seen many closers start right in on their sales presentation without giving the customers any kind of breathing room. This loses sales. The closer has to defuse the customers and get that protective shield lowered if he wants more sales.

I have to say it one more time: The three-step introduction will do the job, everytime. (Note: When the closer is away from the customers he will have more time to analyze and observe them.) The three-step introduction works for the closer in the same manner it works for the customers.

5. First Meeting Closing Traps (Trap Questions)

There are some easy and fun ways to get a customer committed to buy, right from the very beginning of the conversation. These Trap Questions are powerful weapons that can make a sale before the closer even explains the product. The best way to describe them is to give examples:

A. "Mr. and Mrs. Customer, if I could show you how you could save X number of dollars a day or X number of dollars a month for so many months, and at the end of that period of time I gave you back all your money, plus some extra, would you be interested? Now, remember, no strings attached. If I could show you the way it worked, would you be interested?" (Note: The customers will give an answer, but first they will try to ask questions about any strings attached and what they have to do, etc. The closer should ignore these questions and keep saying, "Don't think about that now, but if I could show you the way it works, would you do it? Could you save that much a month to do it?")

The customers will nearly always say "Yes." Now the closer has received a commitment and can use this affirmative answer later against them if he has to. The customers will trap themselves almost every time, if this question is presented properly and with sincerity.

B. "Mr. and Mrs. Customer, let me ask you a question. If I could show you a way to insure your family's future and give you total peace of mind concerning your children's future education, would you be willing to save X number of dollars? If I could completely convince you, would you be a little interested?"

C. "Mr. and Mrs. Customer, would you like to have the very best product for the least amount of money possible? And to know in your heart that you're getting the best service with that product, would you be interested? Just tell me the truth — if it was that clear-cut and simple, would you?"

These three examples of initial Trap Questions illustrate a few of the avenues a closer can use to get the initial affirmative commitment from the customers. They do work. But they have to be delivered lightly, in a soft, sincere and relaxed manner so they don't scare the customers off. The affirmative answer tricked out of the customer will be light and easygoing also, but it can be turned into an unexpected commitment later on by the closer. The customers are not aware of the impending trap and will stay attentive during the sales pitch because they will be curious about the closer's provocative and tricky question.

The closer's next move, after he has received an affirmative answer is to drop the subject of his Trap Question and continue with his regular sales presentation.

A good way for the closer to get from the Trap Question back to his basic sales pitch is illustrated by this example:

"Mr. and Mrs. Customer, all right, let's forget about what I just said for now and let me explain to you how it really works..."

These traps are great tools to get the attention, curiosity and involvement of the customers from the beginning. The closer can devise any kind of Trap Question he thinks will work but he has to ask it gently and sincerely. The trap won't be effective if the customers think it is a joke.

Before we go on to our next topic concerning the first meeting, we should take a look at a summary chart that puts the initial approach to the customer into proper perspective.

The Initial Approach To The Customer

1. THE FIRST APPROACH AND HANDSHAKE
2. GETTING IMMEDIATE CONTROL OF THE CUSTOMER BY RELOCATION
3. SEATING THE CUSTOMER
4. THE THREE-STEP INTRODUCTION
5. THE FIRST CLOSING TRAPS (TRAP QUESTIONS)

These five steps are essential if a closer wants to be completely organized and have control over the customer from the beginning. There are a lot of sales short-cuts a closer can use, but if he practices these steps he'll sell more than he ever has before.

Twenty Tips and Tactics That Work:

Candid Information To Use and Remember About the First Meeting

1. Basic Rule — Talk to the customer alone, then step away for a few minutes to think about him and what he said. Analyze him as well as you can and use that information to determine your closing strategy.

2. The customer loves to hear his own accomplishments admired and his name mentioned over and over again. It's all music to his ears.

3. Every customer has a weakness or "hot button" somewhere in his make-up. The customer is well aware of it, so he will be over protective in this area (especially in the first meeting). Sometimes the closer must find this weakness to get any action out of the customer. A sudden increase in objections or excuses from the customer is an indication that the closer is about to touch on the customer's spot. The customer is really only fighting what he knows is his emotional "hot button;" when he feels the closer is getting too close to the sale he will put up his greatest resistance creating the final, last ditch obstacles.

4. To make the customer feel more comfortable, the closer should speak clearly and pronounce the buyer's name distinctly — spell it if need be. This draws the customer nearer to the closer. The closer should remember the customers' names and use them a few times while initially getting to know them. This will develop a cameraderie with your customers. If the closer didn't hear a customer's name he should be polite and ask him to please repeat it. If the closer forgets a name he can use the trick of asking the customer how to spell their name. This way the closer doesn't disclose he has forgotten their name, as he goes through the motions of writing it down. This may all seem very basic, but it has to be done correctly to improve your chances of getting a sale.

(Note: There is a school of thought that says a first-name basis is *too* friendly; if the closer is too friendly he might let the customer off easily and lose a sale. This thinking does have some merit, but if the closer has built up a good rapport with the customer, first names should always be used. A lot more pressure can be applied to the customer by a closer who gets familiar and uses first names than by a closer who is formal and uses only last names.)

5. The customer who talks all the time will eventually tell everything about himself, his family, his home life, business, etc. The closer should get the conversation going, then sit back and take mental notes. They will be useful as future ammunition.

6. The closer should treat every single customer as though he were the last one he will ever get. The successful closer must always give one hundred and ten percent to his own future, and that future lies in satisfying his customers.

7. When the initial conversation is going on between the closer and the customer, the closer should never let the customer's small talk go off in the direction of some far and unknown horizon, or the closer will lose control. The closer should encourage small talk but he shouldn't let the customer talk too long — the sales presentation will end up vanishing in the background somewhere.

8. When the closer first meets the customer he should be alert to any little thing the customer might say, that both the customer and closer could relate to. Example: "Mr. Customer, I understand you're from upstate New York. That's where I used to go fishing with my father; it's beautiful country you are from, I envy you." This kind of statement can work magic on opening up the customer.

9. The closer should never say, "I'm going to be your representative," or "I'll be your salesman," to a customer. The customer already knows this and a stupid statement will only scare him more than he already is. The closer should meet the customer as an equal and then go to work. Both the closer and the customer will feel more comfortable. It's a good idea not to broadcast, "I'm a master closer" to the customer, but rather to project yourself as a regular guy and more as a friend.

10. It takes only two individuals to make a sale, and both parties have to have trust, respect, understanding, and some friendship between them if any type of contract is going to be signed and honored.

11. If the customer is a referral from another customer, the closer should use a soft-sell approach, and go lightly until he understands the situation thoroughly. It's easy for a closer to trap himself if he proceeds to give a sales presentation to a referral without finding out some facts first. Don't assume that the referral customer is automatically an easy sell just because someone liked you enough to refer him.

12. If the closer has a team customer and only one member of the party is present (the husband or wife is absent; this is sometimes called a "one-legged unit") the closer should just give a brief and informative sales pitch. The closer should use a lot of personality and enthusiasm, touching on the highlights of the product, always keeping it simple. This information should spark enough enthusiasm in the customer to make him pass along the sales pitch to the absent party. After giving the brief presentation, the closer should simply re-schedule the customer for another time, when both parties can be present for the full sales presentation.

(Note: This is very important for a closer to remember regarding a husband and wife team when both parties are not present for a full sales presentation. The closer might be able to sell one of the parties, but the chances for a cancellation are tremendous. The reason for this is basic: When the buying party gets home and tries to explain the new purchase to the other party, tempers and friction usually materialize because the party at home didn't have a chance to get involved. So the buying party will try to cancel, just to have some peace at home. Basically the party left out of the buying decision wanted to give some opinion, or knew the family's financial situation better or didn't like the whole idea in the first place — all these negative reasons cause unrest and unwanted pressure until the buying party ends up calling the closer to cancel his purchase or contract.)

13. If the closer has a customer who has been drinking heavily or a customer who is in a big rush to go somewhere else, the closer should be polite and try to re-schedule a new meeting time. The closer should not waste his time when these negative factors are present.

14. If a closer ever asks a customer to buy his product without first programming him, or giving enough product information — the answer will always, and I mean *always* be "No." The closer must carefully shepherd the customer through the whole sales presentation, feeding him organized, understandable product (or service) information, to achieve a positive buying answer. All the little questions and tricks the closer uses will lead up to a great and well-delivered presentation. It's just like a staircase: to get where you want to go you can't miss one single step.

15. If the customer looks scared or overly nervous the closer can "break the ice," with one maneuver: The closer should walk right up to the customer, look very serious, and say, "Which one do you want to buy?" or "How many do you want?" or "Did you call me?" This approach will throw the customer off balance for a second. The closer should immediately smile sincerely and say, "I'm just kidding, my name is John, may I help you?" or something to that effect. This approach works and will help break down that invisible defensive customer shield.

16. If a closer feels uncomfortable with his customer, for any reason, he should politely excuse himself, go somewhere alone for a few minutes and rethink his approach. The closer should try to figure out the problem that exists, then return to the customer with a new and better attitude.

It is easy to get upset if a customer has a chip on his shoulder or is rude, but the closer has to control his feelings and show professionalism at all times if he wants to close a deal with this type of neurotic buyer. (Note: Being a master closer isn't always easy.)

17. Another way for a closer to deal with a customer who makes him uncomfortable is this: The closer can frankly tell the customer that he feels somewhat awkward. The closer should ask the customer for his help in trying to resolve that feeling. For example: The closer can say in a nice, friendly manner, "You know I've never been around South Texas people before, and I'm not sure how to deal with you," or "This is the first time I've ever been in a coal mining community and it sure is different from where I'm from." Statements like these that fit the closer's situation will work wonders on the customer if delivered with a tone that reflects, "I need your help." The customer will usually come to the aid of the closer every time. The customer will give local information, tell stories, and generally open up. (People love to help other people who sincerely ask for it.) The closer ought to use this approach whenever he can; it's a winner.

18. The closer should never be afraid of the customer. Remember, the customer needs the answers the closer has. Besides, the customer is just another ordinary man. The closer should approach the customer with self-confidence and belief in himself. The closer should walk right up to the customer with pride — pride not only in his product but in himself. Then the closer should look the customer straight in the eye and say to himself, "I'm going to get a sale, I'm going to win."

19. Here is a great way to disarm the customer on the first meeting that is fun and easy. The closer should approach and greet the customer in a joking, slightly confused, disoriented manner. This approach will catch the customer off balance because the customer expects a more serious and professional closer. All this "bit acting" on the closer's part will make the customer feel he is not threatened, and he will smile and let his guard down. (It's the good old "country fox" trick, but it works.)

20. When a closer first meets the customer he not only has to take the lead, but he has to give and understand more than the customer, he has to appreciate more, he has to think more and he has to love more.

Note: There is no certain time or set place in the sales presentation to actually close the customer. The master closer is continually (from the first second he says "Hello" to his customer, until the sale is made) going after the sale with every question and statement he can think of. The master closer knows that every single "Yes" or positive response he gets from his customer is a step that much closer to getting the sale consummated.

This concluded my lesson covering the first meeting of the closer and his customer. Sam said I had just started to learn about sales closing in its actual form and this lesson was only the first step towards perfecting the final close.

Well, I knew one thing: I had learned so much up to now that I was excited about studying the additional tidbits Sam was going to teach me. I think Sam knew how I felt.

Chapter Seven

THE SALES PRESENTATION:
Explaining, Showing and Demonstrating the Product

- A. The Pre-Demonstration Pitch: Programming the Customer and Creating Interest

- B. Presenting the Product: Show-and-Tell Time

- C. In-Home Sales Presentation: The Do's and Don'ts

- D. Pressures, Tricks and Traps: Special Notes to Remember

Chapter Seven

THE SALES PRESENTATION:
Explaining, Showing and Demonstrating the Product

One morning Sam asked me if I was ready for another sales lesson. Since we had just studied "the first meeting" between the closer and the customer, he said we were now ready to go over the next important step, the actual sales presentation.

I told Sam that anytime he wanted to teach I was more than ready to listen and learn. Sam smiled and began to tell me some amazing stories about sales pitches and he didn't miss a trick.

Sam said the first thing a closer has to remember about his sales presentation or his product demonstration is that everything is brand new and unfamiliar to his customer. A customer may have heard a thousand sales pitches before, and may have purchased hundreds of different products, but it will be the very first time he has ever heard *this* closer's presentation. Therefore, the closer must keep his sales pitch simple, understandable and well organized.

The Pre-Demonstration Pitch:
Programming the Customer and Creating Interest

Before the closer jumps right into his basic show-and-tell presentation, he has to give a pre-demonstration pitch (also called a warm-up pitch, point pitch, or qualifying pitch.) This gives the closer some time to program his customer, get him more relaxed and less defensive. (Note: The customer is not aware of this programming process. It is accomplished through casual conversation, with the closer in complete control.)

Programming develops the customer's thinking in a way that the closer can manipulate and direct toward the final close. In other words, programming introduces the customer to the basic product information so the customer can keep this information in mind during the rest of the sales presentation. For a customer to remember any sales information, it has to be repeated several times during the sales presentation, and the pre-demonstration pitch does just that. (Important note: When speaking to a group of customers, the closer must involve every member of the party in the conversation. The closer cannot forget one single member in the party, or that member will be the pin for the closer's bubble. It happens everytime. No one likes to be left out and any member of the customer's party who feels that way will try to kill a sale.)

To illustrate exactly how customer programming works, Sam outlined the following steps. These steps are flexible enough to adjust to different products and situations, but the basic pre-demonstration function is the same. (Note: I don't care what you sell or how you sell it, the customer *must* be programmed to buy.)

Five Steps to Programming The Customer

1. The Closer is special.

The closer should not let the customer think that he is just another average closer, or one of many in the sales office, because a customer doesn't want to do business with someone who is mediocre or low on the company totem pole. To make any kind of special deal (and all customers want special deals) the average closer will have to go to someone else who is higher in the sales organization. Also the customer knows that he won't really be talking to the "top man" and will feel he isn't getting the attention or the best deal he deserves.

The first thing a closer should do is tell the customer that he is in management, or that he is the top closer. (Note: Don't be arrogant, act in a humble and personable manner. The customers love it.) I am not suggesting the closer should lie to his customer, but he'd better be more than "just one of the sales boys" when he's pitching. A lot of closers don't realize how much this one small detail can hurt a sale. If the closer presents himself as someone special, people he deals with will feel special too. It's simple, and it's true. The customer will feel he is getting that little extra attention other customers miss. With this kind of thinking on the customer's part, the closer can successfully sell the customer.

(Note: I know sales people who don't say they are the top closer or brag about their important position, but they build themselves up in other, more discreet ways that have exactly the same effect. For example: The closer will say, "I've been with the company longer than anyone," or "The president of this company and I grew up together." All of these statements have the very same meaning to the customer — that this closer is someone special, someone a cut above the other closers.)

2. The Closer's Story.

The closer should tell the customer something about himself and his family. This brief background information should explain why the closer is working for his company and his future plans. This must be told as an interesting and unique story to keep the customer's attention and interest. The closer can make it a happy tale or a tragic one, whatever suits the situation. But it had better be believable and told with sincerity.

The main purpose of the story is to show the customer how positive the closer is about his own company or product. If a customer does not believe the closer would buy the product himself, he won't buy either. I can guarantee that. The closer has to show emotion and try to discuss common problems he and his customer might have. This will add a great deal to the closer-customer common bond, and help the customer feel more at home with the closer.

3. The Trap Set-Up.

The following example is a good pre-demonstration trap pitch or trap set-up for the customer.

"Mr. Customer, before I really start talking, before I try to give you a big sales pitch, let me say something. It might sound funny, I guess, but did you know that with our product, we would be able to sell every single person we talked to, I mean every single one, if it weren't for three reasons. Some people don't understand what we're doing; some people don't believe what we're doing; and, some people just can't afford it. And that's it — we would sell everybody, if it weren't for those three reasons." (Note: Don't stop at this point. The closer can't break the train of thought he has just created or the trap won't work.)

"What I'm going to do, Mr. Customer, is this: I'm simply going to tell you what we've got, give you the very basics — not a big sales pitch, or anything. I'm going to show you the best deal in the house and I'm going to get it for you at the best price I can, better than anyone else. What do you think, is that fair enough?"

This down to earth pre-demonstration pitch will do several good things for the closer. The closer has told the customer if he doesn't buy he is stupid and can't understand, or he thinks the closer is a liar, or he just plain can't afford it. What kind of answer do you think the customer is going to give to the closer's question, "Is that fair enough?" The customer will (through programming) always say "Yes," and that is what the closer really wants.

Something else happens that is also good for the closer: The customer understands he won't get some fancy, elaborate sales presentation, but rather a man-to-man, bottom-line, take-it-or-leave-it pitch. The closer has put the customer in a position of having to say "Yes" or "No," and has avoided the trap of "I'll think about it." This pre-pitch works if properly delivered, with sincerity and believability.

4. Thought Questions.

The closer should inject occasional "thought questions" as he moves closer to talking about the product. These questions have to be directed toward everyone in the customer's party, if there is more than one, so the feeling of equal participation exists. The closer can get to know the customer's thought processes through the answers he receives, especially if he listens to the customer's children. Kids are a great way of getting information the adults want hidden. Two thought questions are illustrated here, so the closer can see how they work, and get a general idea of how they affect the customer's thinking.

"Mr. Customer, I want you and your family to think about something. Did you know that one thousand of your neighbors have already bought this product? Now there has to be something good about it, right? No one has a thousand idiot neighbors, do they?" (Note: The customer will laugh, thinking that statement is funny. At least he is thinking, and he knows he isn't the first "guinea pig" customer.)

"Mr. Customer, you know we've built this office and this huge complex, all the roads, the country clubs, the golf courses, swimming pools, houses, everything, without one penny from you. Do you know why we got you here if we've already done all of this? Well, I'll tell you. We know we can build roads, put up street lights, build lakes, swimming pools, clubs, the whole works. But we've tried and tried and tried and we can't yet build one of *you*, a person, and this is what our company is all about — people. It takes people to make our product work, and the better the people, the better it works. That's why we've asked you to come, because we need you and your family. We are only as good as our people."

(Note: The closer has just planted an ego seed in the customer's mind, plus he has effectively involved the customer's whole party.)

There are hundreds of thought questions the closer can use to plant information and to activate the customer's mind. The main thing to remember is to use logic with a warm, personable presentation — and listen for the complete answer. Don't ever try to second-guess a customer.

5. The Company and Product

The closer must present his company and his product to the customer in the best possible light. The closer should tell the customer how many years the company has been in business, about its credit rating, financial standing and all the highlights that demonstrate the company's dependability. The closer should build his company and its product up in the mind of the customer, using controlled enthusiasm and pride.

All this information will provide the customer with the basic facts necessary to make a buying decision. (Note: Too many facts and company brochures will only bore the customer. The point the closer wants to make is that he works with a proven, dedicated company.)

There is another goal — a personal one — the closer can achieve by aggressively pitching his company: self respect. (Note: In an earlier chapter I mentioned that the closer *is* the company, in the customer's mind.) The closer might be down, or depressed; he might be broke, or maybe he's just gone through a divorce — or anything else that's negative. The company product pitch can do wonders to help the closer get himself out of a negative attitude rut. All the closer has to do is promote his company with enthusiasm. The closer must convey the feeling that his company is successful and positive — it's growing and on the way up. Since the closer is a part of that company, he is, therefore, also successful. He's on his way up too. The closer is the company and his strength should spring from that fact. (Plus he has himself, the Lord, and the product he's pitching.)

There is no reason for the closer to ever show signs of depression in front of his customers, especially when his company is successful because that company's success also makes him successful. No matter how you are really feeling, if you combine your company's success with your own self-confidence, and self-respect, it will make a favorable impression on your customers everytime.

Sam said there is no time limit on the pre-demonstration pitch. He said sometimes a closer will ask one or two insignificant questions and then go right into a full-scale sales presentation. Then there are other times when the "pre-pitch" can last for an hour or more. It's all up to the closer, Sam said, to determine when his customer is attentive and interested, and then to take the appropriate action.

The following is a brief summary of the five steps in a pre-demonstration pitch Sam taught me. (Note: The pre-demonstration pitch begins when the closer and the customer are seated and comfortable.)

Step 1. The Closer Is Special. The closer should tell the customer he is someone special; this makes the customer feel special also, and helps the closer achieve more control and authority.

Step 2. The Closer's Story. The closer should let the customer have some personal insight into himself, not only to establish trust and a common bond, but to find out helpful personal information about the customer, to better close him.

Step 3. The Trap Set-Up. The closer needs to drop this type of time bomb early in the "pre-pitch" to get an affirmative answer from the customer. This "pre-pitch trap" will work for the closer if he uses it properly.

Step 4. Thought Questions. The closer uses these little questions along the way to find out information, plant ideas, and maintain customer participation. These little thought questions will eventually build up to a big affirmative buying answer.

Step 5. The Company and Product. The closer needs to introduce the customer to the company and the product for the first time here. This orients the customer and provides a foundation for him so he can understand the sales presentation as it continues.

Sam showed me some notes on the pre-demonstration pitch. He said these reminders are important to the closer if he intends to successfully use a pre-demonstration pitch.

Pre-Demonstration Pitch Notes

1. The closer should be able to pre-qualify (make a judgment about the customer's financial capabilities, personality make-up, and degree of product interest) the customer to some extent after he has briefly talked to him. (The length of time is up to the closer.) The closer should think about the right price range for the customer and set up his demonstration to reflect that "price area." The closer should always direct the customer to the lower-priced product first and let the customer go up the price scale if he wants to. The closer should be able to adjust and re-figure his price range quickly if necessary. (Note: The closer still has his basic game plan, but at the same time he has to be flexible enough to incorporate any new information the customer himself might contribute.)

2. If a woman or girl in the customer's party is attractive, the closer should mention it. There is no need for embarrassment, or shyness on the closer's part. For example: "Mr. Customer, I hope you won't get angry with me, but with all respect, your wife (or daughter) is one of the prettiest ladies I've ever seen. My wife would kill me if she heard me say that, but I really mean it. You're a very lucky man." This kind of statement, if said sincerely and with the proper delivery, will get the closer a sale.

3. If the closer doesn't know an answer to a question — or sometimes if he really does — he should tell the customer, "Mr. Customer, that's a good question. You're the first person who ever asked about that. I'd like to know the answer myself. Excuse me and let me go find out."

This will show the customer he doesn't have a know-it-all closer. It will also build trust and respect between the customer and closer. The customer will feel that the closer is honest by admitting he didn't know something, so the customer will tend to put more trust in the closer's future statements during the sales presentation.

4. *Always* build self-confidence in the customer throughout the pre-demonstration pitch and the sales presentation. Work on his ego, his achievements, his family's future dreams — anything that builds positive thoughts. The customer will need this self confidence and fortitude to make a buying decision when the time comes and it's up to the closer to develop that mood in him. The closer should remember that all the little positive ego boosts along the way will help this process. But they have to be delivered and developed by the closer with sincerity.

5. If the closer feels physically ill or has a hangover from the night before, he should simply tell his customer the truth. For example: "Mr. Customer, last night we had a company party and I am not at my best today, so please forgive me." He will automatically think he caught the closer off guard and will, in turn, let his own guard down.

This is the perfect place to use reverse psychology. The closer should give a negative pitch and ask for the customer's help (now and then), during the sales presentation. For example: "Here, Mr. Customer, would you please hold this material for me? I am not feeling that well." Or "Mr. Customer, did they just page me, did someone call me?" or "Mr. Customer, I apologize, but what did you say?"

The customer will join right in and become more involved than he meant to in the first place. Before anyone knows it the customer will be saying, "You know, this doesn't look like a bad deal after all." This maneuver is a great way to get the customer interested, and then sold — not through a great sales presentation, but because the closer let the customer feel like part of the team. This also works because greedy customers may think they can get a better deal out of you in your weakened state.

6. The closer should show the strength of his company to the customer through facts, sales plaques, awards, sales material, etc. There are times the closer has to use all of the sales information he has to close a customer; other times he doesn't have to use any. The important thing for the closer to know and remember is how to use these facts and details when he has to.

7. The closer should tell his customer he is going to get some "inside information" other customers won't have.

The customer must know he gets this inside information and V. I . P. treatment because the closer is in some way "special" (a staff member, a top closer, a manager, etc.). This draws the customer closer to the sales situation and makes him much more interested in what is going on. It's just one more step closer to the sale, compliments of the closer.

> Note: There is no certain time or set place in the sales presentation to actually close the customer. The master closer is continually (from the first second he says "Hello" to his customer, until the sale is made) going after that sale with every question and statement he can muster. The master closer knows that every single "Yes" or positive response he gets from his customer is a step that much closer to getting the sale consummated.

8. The closer can get very close to some customers and guarantee himself a sale almost every time if he uses a version of the following "special approach statement":

"Mr. Customer, the reason I'm going to explain the product to you and not one of the other salespeople is because the regular salespeople didn't really want to spend any time with you. They think maybe you can't afford the product or something. I don't know about your finances and I don't care. All I know is that I would love to show you what we're doing and help you in any way I possibly can. So just forget about them, because now you are with me."

This kind of "special approach statement" should be used on less affluent customers, minority customers and those who seem depressed or unhappy. This approach will usually get the customer angry — not with the helping closer, but with the other salesmen. However, it will generate a sale, if there is any way the customer can afford the product. This approach has to be delivered with tact, a lot of understanding and sincerity.

9. Sam told me he once knew a closer who used to say, "Look 'em straight in the eye and lie your ass off." That's very cute and macho-sounding, but the master closer has to learn that truth is a million times stronger than a lie. The truth can exert as much pressure on the customer as the closer needs. The closer can push a customer around, pound on him and beat him senseless with the truth; if the customer knows it's the truth, he will usually take the punishment. The truth is the only pure, one hundred percent guaranteed closing weapon the master closer possesses and he'd better build on it, use it and honor it, if he wants to be the best. And that's the truth.

10. The closer should always change places with the customer, in his own mind, during the pre-demonstration pitch. By attempting to share the customer's viewpoint the closer will be able to better build a bond of common understanding.

11. The closer must become people-oriented. The closer should be aware and alert to all of the needs surrounding his customer. The customer will say things and do things that tell his whole story, if you let him. The closer just has to watch, listen and think.

12. When the closer is giving his "pre-demonstration pitch" or sales presentation, he can't let anything else distract him. The closer must be aware of his customer's actions and reactions all the time. The closer should be able to tune in or tune out any exterior elements, such as ringing telephones, interruptions, delivery boys — let someone else deal with these things — the closer's main concern should only be his customer and a sale, nothing else.

13. The closer has to acknowledge he will *always* have objections and excuses from each and every customer. There will always be more "No's" than "Yes's" but it's all part of the game. These little hurdles make him a master closer instead of a common salesman. If the closer didn't have to overcome tough objections, anyone could call himself a closer — even a mere salesman.

14. If the customer gets ahead of the closer with a question unrelated to what is being discussed at that moment, the closer can put the conversation back on the right track by saying, "Now, Mr. Customer, you just jumped to page seven and I'm only on page three. Please slow down and give me a chance to catch up — you're going too fast."

This will not anger or offend the customer — in fact, it will flatter his ego making him feel as if he must be smarter than the average people you are accustomed to dealing with. A tactful way to maintain control.

15. All through the pre-demonstration pitch and the sales presentation the closer has to constantly build value for and in his product. This is the only true way the closer can justify the product's price tag. The closer has to establish this value through a slow and deliberate presentation, explaining the merits and potential of the product. If you play it correctly, when the customer finally hears what the price is, he won't have a heart attack.

16. The closer should never depersonalize his "pre-demonstration pitch" or sales presentation. The customer is not a number and never will be. He is a human being with feelings and any closer who forgets this, isn't going to stay in the sales field for too long.

17. The complex matter of the sales presentation can be summarized in three simple steps: First, build value in the product; second, compare the product with others in the same field; and third, sell the product.

18. The closer can make some valuable personal observations about his customer if he studies the customer's handwriting. Sam taught me a few basic pointers on this subject:

A. If the customer's handwriting is neat and meticulous, he probably relates well to these traits in others. If your private office is disorderly and looks like a disaster area, you are better off closing this customer in the conference room, someone else's office, or in a quiet part of the showroom.

B. If the handwriting is sloppy and inconsistent, there is a good chance this buyer won't mind a little disorder in your office and may even be able to relate to you more because it might remind him of his own office. If your office is neat, this buyer won't mind and may even respect you a little more because you are not as messy as he is.

19. The closer has the right to know if his sales presentation is being taped by a customer. If the closer notices he is being recorded he should politely ask the customer why. It is generally unwise to proceed under these circumstances because this customer has a high liklihood of turning into a nightmare experience further down the road. You should send these types to competitors that you don't like and let them suffer.

The master closer is a professional with his own techniques and format; he has a right to protect those secrets from anyone, especially a customer carrying a tape recorder.

20. If the closer has delivered the pre-demonstration pitch correctly, he should be able to tell where he stands with his customer. The closer should be aware how the customer relates to the product and also to him. The closer will also have a good idea of how far to proceed with the sales presentation before he starts closing in on the customer for the sale. All of this information becomes available to the closer if he just gives a good, comprehensible "pre- demonstration pitch."

Sam told me to remember that the pre-demonstration pitch is the beginning of the total sales presentation; it directs and channels the customer toward the actual presentation. Sam said that since I had been introduced to the "pre-pitch," and I knew how the closer utilized it, I was now ready to study the product presentation itself.

PRESENTING THE PRODUCT:
Show-and-Tell Time

Sam always told me the purpose of the sales presentation is to describe, demonstrate, explain and show the product or service in the most positive way possible, so the customer will want to buy it.

The total sales presentation has three basic parts, he said.

• The first part is the pre-demonstration pitch.
• The second part is when the actual product is being presented.
• The third part is when the closer asks the customer to buy the product.

I had just completed studying the pre-demonstration pitch (Part I), and Sam said it would be a good idea not to take a break at this point but to continue right into the actual product presentation itself.

To explain the sales presentation properly, Sam chose an undeveloped square acre of land as an example, presenting and showing it in "progressive steps." All the presentation maneuvers, techniques and tricks that will be illustrated and explained here can easily be adapted to other sales fields. All the closer has to do is understand the steps and procedures of product presentation, then incorporate them into his own sales field.

Sam said the most effective way to demonstrate the product presentation is to show how the steps work, individually, and then how they fit into the overall sales presentation. Each of the twelve steps are outlined in a progressive order leading to the final closing question.

Before studying the steps to a presentation Sam said there are two very basic rules (Fundamental Facts) a closer must understand.

The first is the "Rolls Royce Rule" (primarily for the closer's benefit); the second is the "Seeing is Believing Rule" (mostly for the customer's benefit). Without knowing these two rules, a closer cannot expect to give a complete and successful sales presentation, much less get the sale.

The Rolls Royce Rule

This rule states that sales are made by closers, not by a company's advertising department.

Suppose a young ad executive comes up with a "different" idea for selling. Instead of hiring closers to get the job done, he hires a number of sweet-talking, attractive women, dresses them in beautifully coordinated outfits and gives each one a Rolls Royce. Then the eager beaver executive assembles some potential customers and sends them on demonstration tours with these lovely women as guides. After the tour is complete, the beautiful guides bring the customers back to the company's sales office where they meet salesmen who then try to persuade them to buy the company's product.

This type of selling might sound good on paper, but in cold, hard reality it won't work because the good-looking guides are not *closers*. True, the guides give the customers some product information during their canned presentation pitch. But this type of sales presentation falls apart because the guides never get to know or understand the customers. They are not expected to learn the customers' feelings, know their characters or listen to their dreams and ambitions. The beautiful guides don't have the opportunity to stay with the customers during the whole sales presentation, making it impossible to establish the important salesperson to customer rapport. To the tour guides, their customers tend to turn into numbers and not real people.

Selling in this manner can never match the basic one-on-one relationship that exists when the only parties involved are the closer and his customer. *Every customer needs personal attentiveness, individual treatment, plus genuine interest.* The closer addresses these needs. The closer knows how to make the customer feel appreciated and downright special. Without these personal elements the customer is nothing more than a percentage point on a piece of paper, someone's sales quota, or data in a computer.

A smart company must hire closers instead of tour guides or plain salesmen to sell its products or services. The closer maintains his customer's interest during the entire sales presentation; he knows his customer inside and out. The closer understands his customer's needs and maximizes his buying capabilities. He develops a well-founded and trusting friendship with his customer.

All these feelings, thoughts and emotions the closer establishes will affect the customer when the final buying question is asked. The Rolls Royce, the beautiful women and all the advertising gimmicks can't compete with a determined and confident closer, one who stays with his customer from the start of the presentation until the sale is finally made.

(Note: The next statement is not a contradiction of the example above. That illustration was given to make a strong point concerning the "one-on-one" closer-customer relationship.)

A "tour guide-closer" type of presentation *can* work *if* it is executed properly and in a professional manner. This type of "team-work" selling can be very effective if the tour guide and closer are well organized. The team has to educate the customer about each member's respective role in the total sales presentation. For example: One team member tells the customer that he will demonstrate the product and the other team member will explain the financing and paperwork involved. Each closer or team member specializes in a particular area of the overall sales presentation. This simple explanation will keep the customer from getting confused during the presentation, and give him some understanding of the team's working arrangement.

This type of selling is not only fun but very powerful when used on a customer. Both team members get to support each other's statements and each member gives the other strength. The team can bounce the sales presentation back and forth between each other, with the customer always in the middle and off balance. This team action keeps everyone (especially the customer) excited and interested in the product or service. The main thing to remember about team selling is: Each team member must know exactly what the other member is saying or going to say to the customer. If the team members don't have their game plan down pat and well organized, one member might say something to the customer that would overlap or contradict what the other member has said. This scenario only leads to confusion and distrust on the customer's part, and ultimately a lost sale. Coordination is the key here.

Seeing is Believing Rule

The closer must remember that the pre-demonstration pitch was the very first time the customer was exposed to the closer's company and to its product. In the presentation pitch the closer gave a simple overall picture to his customer of his product. The closer also set up a starting point or foundation on which to build the rest of his sales presentation. (Note: The closer, and it cannot be expressed enough, has got to keep his sales presentation direct and simple, so the customer can follow it, understand it, and then take positive action in the form of a decision to buy the product.)

With the pre-demonstration pitch completed, the closer is now ready to go directly into the physical presentation of the product itself. In other words the closer lets the customer actually see, feel, smell and touch the product. The closer shows the product in its physical form and presence, involving the customer in a "seeing is believing" situation. All the "sales table talk" is finally being backed up through a visual and physical product presentation. Example: "Mr. Johnson, I've been telling you in the sales office how beautiful the view of the valley is from this particular piece of property. Now you can see for yourself — isn't that view magnificent?"

These two basic rules make up the foundation of the total sales presentation. With those under my belt, Sam said I was ready to study the "Twelve Production Presentation Steps," that lead to the pre-closing questions and the close in the next chapter.

(Note: Remember that one acre of undeveloped land will be used as the example product for the "Twelve Steps.")

Step 1: Setting The Stage:
Getting The Customer Physically Involved.

The closer should tell his customer interesting stories about the area surrounding the acre of undeveloped land. He should build narratives around special landmarks — lakes, streams, cliffs, caves, old houses, barns, or just beautiful views — anything the closer feels will spark the customer's imagination and buying interest.

The closer must present a comfortable and intriguing picture for the customer so he can begin to establish a personal attachment to the land (the product). The closer must carefully set the stage; the customer himself will inject the product into his dreams and future plans. If you prepare the customer properly, his subconscious mind becomes actively involved and begins to consider the product (an acre of land) as his own property, before he has even consciously decided to buy.

This type of showmanship on the closer's part will also help build the product's value in the eyes of the customer.

The closer should always try to make his stories thought-provoking, active and to the point. He should show his product with controlled enthusiasm and excitement because the mental and physical involvement he inspires will produce positive reactions in the customer's behavior. The closer's enthusiastic actions will keep the customer alert, attentive, and get his imagination and adrenalin flowing. The closer should try to somehow get the customer physically involved in the product presentation (walking the land, driving a demonstrator car, working a piece of machinery) so he becomes a part of the presentation. This makes the seller's final closing question easier for the customer to answer.

I am going to repeat this following reminder so you don't forget it, a few times throughout this lesson:

Note: The closer must observe, listen to and learn from his customer continually throughout the total sales presentation to gather customer information. He will need that information later as ammunition against his customer when going in for the close (the Kill).

Step 2: Learn From The Customer.

One of the best ways for the closer to establish a personal relationship with his customer during the product presentation is to learn, or at least act like he has learned, something important from his customer. The information doesn't have to be related to the product although it would be more effective if it were related. The customer must believe the closer has genuinely gained some new knowledge from him and that the information is sincerely appreciated.

This kind of "appreciate the information" maneuver on the closer's part will build up the customer's confidence by flattering his ego and letting him know his thoughts have merit and are respected by the closer. For example: "Mr. Customer, I didn't realize that, thank you for enlightening me," or "Mr. Customer, I've been trying to find that answer for a long time and you're the first person who has known it — thank you."

The customer will then become even more attentive to the closer's product presentation, because he will feel his "new" information has put him on the same level as the closer. The customer won't feel as though he is just receiving information from the closer (a one-sided scenario) but that he is actually assisting and contributing as well. The customer will feel he is a part of the closer's personal inner circle and not just any regular, ordinary customer. This is especially successful when dealing with investments. Customers love to give brokers their view of the market, economy, international politics, etc.

Note: The closer must observe, listen to and learn from his customer continually throughout the total sales presentation to gather customer information. He will need that information later as ammunition against his customer when going in for the close (the Kill).

Step 3: Find Out Who Handles The Money:
Who's the Leader or Who Wears the Pants.

The closer should determine who is the leader, the decision-maker and the money controller in the customer's party (the husband and wife team). It could be the husband, the wife or both equally. But no matter who (or what combination) it is, it's the closer's job to find out so he can direct his main sales attack (product presentation) toward that individual.

The same is true of large customer groups as well. For example: In a party of four couples there will nearly always be a leader. The closer has to know and recognize the central figure if he wants to get a sale, period. If the closer can't recognize the leader then he will pitch the wrong members of the team, and appear foolish — the customers know who their leader is, and they will lose respect for a closer who misjudges them so badly. The closer must always be alert to avoid this fatal mistake.

There are several ways the closer can spot a leader. The following rules will be a basic guideline to help determine who handles the money.

Rule A. The person in the customer's party who asks the most questions, talks the most and seems to have the most interest in the product will most likely be the leader. The closer should keep in mind that this is not always and absolutely true. For example: In some groups, such as families, the oldest son will often try to demonstrate his intelligence by asking a flood of product questions to try to impress the closer and his dad. In truth it will be the son's father, the fellow who is just sitting back and listening, who actually controls the family's money. He's the one who makes the final buying decision and not his action-packed son. In large customer groups, one member of the customer's party may do all the talking and appear to be the leader when in reality he may just be trying to impress his friends. In many cases the talking and active customer turns out to be broke, and the silent, reserved customer is the one with the financial capability to purchase the product.

When the closer is confronted with this type of sales situation, he should ask himself, "Who is the most sincere or reserved or interested person in the whole group?" When you figure out the answer to this question you will almost always discover the party's real leader. The closer knows he has to constantly read between the lines, defining and analyzing everything being said and done or not said and done.

Rule B. The closer can determine the customers' leader by observing the individual's physical actions. The closer should notice which members of the party are nervous, which ones are always looking around the sales office, which members are whispering to others. These little physical actions will tell a great deal about the members of the party. By observation the closer can pretty accurately identify the leader.

The leader is usually the one all the other members look at most. The members consciously and subconsciously look to him for guidance, direction and approval. Whether he is a silent type or a visible and verbal leader, the closer can identify him if he just observes and thinks.

Rule C. The closer can force his customers to identify their leader through the following two maneuvers:

(1) The closer should direct all important questions to one member of the customer's party. If that person turns out to be the leader, then everything is fine. But if he isn't then the person the closer is addressing will look to the leader for help sooner or later. The closer's questions will make that customer uncomfortable because he knows, in his own mind, he doesn't make decisions, and will seek out the stronger member for support. From that point on the closer will know exactly who to talk to.

(2) The closer can jokingly ask the whole group, "All right, I give up — which one of you is the leader?" This question might sound silly, but it works. The closer isn't really looking for a sincere answer; but he is watching to see which member blushes, puts his head down, or gets embarrassed. Also, when that silly little question is asked, most of the members will look directly at the money man. It might only be for a split second, but they will look at him, just to see his reaction. The closer has to watch everyone's eyes and pay sharp attention or he might miss the clue.

By using these silly questions the real leader can be discovered. Then it's up to the closer to follow his planned sales presentation, and direct it toward the real decision-maker.

Note: The closer must observe, listen to and learn from his customer continually throughout the total sales presentation to gather customer information. He will need that information later as ammunition against his customer when going in for the close (the Kill).

Step 4: Tell The Customer you (The Closer) Own
The Same Product, Or Would Like To.

A good way for the closer to make customers feel more confident and secure about the product being sold is for the closer to tell customers that he owns the product or service, or would like to soon buy it himself.

For example: "Mr. Customer, this property is the best and most beautiful piece of land I've seen in over two years. I'd buy it myself but I have my money tied up in another piece of land. I even tried to call my brother so he could buy it, but he was out of town and I couldn't reach him. If you really like the property and you're sincere, I'll let you have it for the same price I was going to quote my brother, and on the same terms. In other words, I'll let you buy it at the same price I could have gotten it for myself. Please don't let anyone know about this, as it will not make our company look good if people find out we have reduced our price this much.

By telling the customer the closer couldn't afford the land, he shows the customer he is human too and has financial limitations. This pitch also demonstrates that the product is good enough for the closer to buy, thus making the customer feel more confident about making a buying decision.

This speech must be delivered with total sincerity and smooth showmanship on the closer's part or the customer will see right through it and become turned-off as soon as the closer opens his mouth. This statement will work wonders if the customer believes it, and it's up to the closer to make him believe it's true.

Note: The closer must observe, listen to and learn from his customer continually throughout the total sales presentation to gather customer information. He will need that information later as ammunition against his customer when going in for the close (the Kill).

Step 5: Demonstrating The Product.

When the closer actually touches and handles his product, he must have a genuine sense of respect and reverence for it. This doesn't mean the closer should go overboard and treat a common rock as a perfectly cut diamond or a piece of steel as if it were a rare porcelain sculpture. But the closer should give his customer the very best show he can muster.

The closer should prepare himself for the act of physically presenting his product to the customer. This presentation must convey that his product is the best, the finest, and the greatest in the whole world. The closer cannot afford to show his customer anything less than the best. The customer must feel this specialness, this respectfulness that the closer inspires for his product because that feeling will excite him, keep his attention and make him realize he is seeing the best.

Even if the product is a bucket of mud, the closer should present it in a velvet cloth, saying, "It's the finest, richest and rarest mud in the entire world." The closer has to convince the customer that his product is the finest among all of the competition in this particular category, period.

Here are some special pointers the closer has to remember when demonstrating a product:

(a) When a closer shows a car, or piece of machinery, etc., he should touch it or hold it gently, and avoid pointing at the product or slamming a hand on it. (Note: There are times when the closer has to handle the product roughly to demonstrate a point, but we are not talking about that now.) The product should be handled gently and shown respect; the customer will then be more inclined to believe that the product is worthy of respect.

(b) The closer must demonstrate his product in a simple and easy-to-understand manner. The presentation should have a smooth tempo so the customer can keep pace with the closer. The closer should not talk or explain his presentation so fast that he loses or bores the customer. This will only confuse the buyer and force the closer to repeat himself, leading to more confusion and frustration for both the closer and customer.

(c) When the closer turns a dial on a vacuum sweeper or walks a piece of real estate or demonstrates a new car, he should do it slowly and deliberately, taking enough time to let the product soak into the customer's subconscious.

(d) The closer should point out the most impressive and surprising new features of the product last as a kind of "icing on the cake" for his customer. In other words, the customer has heard and seen all of the basic and familiar strong points about the product. But then, as a final touch, the customer learns about all the goodies, the deluxe extras, the specials that make this product the top of the line. The closer, by showing the extras last, has brought his product presentation up to an even higher level of interest — a level that signals the high point of the product presentation and the beginning of the closing questions.

Note: I would like to again remind you that there is no certain time or set place in the sales presentation to actually close the customer. The master closer is continually (from the first second he says "Hello" to his customer, until the sale is made) going after the sale with every question and statement he can think of. The master closer knows that every single "Yes" or positive response he gets from his customer brings him a step closer to getting that sale consummated.

When demonstrating his product the closer must show genuine pride. This pride and self-assurance the closer projects will be noticed and respected by the customer, and will sway the customer in a positive way. Through showmanship, enthusiasm and pride the closer can make both himself and his product appear to be the best in the world; the customer will relate to this attitude in a second, and appreciate it.

For example: "Mr. Customer, it's just like I told you, back in the sales office, you will never see a more beautiful view, more majestic trees, or a more peaceful setting than this piece of property has to offer. I don't care if you look all around the country, this property is the finest and I think you can see that. Furthermore, the price will fit into your budget. Now you can see why I was so excited and enthused about showing you this acre of land."

Note: The closer must observe, listen to and learn from his customer continually throughout the total sales presentation to gather customer information. He will need that information later as ammunition against his customer when going in for the close (the Kill).

Step 6:

(A) The Closer Should Get Physically Involved With His Product; (B) How To Make The Customer Feel More Obligated.

(a) The closer can create interest in his product and more of an obligation to buy if he becomes physically involved with the product and "gets his hands dirty." When a closer shows his customer a product he should touch, pick up, pat and hold it. If he projects a standoffish attitude concerning the product, so will his customer. The customer will think to himself, "If *he* doesn't want to handle and demonstrate his own product, then why should I?" If this feeling exists there won't be any sale, period. The closer has to lead and inspire the customer to get him involved. He can't do it by sitting on the sidelines praying for the sale to occur.

(b) "The extra mile trick" will get a customer more involved in the product presentation and create a feeling of "obligation to buy." When the closer is involved with his product presentation physically, he should tear his shirt sleeve or step in some mud or "bump" his head or get some grease on his clothes — anything to get the sympathetic attention of the customer. He will see that the closer hurt himself or had some misfortune when he was presenting his product to him and will feel the closer went that extra personal mile for his (the customer's) benefit.

This product presentation trick is so simple it works everytime. Most customers will immediately feel sorry for the closer because of the misfortune and become more deeply involved with the closer personally because of his efforts and concern. This will bring the closer and the customer closer together, creating the total customer-closer relationship the closer needs to finalize a sale.

Note: The closer must observe, listen to and learn from his customer continually throughout the total sales presentation to gather customer information. He will need that information later as ammunition against his customer when going in for the close (the Kill).

Step 7: Planting Seeds Of Imagination In The Customer's Mind.

During the product presentation the closer should tell the customer where actual improvements (water mains, roads, street lights, etc.) are going to be built on the acre of land we are using as an example. The closer has to take the lead at this point and draw an attractive picture of the raw, undeveloped acre of land being sold. The closer always has to plant "positive ideas" and "possibility seeds" throughout the product presentation for customers to feed on. (For example: "Mr. Customer, wouldn't the front of the property look beautiful when it's landscaped just the way you and your family have always dreamed?" or "Mr. Customer, wouldn't it be nice to build a sun deck over there to take advantage of that magnificent view?")

The customer will enhance this picture and paint it with his own multi-colored visions and dreams. If the closer properly motivates his customer the buyer should become more involved in the presentation each minute.

The closer has to constantly plant positive suggestions and stories about the product before the customer's imagination is truly activated.

A customer can imagine the thrill of owning a new car or swimming pool more vividly than the closer can convey. But the closer has to steer the customer's thoughts toward the product being sold and then show how the product would benefit the customer and his family. Then the closer should sit back for a moment and watch how the customer will start closing *himself* through his own special and private dreams. It's an amazing yet common reaction on the customer's part, and it works. But the closer must always use calculated showmanship with enthusiasm when he is planting the "positive suggestion seeds."

Note: The closer must observe, listen to and learn from his customer continually throughout the total sales presentation to gather customer information. He will need that information later as ammunition against his customer when going in for the close (the Kill).

Step 8: Put The Customer In The "Driver's Seat," Get Him Involved Both Physically and Psychologically.

Throughout the total product presentation the closer must stimulate the customer into visualizing himself as the owner of the product being sold. The closer has to describe the product's uses and advantages (but not in too much detail, because this will only bore the buyer) so his customer will "daydream" about how the product will fit into his life. The closer can spark this "customer imagination" through the use of the most basic sales procedures. For example: If a closer is selling cars, he should put his customer in the driver's seat and let him drive around, flattering the customer (working on that old ego) by telling him how sharp and natural he looks behind the wheel of that particular car. If a closer is selling a vacuum cleaner he has to use a convincing demonstration to show his customer the advantages of his product, allowing the customer to actually use the vacuum himself. If a closer is selling stocks and bonds, he needs to point out the return on investment to be made and all the future potential appreciation.

No matter what a closer may be selling, he must always show the best possible advantages of his product, plus all the benefits his customer can and should come to expect.

The closer has to build an understandable and positive picture for the customer to see; and he has to constantly work on the customer's never ending ego and future-ownership pride. All these characteristics are basic and proven — sales wouldn't be made without them. Any rookie salesman knows them — they are rituals that have to be performed to get a sale. These sales procedures are the groundwork for any product presentation, but this book will not dwell on these fundamentals. That information can be found in any ordinary sales book on the market.

This book goes beyond those fundamentals, just as a closer goes beyond a regular salesman when giving a product presentation. You will learn how to create a magical happening, a closer's phenomenon called "customer imagination" and understand precisely how it works. The closer must get the customer involved, both psychologically and physically, during the product presentation. That is a fact. But the closer will do something extra special, something salesmen don't know how to do or just don't do, and that is this: The smart closer will not only put his customer in the driver's seat and encourage him to visualize himself there, but he will actually make the customer believe he belongs there, and he deserves to be there. The closer will not only build a dream for his customer, but he will make his customer believe that dream with all his heart. The closer leads the customer into believing, deep down in his gut, that he not only would use the product being sold, but that he really needs it. The closer establishes this customer feeling in one simple way. He makes the customer believe in himself, feel confident about himself and like himself. The closer accomplishes this through compliments, courtesy, respect and a real and genuine interest in the customer.

Note: The closer must observe, listen to and learn from his customer continually throughout the total sales presentation to gather customer information. He will need that information later as ammunition against his customer when going in for the close (the Kill).

Step 9: Playing The Older Customer Against The Younger Customer Or People Against People.

When the closer is demonstrating or showing his product to an older customer, he should casually mention, "Mr. Customer, you know I show this product to a lot of people and in doing so I've learned something very important: the younger customers — the folks who haven't been around much or haven't gone through all the hard times you have — don't really appreciate or understand my product and its advantages. I guess what I mean is, the younger buyers just haven't grown up enough to really know what is good for them, or what's really beneficial for them. Mr. Older Customer, you know what I mean, don't you?" At this point the closer should shut up and wait for the older customer to answer (and he will). The older customer will, in most cases, automatically say "Yes, I sure do know what you are talking about." (Note: This spontaneous response comes from a natural feeling that exists in nearly all older people. Older customers tend to think most younger people don't have the same respect and understanding for things that they have.)

By agreeing with the closer, the older customer has actually stated that the younger generation doesn't know all the things he does and they aren't smart enough to see a good deal when presented with one like he does, so ... (Bang, Presto): The older customer, without even knowing it, has just trapped himself with his own answer — an answer that was set up and developed by the closer from the beginning with his sly use of "The Statement and Question Trick." The older customer has given a positive answer to the closer which the closer can turn around and use against him when the closing process begins. (For example: "Mr. Older Customer, do you remember what you said earlier, about how younger customers don't appreciate this offer or product because they haven't been through the hard times? And do you remember all the situations you've been through, the problems you've overcome that the younger people haven't ever had to face yet? Do you realize all the advantages you have over them, because you have already experienced so much and have much more knowledge than they do? Well, let me ask you this, with your background and know-how, surely you know the benefits of my product. I know that you can't sit there and tell me "no" you're not interested, when you actually know, deep down, what this product can do for you, am I right?")

The secret to this "Statement and Question Trick" is for the closer to continue (without missing a beat) with his product presentation as soon as he hears the older customer's answer. In other words, the closer should never stop or pause after the older customer gives his answer, because this statement is only being used as a trap (a seed thought) for the older customer. In fact, after the older customer gives his positive "Yes" answer, he may think to himself, "What in the world have I just said? What have I just gotten myself into?" But it will be too late, the closer has sprung the trap and the point has been made.

This "Statement and Question Trick" will work exactly the same way on younger customers. The "statement" made by the closer simply has to be reversed, turned around. The closer should tell the younger customers how the older customers don't appreciate or know what is going on in today's world, and that the younger customers have the foresight and opportunity to take advantage of new offers or products that older customers just don't understand. The closer should plant the "ego seed" the same way for the younger customer as he did for the older customer. This "Statement and Question Trick" will work on either customer, older or younger; the only thing the closer must remember is to continue on with his product presentation and let the customer's answer soak in and work on the customer's mind, all by itself. (Note: The "Statement and Question Trick" can be used to attack or compare people from different parts of the country, different cultural backgrounds, etc.)

Note: The closer must observe, listen to and learn from his customer continually throughout the total sales presentation to gather customer information. He will need that information later as ammunition against his customer when going in for the close (the Kill).

Step 10: The 'Plain Jane' vs. The 'Top Of The Line'.

(Note: This is one of many example steps that can be used throughout the product presentation to explain the many benefits of the closer's product and make the product's future potential and value easy for the customer to understand and relate to. This example can be easily adapted to any product or service.)

The closer should tell the customer he is getting in on the ground floor (the best place and time to buy) regarding the undeveloped acre of land. The closer should point out the advantages of purchasing the property before any improvements are put on it, so the customer will not only save money but make additional money after the property has been developed and has "value added."

The closer can illustrate this point to the customer by using the following example. "Mr. Customer, this undeveloped acre of land that we're looking at is exactly like a 'Plain Jane' car — it doesn't have any special equipment on it or any extras at all. That's why you can go down to your local car dealership and buy this type of automobile at the lowest possible price. Isn't that correct? All right let's say you take this 'Plain Jane' and you put steel belted tires on it. Then you put leather upholstery in it; you put a sun roof on it, a tape deck, power steering and power brakes — the works. Now, all of a sudden, you don't have a stripped-down model anymore, do you? Now you've got an expensive top-of-the-line model that costs a whole lot more than the 'Plain Jane' we started with, and it's still sitting on the very same 'Plain Jane' frame. Mr. Customer, this undeveloped acre of land is exactly the same as the 'Plain Jane' car. All you have to do is use your imagination a little and I think you can visualize what this property will look like when it's improved, and at the same time, Mr. Customer, what the appreciated value of this land will be. It's just that simple."

Note: The closer must observe, listen to and learn from his customer continually throughout the total sales presentation to gather customer information. He will need that information later as ammunition against his customer when going in for the close (the Kill).

Step 11: Tell "Other-People Stories" And "Third-Party Stories"

The closer can pressure the customer, make a point to the customer, or explain a "good deal" or "the right opportunity" to the customer by using people stories. For example: (This is an "other-people story" used to explain a "good deal") "Mr. Customer, the reason this property is for sale at this unusually low price is because the people who bought it a few months ago had to make a sudden move to another part of the country due to a job transfer. The property hasn't been re-priced or appraised yet, so you can buy it at the same price the other family did because they just want to get their original money out. In other words, you can purchase the property for the original price." Or, "Mr. Customer, another family was going to buy this property two months ago, but they decided that they wanted more acreage. In all the confusion the land hasn't been put back on the market yet and because of this mix-up it is the only plot in this area still available.

The closer can also use "third-party stories" to put added pressure on his customer. For example: Mr. Customer, I had another customer just like you — in fact, you remind me of him. About one year ago he said that he wanted some property for his family so he could take them out in the country to go camping and build a vacation home someday. You know, he wanted a place to just get the family together. But first he said he had to look around and think things over and then he would let me know about the property. Well, I found out three weeks ago he never did buy any vacation or investment property — he died of a heart attack at his young age. He never did have an opportunity to get close to his family like he was telling me he wanted to, and I want you to know I feel that if I had encouraged him a little harder or used more persuasive salesmanship I could have maybe helped him make his dream come true. But I didn't and now it's too late. Mr. Customer, I'm sorry to bring up such a sad example but these things do happen and we see a lot of these types of stories.

The customer generally does not feel very pressured by "third-party stories" or "other-people stories" told by the closer. That is the beauty of using these types of stories. But in reality the customer will see the parallel and start thinking about buying. The closer can use this simple tactic all day long and get positive results.

But, third party stories have to be told with complete sincerity and effective showmanship on the closer's part. The closer can't make the story seem ridiculous or silly. It has to make sense and be believed by the customer to have any effect. The closer can explain away objections, problems, incidents — just about everything, by using "third-party" and "other-people" stories — but he has to make doubly sure that they directly relate to his customer and the sales situation he is confronted with.

Note: The closer must observe, listen to and learn from his customer continually throughout the total sales presentation to gather customer information. He will need that information later as ammunition against his customer when going in for the close (the Kill).

Step 12: Tell Customers They Are The Best.

Important: The closer should, at some point in the latter half of the product presentation, tell his customer that he is one of the finest people he has ever talked to. (Note: The closer should not make this statement during the closing part of the sales presentation because it will be too late to give out compliments at that point. Any complimentary statement at that time would only sound phony to the customer.) The closer should make a statement something like this: "Mr. Customer, what I'm about to say might sound like a sales pitch, and please forgive me for making it sound that way, but, in all sincerity, you and your family, whether you buy my product or not, are some of the best and most likable people I've ever known. I really mean it. It's truly a pleasure to talk to folks like you. It makes my job a whole lot more pleasant."

After the closer makes this statement he should act a little embarrassed, to insure the customer believes he was honestly speaking from the heart. Then the closer should continue with the rest of his product presentation, not waiting for any kind of response. The closer shouldn't dwell on the subject but simply let it linger and soak into the customer's mind. Then when it finally comes time for the closing questions you can be sure the customer will think about this genuine compliment and react in a positive and receptive manner. (Note: Remember, no one can dislike someone who they believe really likes them.) This complimentary statement the closer made will bring the sale that much closer. Customers tend to melt in the closer's hands if this statement is delivered with tactful sincerity and if the customer honestly believes it.

Note: The closer must observe, listen to and learn from his customer continually throughout the total sales presentation to gather customer information. He will need that information later as ammunition against his customer when going in for the close (the Kill).

Note: I would like to again remind you that there is no certain time or set place in the sales presentation to actually close the customer. The master closer is continually (from the first second he says "Hello" to his customer, until the sale is made) going after that sale with every question and statement he can muster. The master closer knows that every single "Yes" or positive response he gets from his customer brings him a step closer to getting the sale consummated.

Sam said this ended "the twelve product presentation steps," but there were three important notes I should remember concerning these "twelve presentation steps."

Note 1. Taking the Customer's Temperature. The closer should know exactly where he stands with his customer at any given time during the product presentation. He should also know how close his customer is to making a buying decision at any point during the presentation or demonstration. The closer can always find this type of information out by taking the customer's temperature. (Seeing how "hot" or close to the sale the customer actually is.) This is accomplished through questions directed straight at the customer. (Note: It's up to the closer's own discretion to determine what time during the presentation he wants to take this temperature reading.) For example: "Mr. Customer, how do you like the fantastic view from the back of this property?" or "Mr. Customer, what kind of driveway would you build from the main road?" or "How would you landscape the property to take advantage of that huge old oak tree?" Any kind of question from the closer that requires a positive and involved answer on the customer's part will work. The customer will either give an interested and thoughtful answer or an indifferent and unconcerned answer. The thing for the closer to remember is that the answer the customer gives will tell, to some degree, how he feels about the product, and it will show how close he is to buying. (Note: The closer has to listen intently and be alert to any answer the customer gives. The closer has to read between the lines and pay strict attention not to miss a thing the customer says or the sale could be lost at that point. The closer can tell a great deal, not only by what the customer says but how he says it.)

The closer can, if he feels the customer's answer is positive enough and the customer is ready, go right into a closing question, to get the sale then. But by the same token, the closer can keep right on pitching if he feels the customer's answer wasn't that positive or if the customer wasn't quite ready for a closing question.

Taking the customer's temperature is an easy way to get the customer involved in the product and to find out where things stand at the same time. The closer has to use tact and sincerity when he throws out his temperature questions, but the answers he receives will give him the coordinates he needs to steer in the right direction to get the sale. To put it another way, the closer has to have his finger on the customer's pulse all the time.

Note 2. (a) Customers Want What They Can't Have. The closer should be aware of a basic purchasing phenomenon that is true of every customer: All customers want what they can't have or get. If a closer shows the customer a common or average acre of land and the customer sees another piece of property that is beautiful, but has already been sold or is unattainable for some reason, the customer will dwell on the sold property and say things like, "Now, I would buy that property if it were for sale," or "That property is just what I was looking for, it's too bad that it's already been sold." (Note: Remember, people are people and they want what they can't have. Example: Why does a lovely woman date an unattractive man? Forgetting about money as a factor, the other reason is usually because the man played hard to get and most women love to be challenged socially.)

Note 2. (b) How to Trap Customers by Using This Human Weakness. The closer should set up traps for his customer by using this buying phenomenon. To illustrate this trap-setting maneuver, let's say a closer has a customer and he first shows the customer an average acre of land that looks all right but is nothing special. Then the closer shows the same customer another piece of property (because it's in the same vicinity or for some other believable reason) but this land is beautiful, with a great panoramic view for the exact same price. Now the closer tells or suggests to the customer that the beautiful view property has already been sold (in truth it hasn't, it's still for sale) and that the first property they looked at is the next best thing to buy. This is when the average customer will start making all of his positive and serious declarations and statements about what he would have done, saying that the view property is the only one he really wants and if it was for sale he would buy it immediately. This kind of statement is what the closer wanted to hear in the first place. Now, all the closer has to do is give a mediocre presentation concerning the first property (the average one), while still referring to the view property in an off-the-cuff manner, such as "Mr. Customer, you know, that view is fantastic, no wonder it has already been sold. I just wish we could have been here sooner so you could have owned it."

From this point on the customer will think that he's off the closer's hook because the property he really likes is gone. So the customer will continue to rave about the view property, its potential, its character, and all of its possibilities, not knowing he is only getting himself boxed in and trapped deeper by the minute. After the presentation is over the closer should excuse himself for a few minutes and go look at his property listings (or inventory). Then with excitement and enthusiasm the closer should tell the customer that upon checking, he found out that the view property was indeed sold, but the owner had just traded his equity into a piece of lake property (or some other believable reason). So now the customer can buy the property he wanted so badly at the exact same price quoted for the mediocre acre. The closer should then start writing up the order, without waiting for any customer response or objections. The closer should assume the sale is made and in most cases it will be a solid sale.

Note 3. Customers Talk to Customers. Some customers will always try to mingle with another closer's customer so that they can compare notes and information (whether it's in the restroom of a sales office, on the parking lot or at the refreshment center). Even if the customers don't know each other, they will try to talk to each other. The customer wants to know if the product presentation he is hearing from his closer is the same as the presentation being given by another closer. Customers are basically skeptical and they need this type of reassurance and enjoy checking up on their closer. The closer should recognize this and attempt to keep his customer away from the other closer's customers, without his customer being aware of what he is doing. The reason for this separation of customers on the closer's part is this: Customers will talk, exaggerate, and make up stories regarding their closer and the product to make themselves look sharp and knowledgeable about the whole sales situation in the eyes of the other customers. Customers want and need to project an air of confidence and strength to other customers (new-found friends). This is because they can't show this type of attitude around their own closer, as he is in charge and in control. So the customer lets the pressure off by talking (gossiping shamelessly) to other customers and in doing so lets the other customers know little "thises and thats". The little "thises and thats" comments between customers can kill a sale for a closer faster than anything else, and the closer will never know what happened.

Remember: Any kind of statement (or gossip) from a talkative, gossiping customer that contradicts something in your presentation could blow away one sale or more.

The closer should keep his customer to himself and protect his own product presentation from outsiders. The closer must have total control; any negative conversation or question from another customer could destroy the closer's control.

The customer separation can be achieved tactfully by the closer if he tells his customer he is not normally in the sales department, but is in management or on the staff, etc..., and that he (the customer) will be given special product presentation facts and prices other customers won't have and don't have to know about. The closer should then explain that for this reason the best thing to do is for the customer to stay right with him and keep all the special prices and product information to himself.

Since my lesson on the "twelve product presentation steps" was completed, Sam said I could proceed into my next subject of study: the "in-home sales presentation." Sam told me the best way to study the in-home presentation was to look at it in the form of a "do's and don'ts" list. Sam said, "When closing sales, whether a closer is in his sales office or in the customer's home, the basics never change." The closer has only to adapt his presentation to fit the situation and environment. The most important positive factor the closer has going for him when he is in the customer's home is that he (the closer) can tell everything about the customer's lifestyle (the way a man lives will reflect everything about the man) and adjust his presentation accordingly.

When the customer is in the closer's sales office, the closer has to judge the customer's lifestyle only from observing him personally without the advantages of seeing his usual living habits. The "in-home sales presentation" is always educational because every house and every customer has something different to offer, and every simple call the closer makes only adds to his professional character and knowledge.

In-Home Sales Presentation:
The Do's and Don'ts

1. Do: Go empty-handed. The closer should always go to the customer's door empty-handed, without any of his sales material. If the closer took all his sales equipment with him and the customer peeks out the window from behind a curtain or just opens the door, the sight of a closer with all his sales baggage will only scare the customer and make him more tense. (Note: When the closer goes to the door empty-handed, he looks more relaxed, unpressured and at ease, thus making the customer feel, to some degree, the same way. When the customer comes to the door, the closer should just give a simple, pleasant greeting, introduce himself, and then after an exchange of positive comments, excuse himself so that he can go back to his car to get the necessary sales material. For example: "Mr. Customer, good morning, my name is _____ and I'm with _____ company. I hope I'm not too early for our appointment. (response) My watch runs a little fast. By the way, you have a beautiful home and yard, I bet you spend a lot of time and work on it. (response) Would you excuse me for a minute and let me get my material from the car?"

> Note: I would like to again remind you that there is no certain time or set place in the sales presentation to actually close the customer. The master closer is continually (from the first second he says "Hello" to his customer, until the sale is made) going after that sale with every question and statement he can muster. The master closer knows that every single "Yes" or positive response he gets from his customer brings him a step closer to getting the sale consummated.

2. Do: Get the customer involved. For example, if the closer is selling steel siding, he should get the customer to help with some of the measuring of the house or get the customer to come outside with you so he can point out this or that about the house. The more interaction with the customer, the better. This tends to get the customer enthused and more excited about working with you on his home improvement. Remember: If they like you they'll probably want to deal with you, even if you are more expensive.

3. Don't: Go into the customer's home and try to gain control by talking first and sitting in the customer's favorite chair. This is an old pro's trick and it stinks. The customer — I don't care who he is — will be offended and resent the closer. Plus the sales presentation will get off on the wrong foot. (How would you like it if a stranger came into your home and sat in your favorite chair?) The closer should ask politely where he can sit and then adjust his chair toward the customer so that a proper, comfortable and understandable presentation can be given.

If the closer needs to use a different room for his presentation, or the kitchen table, or whatever, all he has to do is use some charm and ask the customer permission. And the customer in nearly every instance will go out of his way to help you if you treat him graciously and with respect.

4. Do: Look for objects in the home (bowling trophies, football trophies, awards, hunting rifles, etc.) that tell you something unique about the customer, and then comment on them in a sincere, positive and inquisitive manner. The customer will be more than happy to explain them to you.

5. Don't: Park your car right in front of the customer's house or behind someone else's car in the customer's driveway. By parking the car say, one house away, it gives you time to straighten yourself out, (clothes, hair, etc.) while you are walking to the customer's home. (Note: If there is a newspaper in the customer's yard, pick it up for the customer and hand it to him.) If you are not parked in front of the customer's house he or she won't see you coming, and won't run and hide or not answer the door when you ring. Curiosity will make the customer answer the door and then there you are — surprise! The reason for not parking your car behind someone else's car in the customer's driveway is to show some class and courtesy. Some old pros suggest you block the driveway with your car, a "cute little control trick," (so the customer can't leave before your presentation is over) but the closer will do a lot better and get more sales if he just thinks, "Now, how would I like to be treated?" It works.

6. Do: If you're a white (caucasian) closer and you are in a black customer's home, ask for a drink of water from his kitchen. When you get the glass of water, drink it. This will immediately demonstrate to the black customer that there are no negative racial thoughts or uncomfortable feelings on your part. The sales presentation will be much better and go so much smoother if this one silent race question is killed on the front-end of the demonstration. This "drink the water" trick will do wonders and get the white closer more sales from the black customers than he ever imagined. (Fact.)

7. Do: If the customer needs help doing something around the house while you're there — if time allows — help the customer. For example, if you notice the customer has a large piece of furniture he wants moved but can't do it himself, then help out; the sale will be that much closer and easier to get.

8. Do: When the sales presentation seems to be at a standstill or lull, ask the customer if you may use the phone and make a real or fake phone call to your office. Then act as though you have other appointments waiting and business is going fine. This little act will get the ball rolling again, stir up the conversation.

This "Do and Don'ts" list for the in-home sales presentation has to be coupled and worked in with the basic product presentation steps so that the closer feels just as comfortable in the customer's home as he does in his own sales office. (Note: The only difference is that in the sales office the customer is the closer's guest, and in the customer's home the closer is the guest. But with all the sales information the closer possesses he should always be in full control in both locations. That's why no matter where in the world the customer is waiting, the closer should still be able to close that sale.)

Pressures, Tricks and Traps:

Special Notes to Remember

1. The closer has to adjust his total sales presentation so it has a tempo that will be acceptable and understandable to his customer. The closer should keep the presentation sharp and crisp, but it has to be delivered with the customer in mind. (For example: Older customer — slower and more deliberate; younger customer — excited with more enthusiasm; hard-of-hearing customer — a little louder and slower.)

2. Important — Sell the things the product (or service) will accomplish and do, more than selling the product itself. It's easier to sell a dream than it is to sell a physical object. The closer should not only sell the product, but must sell beyond the product itself — selling the future benefits the product can offer. (Note: The customer will do most of the dreaming once the closer plants the "imagination seeds.")

3. When something special and exciting happens during the presentation, comment on it and put it into the sales presentation. If while driving some customers to show them real estate, a deer runs out from the woods, the closer should point it out and build a story around it that will assist the sales presentation; or if a closer is selling boats and he's out on a lake with his customer when a school of fish swim by, the closer should get excited and spontaneously work this into the presentation.

4. During the sales presentation, if the closer hits a lull, goes blank, or has a dry period (silence), he should ask the customer a question and let him do the talking for a while so the closer can regroup, think and rest. The closer should ask a friendly question that he knows will take the customer some time to answer. This not only gives the closer a breather, it keeps the customer active and involved.

5. The closer can put another couple (who he personally knows) with his customer and act as if both parties are new customers. Then, when the closer is giving his sales presentation, the "customers" he knows personally can ask all the right questions and act as though they are buying the product. The real customer will most of the time follow suit and purchase also, never knowing that the whole presentation was staged. This practice is not recommended, but as Sam taught me everything he knew about closing, I am going to tell you everything I know without editing or making any moral judgments. Your own ethical feelings will have to dictate how far you will go to close that sale.

6. During the sales presentation the closer should drop hints about inflation, a new price list coming out next week, the limited supply of the product, or anything that makes the customer aware that he can't wait forever to buy, without suffering some downside.

7. If a customer doesn't have time to hear a closer's complete sales presentation (a legitimate excuse), then the closer should simply reschedule the appointment and make another date. The closer's time is money and he shouldn't waste it on a customer who can't take the time to hear the whole master-presentation.

8. When a closer is with his customer he should be friendly and polite to everyone he meets, even if he doesn't know the people he is being friendly and polite to. This will at least create the impression to the customer that he is well-known and well-liked.

9. The closer should be sure that his sales presentation is not boring; he should tell interesting stories that help illustrate points he wants to make or describe, and stories people can relate to.

10. When a closer has a new customer with him and he sees one of his satisfied customers from past dealings, he should stop and say hello to him and see how he is doing while his new customer is present. This will make the new customer (the one who hasn't bought yet) feel more comfortable and at ease with the closer, because he will think about himself after he buys and feel better knowing that after the sale the closer doesn't just forget him.

11. When the closer is giving his sales presentation, he must pay attention to both members (husband and wife) of the customer's party. The closer has to be a perfect "balancer" when throwing out questions. That is, he (the closer) has to ask both husband and wife an equal number of questions and get an equal number of responses, so each customer will feel equally involved in the presentation. If one person is feeling left out then the sales presentation could be dead.

12. The closer has to nearly always lead the customer toward the product he (the closer) wants to sell. For example: "Mr. Customer, I think you really need this larger model to accommodate your entire family. Then everyone can be more comfortable." The closer has to use some tact when he is leading so the customer winds up thinking it was his idea in the first place to choose that particular model. If the customer feels pushed into something the sale could be lost very easily.

13. When the closer is giving his sales presentation, he should ask the customer's kids questions and get them involved in the product also. Kids are great allies for the closer because they always slip up and tell secrets about their parents. These slips add to the closer's information pool about his customer, so when it becomes time to close the closer has additional ammunition he may need to get the sale.

14. The closer should never monopolize the sales presentation. It has to be divided with some conversation from the closer and some opportunity for feedback from the customer, but not necessarily evenly. This will make the sales presentation more of a team effort and not one party talking at the other party.

15. The closer should always express positive thoughts when talking to the customer. For example: "Mr. Customer, now that color would look good on you," or "Mr. Customer, can you imagine what this product will do for your business? Why, you'll not only be the biggest supplier in the state, but most likely in the country."

16. The closer should always use the word "when" in talking to his customer, and not the word "if" or any other negative word. For example: "Mr. Customer, when you and your family build your vacation home on this acre of land, I promise you, that will be one of the proudest days of each member of your family's lives."

17. If the closer even once thinks about his sales commission during the sales presentation, he is dead. That greed and money sign will show right through to the customer, and the customer will read it like a book every time. (Fact.)

18. During the sales presentation the closer shouldn't downgrade his competition. The customer will not think much of this kind of sales approach as it doesn't show much class on the closer's part. The best thing for the closer to do is to talk up his product and just put himself above the competition. The closer can even tell his customer that he respects his competition but their product isn't even in the same league. Customers will prefer the more self-assured approach over the negative, mud-slinging approach.

19. When the closer calculates with a pen and paper, it actually has a type of hypnotic effect on the customer. This is because the customer doesn't know what final price or other piece of information the closer will finally come up with. So all the anticipation and thoughts of the customer are directed toward the closer's pen. The closer can use this tactic very effectively if he writes with deliberate strokes and smoothly, always keeping the customer guessing about the outcome of the figuring.

20. To lighten things up a bit you can break the ice by saying something like, "Mr. Customer, my product is absolutely free, but you had better pay attention because my sales presentation costs ten thousand dollars."

21. Remember, customers will always have champagne taste with beer budgets; the closer has to show the customer how he can obtain the champagne and still stay within his budget.

22. The closer has to take action first if he wants his customer to follow. For example, if a closer has a customer in his car and wants that customer to get out and walk across a piece of real estate, but the customer doesn't really want to get out of the car, the closer can get the customer out by simply saying, "Mr. Customer, let's get out and stretch our legs." The closer shouldn't mention the property at this time, but just "let's stretch our legs, it's been a long drive." The customer will follow almost every time, and once the closer has him out of the car he can then show him the property.

23. Remember — If the closer has sold the woman, in 98% of the cases the sale is made. The man will buy if his wife wants the product badly enough. The closer's challenge is to establish that want.

24. Throughout the sales presentation, the closer should ask the customer, "Mr. Customer, can you see the potential of my product (or service)?" The closer has to be constantly planting imagination seeds.

25. The closer should always remember he is an actor and everything around him should support his sales presentation. All the tools he uses are the props so he can put on his performance in a professional manner. That is the only way to improve your odds of making a sale.

26. If a customer says he doesn't have time for a full demonstration, the closer should tell his customer he wouldn't be doing him or his family justice if he didn't give the complete sales presentation, "You deserve the best and I would like to give you the best."

Sam said this ended my lesson on the sales presentation, and I was now ready to study closing — the art of getting the sale. Sam said that before I continued, I should remember this one thing about sales presentations: When the closer is giving his product presentation he should always be constant in his delivery. In other words, the closer should arrange and organize his presentation so it continually moves towards the closing question and the sale. The closer shouldn't "zig-zag" (sporadically jump from one subject to another) or confuse the customer with unrelated material and information. The closer should stick to his product (or service) presentation game plan, and divert only when he has to make a special point concerning the product (or service).

The product presentation has to make sense to the customer because the customer not only has to follow what is being said, but also has to fully understand it. If this basic "presentation reasoning" is not used by the closer, then he won't sell, period.

The product presentation is the factual proof (product information) given to the customer so he will have enough useful knowledge to make a buying decision. It is essential that the product presentation be well organized and have continuity, because all the product information is being molded, channeled and aimed at one final goal: a closing question that will get an affirmative answer.

Chapter Eight

CLOSING THE CUSTOMER

- A. The Word "Close": What It Means

- B. Regrouping the Customer After the
  Product Presentation

- C. Closer's and Customer's Attitudes:
  What Each One is Thinking

Chapter Eight

CLOSING THE CUSTOMER

It was the latter part of August and this particular morning was beautiful. Everyone at Green Vista Estates was in a great mood except for Sam. He seemed to be extra quiet and serious for some reason. I asked if everything was all right. He just smiled and said everything was fine. So I went on doing my duties and paid no more attention. Later that afternoon, Sam came over and told me he had something very serious he wanted to talk about after work. This was unusual because Sam and I usually talked about sales and selling, as well as other things, during the working day, never after the job. When I got off work, we sat down together on the old hotel's back porch steps that overlooked a beautiful valley.

Sam asked me if I had understood all the lessons on sales closing he had taught me up to this point, and I said, "Yes, I think so," wondering to myself if he was going to start talking about the lesson on product presentations again. But he didn't. Instead, Sam pointed out to the valley and proceeded to tell me some down-to-earth, old closer's philosophy. He told me that everything in this wonderful world had a special meaning. There was a beginning and an ending, and a true reason for being.

Sam looked at me with tears in his eyes, and said that he was about to take me through the most important and serious sales lesson I would ever have. He said my next lesson would be the culmination of everything I had learned so far. Sam said he would explain this lesson only once, so I had better pay close attention and not miss a single thing. He also told me that this was going to cover the essence of selling that most closers do not completely understand or take the time to study at all. He said this lesson would be the very heart and soul of all sales presentations, regardless of the product (or service). Sam told me he thought I was now ready for this very special lesson in sales.

So I sat there, as the sun was setting over that very peaceful valley, and listened to my older friend explain the lesson that controls literally everything in sales: the lesson was about "closing."

The Word "Close":

What it means

Sam said the very first thing to learn about closing, before actually going into the study of closing customers, was to know and understand exactly what the word "close" means as it relates to sales. The best way to know exactly what it denotes, he said, was to see it through an illustration that not only demonstrates how the word "close" works, but also shows all the ingredients that go into the word to make it function.

NOTE: When illustrated, the meaning of the word "close" looks like a box with each side made up of all the ingredients that go into its construction. The closer builds this special "trap box" completely around his customer during his sales presentation, just waiting for the right time to "close" the final door to the trap. Each side could be used as the closing or boxing-in door, but it takes all sides joined together tightly and united at exactly the same time to make the "trap box" work. In other words, getting the boxed-in customer to say "Yes" when asked to buy.

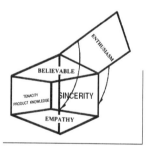

THE WORD "CLOSE" ILLUSTRATED

"The Trap Box"

Sam said the word "close" simply means the final act of a closer, through the efforts of charm, persuasion, product knowledge and enthusiasm — to convince his customer to buy his product, right then and there. (Note: The closer "closes" when his customer says "Yes, I'll buy," making that tough affirmative decision.)

The "trap box" is exactly what the name implies. It represents all the ingredients the closer needs and uses to get his customer into such a position that when he is finally asked to buy the product, he (the customer) has to say "Yes." The illustration showing the "trap box" makes it easier for a closer to understand how (by using all of his skills and knowledge) he can surround the customer with invincible and invisible walls, and when the time is right, close the final door to the "trap." At this point the closer's customer is sealed in, locked in, boxed in, and sold.

The closer has to remember that all of the steps — from the first meeting, the sales presentation, the pre-closing questions, everything — must be used to build the "trap box" around the customer. If any part is left out, the "trap box" won't be complete. Instead there would be an opening, an essential side of the "trap" missing for the customer to escape through. The closer has to think and plan his total sales presentation with precision and professionalism in order to successfully construct the "trap box." This is a basic rule that cannot be stressed enough.

Everything in the sales presentation should point to and lead to the final "Yes, I'll buy" answer from the customer. The sales presentation has to be directed toward that final goal and nothing else. The closer, by remembering how the "trap box" works and how it is constructed, can direct all sales presentations so they develop to the point where the sale is made (the point where the customer is "closed").

(Note: Sam told me not to confuse the meaning of the words "closing" and "close." He said "closing" was getting your point across to another person and getting that person to agree with you. There was no time limit or time element involved in "closing" — it could take two minutes or all day. But to "close" was *the act,* the conclusion, the one point where the customer is put on the spot to give a positive response to the closer, a "Yes" answer when asked to buy the product.)

Regrouping the Customer After
the Product Presentation

Sam said we should take a look at how the closer regroups his customer after the product presentation is completed.

A. Regrouping the Customer — When the closer has finished his product presentation (the actual act of showing his product) and/or demonstration he should regroup, directing and leading his customer to a comfortable, more quiet location. (Note: While orchestrating this regrouping the closer should try to get as physically close as is comfortable to the customers, enhancing feelings of concern, trust, and caring.) The reason for this movement is to get the customer away from the product and back to the closing table so the closer can sit down with his customer and get to the business of closing the sale. This maneuver can easily be accomplished by telling the customer you still have something to show him back in the sales office or by telling him some realistic story so that he will follow. For example, "Mr. Customer, now let's go back to the office and I'll show you what everything looks like on paper," or "Mr. Customer, let's go inside for a minute and let me show you something about the product that you won't believe," or "Mr. Customer, I have to check in with my sales manager for a minute, so come on in and have some coffee," or whatever appropriate excuse you can come up with.

The closer must get his customer sitting down and back into a frame of mind geared for finances and paperwork, rather than being psychologically geared for the actual product. This "product presentation to the closing table" transition has to be a calm and nonchalant movement so the customer won't panic or start to feel trapped. If the customer feels he is about to be "boxed in," his defensive shield goes up in a second. The closing location could be a sales table or desk in the office, or the kitchen table in a customer's home, or even the closer's car, parked under a shade tree — anyplace that will be conducive for the closer to continue with the rest of his sales presentation. Then, without moving the customer again (the less confusion the better), go right into the pre-closing questions, and ultimately the close.

It should be remembered that a closer could also "close" the customer right in the middle of his product presentation, for example, when he is out in the middle of a field showing real estate, or driving around with his customer in a new car, or showing the customer how to operate a piece of machinery. The customer can be "closed" any place and any time the closer feels he is ready to buy the product. But we're not talking this type of easy sales situation here. What we are talking about is a more complicated sales situation where the closer, after finishing physically showing his product, takes his reluctant and unimpressed customer to a closing table, seats him, gets him coffee or refreshments and then goes on with his sales presentation, heading consistently and smoothly toward the "close." (Note: When the closer is seating the customer back in the sales office after his product presentation, he has to use the very same seating arrangements and control techniques he used when he first met his customer, as fully explained in Chapter 6.)

B. After the closer has seated his customers, he should ask them if they would like anything to drink and then get the refreshments himself, leaving the customers alone so that they have some time to themselves, and can get their thoughts together. (Note: There is a school of thought that says the closer should never leave his customers alone after showing them the product, because it gives them time to talk in private and figure out how they are going to get out of the sales office without buying, or how they can come up with a good excuse for not buying today, etc. This theory has some merit, but it's not completely accurate.) The closer should get up and leave the customers by themselves for a few minutes so they are able to ask each other questions and exchange ideas they wouldn't share in front of the closer. They will like the closer a little more for showing this courtesy and respect. The customers will discuss everything from their personal finances to whether they believe the closer's product presentation story. It really doesn't matter what the customers talk about because the closer should not only be in control, but by this time he should have made friends with the customers and established a close relationship with them. The closer has to keep in mind that he's already about two-thirds of the way through the total sales presentation and that's a little late in many cases to pull a friendship or close relationship "feeling" out of the hat.

C. When the closer is away from the closing table getting coffee, checking the inventory, or whatever, he should observe his customer's actions, to see if they are having a serious discussion or if they are just laughing and having a good time as though everything about the product presentation was a joke. The closer had better know where he stands with his customers when he comes back to the closing table, because that's the time to get down to the bottom line of getting the customers sold.

(Note: The closer can tell a lot about his customers from just watching them as they talk together and remembering the degrees of interest they showed during the product presentation, along with all the things that were said. The closer should decide at this point what maneuver, approach or technique he is going to use to "close" his customers. He's had sufficient time to study the customers and analyze them during the pre-presentation pitch and the product presentation. The closer should have no problem determining their overall make-up and what weak points are vulnerable to his closing attack.)

D. When the closer returns with the refreshments to the closing table (where his customers are seated comfortably) he should project a look of confidence and self-assurance, thinking to himself, these customers are really going to buy the product, period.

The Closer's and Customer's Attitude:

What each opponent is secretly thinking

Sam said at this point the stage is set (back in the sales office with everyone seated) and the two opponents are now ready to go into the final, deadly round (Step III) of the overall sales presentation. It's a good idea to look at each opponent's attitude separately, Sam told me, to see exactly what each one is thinking privately to himself. This is how Sam explained it:

1. The Customer's Attitude. What the customer is thinking about and how he feels as he sits at the closing table waiting for the closer to continue with his sales presentation.

The customer should have a sound overall picture of the closer's product (or service), plus he should understand the product's advantages and benefits due to the closer's pre-demonstration pitch and product presentation. The customer's general attitude at this point could be one of the following or a mixture of all:

A. The customer is sold on the product and wants to buy it immediately, but he doesn't know the price yet. He is anxiously waiting for the closer to tell him.

B. The customer wants to buy and he knows the price of the product, but he can't afford to pay cash at this time, or thinks he just plain can't afford it. So he is anxiously waiting for the closer to tell him about the financial terms and ways of purchasing that will or will not fit into his budget.

C. The customer is undecided. He doesn't know if he wants to buy or not; his mind isn't made up yet — in other words, he's not completely sold. So he sits there waiting for the closer to explain more about the product or he just sits there waiting for the closer to make his next move. (Note: In this case the customer could afford the product if he wanted it badly enough.)

D. This customer is not sold on the product. He doesn't like it and doesn't want it. He's simply waiting for the closer to hurry up and finish his presentation so he can leave and go home.

The closer has to acknowledge and understand one very important fact concerning customers and their attitudes: When sitting at the closing table and waiting for the closer to continue his sales presentation, all customers, no matter who they are, will have a combination of the very same basic thoughts and feelings. They are fear, anxiety, confusion and excitement. These four elements are present and bottled up inside every customer that closers will ever talk to at the closing table. Some of the feelings will be stronger than others, but it's a fact that every customer, whether rich or poor, will have these feelings when it's "sit down time" and "dealing time" with the closer.

Sam said the reason these common elements are found in all customers is easy to explain; at this point in the sales presentation the seated customer really doesn't know what to expect next. He doesn't know what the closer is going to say, or how or when he will ask him to buy. The customer doesn't know if the closer is going to use some "closer's trick" or if he is going to bring in another closer — like the sales manager — to help get the sale. The customer is somewhat tense with a number of possibly negative thoughts running through his mind.

If the closer has done his job properly during the pre-demonstration pitch and the product presentation, the customer should be thinking seriously about buying the product and will possibly have some meaningful questions concerning the product. But if the closer didn't do his job and failed to create enough interest and desire in the customer to own the product, the customer will only be thinking of ways to say "No" and get out of the sales office. The customer's attitude and way of thinking depends on how the closer has done his job. It's also very important to remember that the customer, if not completely sold on the product will automatically be looking for reasons not to buy rather than reasons to buy. It's easier to say "No" and be uncommitted and unconcerned than it is to say "Yes, I'll buy," and then have to take on a new obligation or responsibility. The customer, in most cases when buying decisions are left to him alone, will want to take the easy way out, and that usually means a "No" answer.

The customer will be looking for and trying to come up with what he thinks are legitimate reasons not to buy, reasons for not having to spend his hard-earned money. The customer will want to be able to justify his "No" answer to the closer because he likes him and doesn't want to sound ungrateful or rude. The customer will also be trying to rationalize his "No" answer in his own eyes, so he will feel that by not buying he didn't really miss out on anything.

The customer's attitude after the product presentation is very, very important. Not only because it shows the closer how close he is to getting the sale, but because it gives the closer customer information he needs to know so he can plan and direct his "closing" attack. This information is obtained by observing and listening to the customer's actions and statements, which are all reflections on his general attitude.

Notes to Remember Concerning the Customer's Attitude

A. No matter how much a customer believes or likes the closer, he will somewhere in the back of his mind be skeptical and leery because the customer has sometime in his own past put his trust in another sales closer and gotten hurt.

B. The customer is wondering to himself what exactly the closer is going to do next. So he automatically starts to build up his lead shield or guard again. The closer has to re-relax the customer at the closing table, so he is calm and not defensive.

C. If the customer is timid or unusually quiet compared to how he acted during the product presentation, it could be because he has a question to ask about the product and is too embarrassed to ask it, thinking it sounds silly or that he acted too excited during the product presentation. The customer may feel he showed too much emotion and now he realizes it's time to get down to the business of buying and negotiating so he is re-establishing his defenses. To put it another way, the customer may have gotten carried away with enthusiasm when he was inspecting the product and revealed too much of his hand to the closer, and now he has to act reserved and self-controlled so he won't look like an easy mark.

The closer can take care of both of these problems by merely getting the customer relaxed again, getting him talking (asking the right questions), becoming his friend again and making him feel at ease at the closing table. He must let the customer know that nothing has changed from the first time they met and that no one is going to force him to spend his money if he decides not to buy.

D. When the customer is sitting at the closing table, he ought to know enough about the closer's product to be able to pay attention and know what the closer is talking about. If the customer doesn't understand everything or missed something during the pre-demonstration pitch or the product presentation, that missing information could very easily kill the sale, just because the customer and closer didn't fully understand each other. There was a lack of communication. (Note: It's the closer's responsibility to make sure this doesn't happen.)

E. The customers will be thinking and talking between themselves (husband and wife team) about how they can afford the product. This discussion could cause a problem if one party is sold and the other party is not. One party won't want to spend their money and the other one will. The closer has to watch out for this husband and wife "money fight" and stop it, or the whole sale will be lost because the customers and the total sales situation got out of the closer's control.

F. The customer will tell just about everything about himself through his eyes. He doesn't have to say a word to the closer. For example: If the customer is looking around the sales office in sharp, short and jerky movements, the customer is scared to death and nervously waiting for the closer's next step; or, if the customer is looking out of the window or across the room with a kind of faraway look in his eyes, there is a good chance he is thinking about finances, or the product's advantages. He is probably daydreaming about everything the closer has shown him and said. The customer's eyes and facial expressions pretty much tell the closer the story on how close the customer is to buying, after he has received and gone through the product presentation.

G. If the customer is sitting back in his chair and has pushed away from the closing table with his arms folded, if he is not talking, or is nonchalantly chatting to other customer team members, the closer should know this customer is still not sold. (Note: Customers have to have both feet squarely on the floor and arms on the table, showing interest in what the closer is saying or doing, if a sale is to be made.) The customer who has an attitude of "Okay, I've seen the product, what now?" is not yet sold. The closer has his work cut out for him but that's all right. If the closer does the rest of his job correctly the customer will usually buy.

H. After the presentation, the customer will be trying to regroup to get back to his original game plan of "I'm not going to buy today." The customer will try to get his thinking back on track, the way it was before he met the closer and was introduced to the product. But now it's more difficult because the customer probably likes the closer and knows more about the product. He also now realizes that the product presentation wasn't as bad or rough as he had thought it was going to be. So the customer is now somewhat off balance in his thinking (off guard) and a little confused. The closer has tactfully broken through the customer's defenses and the customer's original "no buy" policy is starting to fall apart. (Note: This is exactly what the customer's attitude should be after the closer's product presentation, if the customer hasn't bought the product already.)

2. The Closer's Attitude. What the closer is thinking to himself and how he feels just after he has given the product presentation and just before he goes back to the closing table to sit down with his customer.

The closer has to know that his customer is sitting on pins and needles waiting for his return. He must calm the customer down before going into the pre-closing phase of the sales presentation.

Once the closer knows the customer's attitude he can plan the next step, properly adjusting his own attitude.

The closer should be thinking that he has the sale (if he gave a good product presentation). He has to assume the customer is going to buy. The reason for this is because the air of confidence the closer shows will unconsciously rub off on the customer when they sit down together. The customer will feel this self-assuredness and automatically become more secure and more positive in his own mind. The customer wants to do business with a winner, a champion, someone who shows that he is a professional and has a product that is the best, not a runny-nosed little salesman who is afraid of the customer, embarrassed about the product, and afraid to ask for the sale. (Note: Some customers will resent the closer's assured attitude and will put up their defensive shield to protect themselves. The closer should be able to spot this nervous reaction from the start and through simple, comfortable conversation and friendly charm convey the message that his confident attitude is not threatening and is based upon a sincere belief in his product. After the customer sees the closer's attitude is based on enthusiasm and sincerity and realizes he is a nice guy, the defenses will come down.)

The closer also has to watch his customers' actions and notice who in the customers' group is talking or acting like he is not interested in the product. This person could become a future problem for the closer, because he may try to talk everyone else out of buying. The closer has to be alert and observe these things so he can plan exactly how to approach the seated customers.

The closer should have the attitude that he has just shown his customer the best product in the world. He couldn't go out and buy a better product anywhere. The closer should take pride in the fact that he represents this product and that he is giving his customer the opportunity to buy it. To really be effective the closer has to not only show this pride but *believe* it. (Note: This does not mean the closer should be arrogant or snobbish, but rather he should display an attitude that radiates the feelings of being on a winning team, or a "Mr. Customer, my product is in a league by itself, it's the top of the line." This is the type of attitude that turns customers on.)

This kind of thinking on the closer's part will maximize sales. It will also make the customer feel more comfortable knowing that he is with a professional that really knows what he is doing. Just as people don't want to be with a dentist or doctor who is a beginner, they don't want to deal with a sales beginner either.

Notes to Remember Concerning the Closer's Attitude

A. The closer should have an irrepressible, thick-skinned, always positive attitude. The closer has to realize that a "No" is not the end of the world, but only the beginning of his job. He should go in to close his customer with nothing to fear. If the customer doesn't buy, then in the final analysis it's his loss not the closer's.

The closer has to remember that he is the one who has to get the customer over his fear-of-buying feeling. The closer can't accomplish this if he shows the fear of asking his customer to buy. Two fears surely do not contribute to a buying decision.

B. The closer has to get himself psychologically prepared to go in and sit down with the customer, leaving only after the sale has been made. To do this, the first thing the closer has to do is clear his mind of everything except his customer and his product. He can't be thinking about his wife, the commission he's about to make, the party he's going to later, or anything else. The closer has to be totally dedicated and committed to getting the sale. If he lets his mind wander when he sits down with the customer, it will show and the customer will feel that if the closer doesn't care enough to show complete interest then why should he buy? A lack of complete interest and focus will kill a sale.

C. The closer must realize that to get the sale he has to use the power of emotions on his customer. To get himself ready for this "final act" in the overall sales presentation, the closer should go someplace alone and psyche himself up for this closing process. (Note: He should use the earlier mentioned mirror technique and get serious with himself.) The closer should know by this time the weak points in the customer's make-up and plan an emotional attack for that sensitive area. For example, the customer's weaknesses or vulnerable points could be his future dreams for his children or his desire to attract members of the opposite sex. Anything that gets the customer activated, excited, and thinking should be used in conjunction with the seller's final closing question.

D. The closer has to psyche himself up into believing that this is his final approach, his last shot to deal with the customer and get the sale. The closer has to be mentally ready for a long and drawn-out battle with the customer, if necessary. He should fight for the sale right now and not allow the customer to get away. He must assume that if they walk out the door without buying he will never see them again.

E. A closer must really understand this one special aspect of "closing" a customer: The act of getting a customer to buy the product, of getting him to make a decision that is good and right for him, isn't always nice and pretty. The closer sometimes has to apply intense and continuous pressure on the customer. The kind of pressure that may occasionally produce tears and other emotions, to get the sales. There are many sales books and schools of thought that look down on tough, hard, aggressive sales pressure. That's their privilege. Sam agrees; he said this kind of closing practice shouldn't ever be the normal procedure a closer uses. But he did tell me that it is a very necessary tactic for the closer to be aware of and utilize when he must.

Pressure closing exists, it's alive and well and it will always exist. Any closer who is not using a little pressure when it's necessary is missing many, many sales.

In wrapping up this attitude lesson, Sam told me I should always remember these standard customer attitudes and closer attitudes, and I would improve my closing average. He said they would help in anticipating and overcoming objections and problems that otherwise would be likely to sabotage the sale.

Chapter Nine

CLOSING THE CUSTOMER:
Advanced Techniques

- A. The Closers Pre-Closing Questions, Statements and Actions: Setting Up the Customer For the "Close"

- B. Closing: The Actual Act of Getting the Customer to Say "Yes"

    1. Going In For the Kill
    2. The Closer Handles and Completely Conquers the Customer's Objections

- C. The Master Closer's "Deadly Rules of Closing"

- D. Important "Closing Notes" to Remember

Chapter Nine

CLOSING THE CUSTOMER:
Advanced Techniques

Sam felt I was ready to study the next most important thing to actually "closing" the customer which was how to "set up" the customer, getting him prepared through product education and programming, for the final closing question where the closer asks the customer to buy his product.

To understand the pre-closing procedure, Sam said that first I had to remember one very important fact: The customer has just finished the actual inspection of the product (the product presentation) and therefore, a lot of the information that he heard in the pre-presentation pitch has probably been forgotten.

So when the closer sits down at the closing table with the customer after completing the product presentation, he has to re-educate, re-orient, re-outline and re-program him. (Note: The closer shouldn't bore the customer with a complete detailed recap of everything; instead summarize, touching on only important product facts that will help persuade the customer to buy.) In other words, the closer has to put all of the parts of the puzzle (the overall sales presentation) back together again, in perspective for the customer. Then the customer will be able to make an easy and unconfusing decision when asked to buy the product. Remember the rule, "If you confuse 'em, you lose 'em."

Sam said the best way to explain and show this process of customer re-orientation and programming was to give examples in three carefully planned and progressive steps. These three steps begin with the first words a closer speaks and continue until it is time (in the eyes of the closer) for the customer to be asked to buy the product.

The Closer's Pre-Closing Questions, Statements And Actions: Setting the Customer Up for "The Close"

Step 1. Get the Customer Relaxed. The customer is nervously waiting for the closer to drop the hammer (ask him to buy) so the customer is defensive and tense, trying to be prepared for anything that might happen. The best thing the closer can do to ease these negative feelings is to first ask a question or make a statement that doesn't relate at all to the product. This will get the customer talking about another subject making him feel more at ease and less defensive. The closing table, the sales office, and the other closers in the general area, tend to scare customers. This is because when the customer first met the closer in the sales office there was no obligation on the customer's part and he was a free, independent "looker" or window shopper. Then when the customer was out of the sales office actually inspecting the product (for example: an automobile) he was still feeling free because he was out of doors and could easily walk away if he wished. It was just himself and the closer on equal ground (at least the customer thought so). But once back inside the sales office surrounded by other salesmen and stacks of selling material, the customer starts to feel the obligation and pressure build because he, the closer, is spending a lot of time with him. The closer, through his product presentation, has indeed invested precious time and energy in the customer and the customer quite naturally feels an obligation to either stop wasting the salesperson's time or to buy something. Here is an example of how to get the customer talking, thus leading to a more relaxed atmosphere: "Mr. Customer, you said earlier that you were in the home construction business. Have you ever built large commercial buildings before?" or "Mr. Customer, your kids said they like to ride horses. Do you have some horses back home or is there a special place the family goes to ride?"

Planned, unrelated questions like these will get the customer's mind off the product for a few seconds and he will start to calm down. It's important for the customer to be at ease because if he isn't, then he won't hear a word the closer says. (Fact.)

Step 2. Re-educate the customer about the product. (Summarize the product presentation with "trial closes".) The closer has to get and keep everyone in the customer's party involved in this conversation. Remember, it can be fatal to a sale if even one member feels left out.

This is the step in the pre-closing process that lets the customer again hear some of the product information the closer had related earlier in the pre-presentation pitch and during the product presentation. This is the "refresher outline" that enables the customer to comprehend the total product and its benefits, so he has enough product knowledge to base his buying decision on when the time comes.

Here is an example of summarizing for the customer, using an acre of land as the model product. "Mr. Customer, let me show you, for just a minute, exactly where we've been and where the property that I showed you was. (The closer is pointing to a map at this time.) Mr. Customer, I told you that the property was only one-quarter mile from the ski slopes. Remember I said that our company was going to build a new country club right on the other side of that mountain we were standing on. Well, (pointing to the map) that's the location where the club will be built, and we were standing right about here — pretty close and convenient, isn't it?" etc., etc.

This kind of showing and telling maneuver, the backing up of facts and statements with maps, sales material, and verbal summaries, reassures and reinforces the customer's belief in the credibility of the closer and the value of his product.

Another example of summarizing: "Mr. Customer, now that you have seen the property and everything that my company is doing to improve it, wouldn't you agree it has potential? If you buy the property and wait two years for all the improvements we are making in this area, can you imagine what that land will soon be worth? You know, every little thing that we do, every amenity, every street light, every addition that's put in, makes that property worth more. Remember that you and your family could come here and use the club, the swimming pool, the lake — use all of the facilities for practically nothing and at the same time own property. We are in the process of doing everything I've told you we were going to do, much of which you saw for yourself during our tour. You were right there with me. Mr. Customer, when we first got together I told you I was going to prove everything I would tell you about my product, and I have. I think you'll agree that when we say it's going to be done or that something is going to happen, you can count on it. Wouldn't you say so? My product is great but it's nothing without people like you and your family because the better the property owners are, the better our whole surrounding area is, and that's a fact. Mr. Customer, you can see the potential here and you know it is real, right? Now tell me the truth, I've been honest with you."

Or say something like, "Mr. Customer, let me put everything together for you. Remember when we first met, I told you that my company knows what it's doing, and that we have the best product anywhere. Well now, I think you can see and understand what I was talking about. Not only have you looked at all the benefits of my product on paper, but you've actually seen them with your own eyes during the demonstration. Wouldn't you agree that my product has a lot of fantastic potential?"

Or say, "Mr. Customer, I told you that my company was putting in underground cables to the property, didn't I? And didn't I say you could see the lake from that property? Well, you could, couldn't you?" etc., etc.

The closer has to keep in mind that he's continually bringing the customer up to a point, a peak, where the customer is excited and enthused enough to be asked to buy the product. (Note: The timing and precise point of asking for the order depends on the judgment of the closer. There is no set rule.)

In this type of conversation, the closer is actually forming and programming the customer's thinking, so that it is discreetly directed toward a positive buying decision.

With a team customer the closer has to keep everyone in the buying party involved in these outlining and summarizing questions and comments.

Step 3. Summarizing up to a point. The closer has to know when to stop re-educating the customer about the product and know when to get aggressive and ask him to buy. The reason is simple. If a closer doesn't know exactly when to ask for the order and keeps right on summarizing while his customer is ready to buy the product then and there, the closer could lose the sale because he walked right past the "magical buying point" where the customer's attitude, emotions and feelings were exactly right and ready to buy. This "magical buying point" is so difficult to detect that it takes super concentration on the closer's part. But that "magical buying point" grows, it gets stronger and bigger the more the customer is sold, thus making it a little easier for the closer to see. Finally, that "magical buying point" is so huge it's right smack in front of the closer's face. If he still doesn't recognize it and continues summarizing, the "magical buying point" will become less visible and weaker until it finally vanishes, and the closer will be left wondering how he missed the sale. You can think you have a sure sale on the way, but if you are too professional acting and too detailed in your pre-closing and closing statements and questions, you can lose the sale and never realize why.

The closer has to understand that there is always a point in the presentation where he will reach the very final approach to getting a sale. The only thing left to do after realizing you have gotten the customer reprogrammed and to this point is ask him to buy the product, and then, if he has objections, the closer has to overcome them and again ask the customer to buy. And again, and again, and again.

When the closer is summarizing he must remember in what direction he is heading and the objective of the whole presentation. It is all designed to point the customer toward a positive buying answer and nothing more.

The closer's pre-demonstration pitch, his product presentation, the pre-closing conversation — the whole package — has one common goal, and that is to "close" the customer.

Sam said the main factors to remember about the closer's pre-closing questions were to first relax the customer, second, to get him re-oriented, and programmed, and third, pay attention so you don't go right past a "closing" opportunity.

Tips and Notes on Pre-Closing Questions

1. Always try to get the customer to agree with you. Use only positive ideas, illustrations or examples when giving your final summation of the product presentation.

2. Set the customer up (get him ready) for the "close" with deliberate and sharply directed questions throughout the pre-closing question and statement process. For example: "Do you see the potential?", "Wouldn't this be nice to own?", "Can you imagine how proud you will be?", "Won't your kids love it?"

3. Remember that every customer has a bit of larceny in him. The closer should plant "greed seeds" and "self-indulgence seeds" throughout the pre-closing process, if necessary. It all depends on the customer. But if you sense the customer is the type who'll act on these seeds then the closer should bait that customer, without hesitation.

4. When the closer is reiterating the main positive points of the product he has to be aware of the customer's interest level. If the customer is not maintaining the same enthusiasm he had during the product presentation, or if the customer starts looking around and not paying as much attention to the closer as he should, the closer has to bring the customer back into the pre-closing process with "shock questions." For instance, "Mr. Customer, what did you say? Oh, I do apologize, I thought you said something." Or, you can change the loudness or tone of your voice. The closer has got to regain the customer's attention and keep it, to get a sale. (Note: You must do this tactfully; if you shock the customer or make him too angry, the sale will be lost.)

5. The closer can build his pre-closing statement on either fear, greed or love. Any one of the three will get the job done.

6. If the customer doesn't believe the closer it's usually because the closer doesn't believe himself. (Fact.)

7. The closer can lead a horse to water but he can't make him drink. Leading him to water is the pre-closing questions and statements; making him drink is the "close." Sam especially liked to remind me of this one.

"CLOSING"! The Fine Art of Getting
the Customer to Say "Yes"

Sam said the time had finally come to study and learn about the delicate art of getting the customer to say "yes" which is *"Real Closing."* He told me that in this very specialized lesson I wouldn't just be hearing all of the same old closing theories or procedures that many so-called sales books talk about and continually repeat. Sam said I would now learn the exact and detailed maneuvers, manipulations, tricks and traps that go into *"Real Closing."* The type of closing practice that leaves a customer not only enthused about the product, but with a signed contract that states he owns that product, period.

Before we went any further with this lesson about the fine art of closing, Sam explained there were four closing statements I had to know. These statements would help me understand the basic foundation of closing, and they would clarify what goes into closing to make it work correctly.

Closing Statement (A): The Customer's Emotion Factor

The main element and most important thing to remember throughout this lesson was the secret key: "CUSTOMER EMOTIONS." Sam told me "CUSTOMER EMOTIONS" were the heart and soul of "closing,", dictating the outcome in every closing situation. He said, logic, comprehension, finances and product benefits all have their merits and contributions to "closing," but they could never equal the "CUSTOMER EMOTION" factor when it becomes time to make a buying decision.

A good thought for a closer to always keep in mind when selling is this: The emotions of a customer will buy more products or turn down more buying opportunities than anything else.

Closing Statement (B): The Closing Attack

I was told one of the first things to do before studying "closing" was to mentally picture a closer's "closing attack" on his customer. Sam explained the reason for this was so I could refer to that mental image whenever I needed, and better understand what was actually taking place during my future "closing" activities. The best way to show you that mental picture is to put it into an illustration.

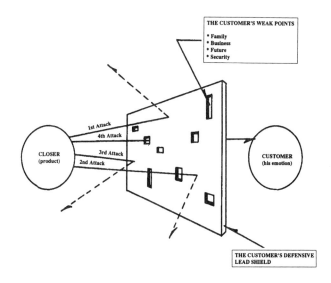

This drawing demonstrates how a closer has to use many "closes" or approaches to finally penetrate the customer's protective and defensive shield. When the closer accomplishes his closing attack and successfully spears the customer (hits his emotional "buy" button) the customer will react almost immediately and become not only more attentive, but more aggressive in his thinking and actions. It's totally up to the closer to control this reaction and steer it toward a "close."

Closing Statement (C):
Timing, When to Ask the Customer to Buy

Sam said "closing" had everything to do with timing. He said there never has been and never will be a set law or time-honored rule that states the exact point or time in a closer's total sales presentation for him to ask the customer to buy the product. But he did say a closer could follow certain guidelines concerning the best time to "close," and be right on the money, nearly every time.

He told me to remember throughout the total sales presentation that the word "timing" was important because it represented the closer's tempo —

how he geared his presentation so it ran smoothly and coherently for the customer.

But when talking about "closing" the word "timing" means a great deal more. It means the very point where the closer asks the customer to buy the product. To find this point, this exact "time" in the sales presentation, Sam said to follow these guidelines:

The best way for a closer to know exactly when to ask for the order is to first recognize in his own heart that the customer actually knows enough about the product to make a valid buying decision. If the customer has just been politely agreeing with the closer, without completely understanding everything that has been said, then he usually will not buy, he's not ready. (Note: If the customer buys the product without totally understanding it, there is a good chance he will go home and cancel later.)

When the closer knows for sure that the customer understands the whole product presentation, it's time for the closer to start looking for a good opening (an opportunity) to ask him to buy. This opening can be discovered or revealed by watching the customer's actions and facial expressions.

Here are some customer give-away signs and signals that will always let the closer know when to strike (ask for the order).

(a) You Know The Customer is Ready ...

When the closer gets through explaining to the customer a detail concerning the product or how financial arrangements are handled and he looks up and sees the customer looking serious and thinking deeply about what has just been said. Next, the closer should, in a positive, soft, pleasant voice say, "Mr. Customer, why don't you give my product a try?" Then of course the closer should be quiet, and wait for the customer's answer. If it's an objection then the closer has to overcome that hurdle and again ask the customer to "give it a try."

(b) You Know The Customer is Ready ...

After the closer has explained some fact about the product and the customer looks at his team member (husband or wife) silently and raises his eyebrows or has a "What do you think about it?" look on his face. The closer should then wait to hear the other customer's answer, and proceed from there to "close." The closer should ask them to "Give the product a try?" If the wife says "Well, honey, it's up to you, I'll do whatever you say," the closer had better interrupt (jump right in) and bring the wife back into the conversation, by saying something like, "Now, Mrs. Customer, remember when you got married everything was fifty-fifty. It's up to you, too." This statement on the closer's part will get a small laugh from both members, but it will get the wife interested and back into the decision-making conversation. (Note: Keep in mind that no one should feel left out, or the sale could be lost.)

(c) You Know The Customer is Ready ...

When the customer leans back for a few seconds in his chair, looks at his wife, shuffles his feet and has that "Well, what should we do?" look about him. The closer should lean forward, getting nearer to the customer and ask him to "Give it a try."

(Note: Remember, the distance between the closer and the customer is a selling challenge. The closer has to get as close as possible to the customer so he maintains that "intimate and caring" effect. This way the customer doesn't feel alone in his decision-making, he's got his good friend the closer right there with him).

(d) You Know The Customer is Ready ...

When the closer is finished showing or explaining something concerning the product and the customer puts his hands on the table and starts tapping his fingers, he is thinking about buying. The closer had better ask him to buy right then. "Mr. Customer, this product would be perfect for someone like you, so why don't you give it a try?"

(e) You Know The Customer is Ready ...

If after the closer makes a statement, everything is completely silent in the room, and the customer gives a slight sigh and looks down at the closing table, the closer should right then ask, "Why don't you give it a try?"

(f) You Know The Customer is Ready ...

When the customer acts nervous (for example, wetting his lips, wringing his hands, squirming in his chair, playing with his hair or a cigarette, continually clearing his throat, pulling on his ear lobe, etc.) he is actually thinking about the answer or objection he is going to give the closer when asked to buy. (Note: The customer knows the closer is going to ask him to buy any time now.) So the closer had better do what this nervous customer expects him to do, and that is go ahead and ask him to "Give it a try." If you don't ask at this point, the customer will get even more nervous which will hurt your selling chances.

(g) You Know The Customer is Ready . . .

When the customer asks a question about something the closer has said already, for example: "Mr. Closer, now exactly how wide is the front of that property?" Then he's not only interested, he is ready to buy. The closer should answer his question, then look directly at the customer, and ask him to "Give it a try."

(h) You Know The Customer is Ready . . .

When the customer has a certain alertness, a certain sparkle, a bright, excited look in his eyes (the same look that a young boy has when he gets a new bicycle — the kind of look a closer can't miss), then the customer is ready to be asked to buy.

(i) You Know The Customer is Ready . . .

When the customer looks downward and scratches his head and turns it a little to one side with a "Well, I don't really know" look on his face, he is ready for the closer to ask him to buy.

(j) You Know The Customer is Ready . . .

When the customer starts demonstrating greater interest and either talks more, leans heavily on the closing table with his arms, gets more involved in what is being said and what is taking place, tells his kids to be quiet so he can hear better, tells the closer to show him how the financing is arranged, asks the closer if he can get some coffee — or anything else that shows a more sincere and genuine interest — it means he is ready to be asked to buy the product.

Sam said there were many, many buying signs and signals the customer will unconsciously show to the closer similar to the ones mentioned here. It's the closer's responsibility to be alert and notice them, or he could lose a sale. It's that simple. When the customer wants to buy the product the closer shouldn't miss the enthused, excited and eager expression on his face and the sparkle that radiates from his eyes. These signs are always dead giveaways of his buying interest.

NOTE: In the examples given so far, the closer always asked the customer to "Give the product a try," not "Buy it, Mr. Customer." The reason for this, Sam explained, is that when a closer makes it easy and creates a friendly, non-pressured environment for the customer, he will get more sales. The word "try" is a great word to use, because it makes the customer kind of feel he is just testing or using the product temporarily and is not really stuck with it forever. The word "try" and other harmless-sounding trick words will be looked at later in this chapter.

Sam said you should always understand that the timing and pacing of a closer's sales presentation is quite important. But that is only part of the successful sales equation. Knowing when to ask the customer to buy is the most important skill for closers to perfect.

IMPORTANT:

There is an old pro's saying that states you can't ask the customer to buy the product soon enough. In other words, the sooner the closer asks the customer to buy, the better. That statement is not true. A closer has to deliberately program and direct his customer toward the "close." He has to continually feed the customer product knowledge, plant imagination and owner-benefit seeds throughout the complete sales presentation, if he expects to sell. Without enough product information and a total under-standing of the product's advantages, the customer cannot make a proper buying decision when asked to, because the customer just doesn't know enough about the product.

If a closer does ask the customer to buy too early in the sales presentation, that could possibly make the customer upset, causing him to put up more of a rigid defense than he had intended. The customer will feel the closer is not only pushy but also arrogant, making it that much harder for the closer to actually "close." By asking the customer to purchase early in the presentation, the closer has only created problems and new objections that were unnecessary in the first place.

The old pro's saying, even though it is not correct, was designed for a purpose: By asking the customer to buy early, the customer will either buy right away (unlikely) or give the closer an objection. Then the closer could overcome that objection and work from this point toward the "close." In other words, the customer's answer and/or objection to the closer's early "closing" tactic would give the closer an insight into what the customer is truly feeling and thinking at that point. This enables the closer to redirect and replan (if necessary) the rest of his sales presentation. The presentation would then be in accord with the customer's objections and thoughts. This early "close" tactic saves the closer time (some customers might buy when first asked) and allows him ample opportunity to pinpoint and concentrate on the customer's problems with the product early in the sales presentation, rather than learning the real objection at the tail end of the presentation, and having to handle (solve) it then.

A smart closer can discover the same thing that the old pro's saying of "ask them early" was designed to uncover, without creating potential customer problems. By having some patience and simply taking the customer's temperature — listening to him talk — the closer can: use small trial closes (pre-closing questions), make positive statements about the product and how it would benefit him, and continually get the customer to agree with what is being said.

This type of sales practice will not anger or upset the customer, as the "old pro's saying" could. The fact is, it will not only achieve the goal of finding out what the customer is thinking and what his objections are, but this approach gives the closer the time he needs to educate and program the customer so when he asks for the order the customer will be able to make an intelligent and positive decision.

FACT: If one closer used the "old pro's" method during his sales presentation and another closer of equal talent used the method of taking the customer's temperature while giving a complete, positive, and well organized sales presentation, the closer who used the "temperature" method would outsell the "old pro's" technique, ten to one.

Closing Statement (D): Basic Do's and Don'ts of "Closing"

(a) DO: The closer should always listen to what the customer has to say. He has to hear the customer out completely when being asked a question or given an objection.

DON'T: Pre-guess. The closer should never read between the lines or cut off the customer's remarks when he is talking. The customer just might say or ask something that is the complete opposite of what the closer is expecting. For example: The customer may say, "Mr. Closer, I don't think that the real estate we looked at is exactly ...." and the closer jumps in responding, "Mr. Customer, I know it's not what you were looking for." Then the customer states, "No, that's not it, what I was going to say is the property isn't exactly what I had in mind, but I really like it and I'm interested in making a bid."

The closer, by cutting in, could not only jeopardize the sale but may create problems or objections that didn't have to exist at all. The closer should always listen and show the customer some respect. Remember, customers "ain't stupid."

(b) DO: The closer doesn't only have to listen to the customer, he also has to understand (comprehend) what the customer is saying or trying to say. The closer has to know exactly what the customer is talking about so he can get the sale. The closer and the customer have to have a "meeting of the minds" (complete understanding of what each one is saying).

DON'T: The closer shouldn't act like he understands the customer's remarks or statements if he really doesn't. This misunderstanding has killed many, many sales. The closer, by not completely knowing what the customer is saying or asking could very easily misdirect his sales presentation and completely miss the customer's main objection to buying the product. Plus the customer will easily see through this "act" and develop the feeling that the closer doesn't care enough about him to find out what he means or is saying. The customer will say to himself, "If he (the closer) doesn't care enough, about what I'm saying, then I don't care about what he's selling," and another sale would be lost.

To overcome this sales situation the closer should politely and sincerely say, "Mr. Customer, excuse me, but I'm not precisely sure of what you're saying. Now what exactly did you mean?" The customer will not only respect this statement but will feel the closer genuinely cares enough to answer thoughtfully. This builds more trust and closeness between customer and closer. (Two important ingredients needed by the closer to "close.")

(c) **DO:** The closer must be aware of everything that is going on around him and his customer during the "closing" process.

The closer has to not only watch his customers' (husband and wife team) eyes giving silent signals to each other but, he has to be aware of other customers, other closers, surrounding circumstances and events that might or might not affect the outcome of his sales presentation and "close." If the closer is alert and prepared for unexpected incidents or activities he can also protect or prepare his customer for the same, thus avoiding problems or objections that are unnecessary. For example: The closer is getting his customer prepared to buy and he notices another closer who is within earshot and on the verge of a verbal battle with his customer. The first closer should tactfully get his customer away and out of hearing range so his sale won't be lost due to the stupidity of the other closer. (Note: Closers should always be courteous and respectful to another closer when he is with his customer, *always*.)

DON'T: The closer should never try to avoid or ignore any kind of positive or negative activity that is going on around him and his customer, especially if he knows his customer is aware of it also. If the closer tries to overlook something embarrassing and acts as though it didn't happen or wasn't important, it could create suspicious thoughts (unanswered questions) in the customer's mind, making the "close" that much more difficult. For example: The customer of closer number one sees the customer of closer number two get up angrily from a table, rip up a contract and storm out of the sales office. This kind of negative activity certainly won't help closer number one sell his customer. So he should say something positive, explain the situation and get his customer settled down and calm again. If he doesn't convincingly describe to his customer exactly what happened, then closer number one could easily lose a sale. To get out of this unpleasant situation, closer number one should say something like, "Mr. Customer, did you see what just happened? Let me tell you the real story behind that." etc. and give the customer the most believable and understandable explanation possible. (Note: Closer number one must make the explanation quickly and clearly and then drop it, so he can get back to work and "close" his customer. If he dwells too long on the negative happening the customer will also, and this could lead to a lost sale.)

(d) DO: When asking the customer to buy the product, the closer should always say, "Mr. Customer, why don't you give it a try?" or "Mr. Customer, let's try it" or "Why don't we try it?" The closer has to make the customer feel comfortable and relaxed, not alone or isolated in his important decision-making. The customer must feel secure and unafraid if he is going to give the closer a positive buying answer. Otherwise, the chances are higher that he won't buy. It's that simple.

The little magic words, "let's," "when," "try," "we," "our," can't be praised enough by closers. These harmless, suggestive words make the total sales presentation easy and uncomplicated for the customer. These magic words don't offend the customer, push him, intimidate or pressure him. All they do is offer the customer a pleasant and painless buying opportunity. (At least that's how it sounds when it comes from the closer.)

DON'T: When the closer is asking the customer for the order he should never say, "Mr. Customer, why don't you buy it?" or "Buy it today," or "If it were yours." Any of these kinds of statements tend to make the customer put up that thick defensive shield again. The customer will not only feel cornered and threatened by these statements, he will feel distant and turned off toward making a buying decision immediately. The reason is this: If a closer approaches a customer with a very direct buying question like, "Mr. Customer, if you buy this property, etc...." the customer will automatically think to himself, "Well, if I do ..." That "If I do" thought will subconsciously lead the customer to figure out a way to delay having to make the decision which will inevitably be in the from of an excuse to postpone it into the future. So the closer sits with one less sale that day because he tipped off and educated his customer, through his "if" and "buy" words, that he was moving in for the close. This scenario for losing a sale is completely the closer's fault.

Sam said the closer has to always keep everything he has learned in the complete sales presentation process in proper order and in total perspective. Closers have to remember all the points, steps and ingredients that make up the three main phases of "closing" (The First Meeting, Ch. 6; The Sales Presentation, Ch. 7; and Closing the Customer, Ch. 8) to be able to master the fine art of "closing." These three phases, Sam explained, have been carefully devised and are in perfect order. If they are studied, practiced, and sincerely utilized, they can and will make any salesman in the world a master closer. (FACT.)

Sam told me that before I begin to learn about "when the closer goes in for the kill," I should realize one very, very important point: The closer has to make his customer (gradually and deliberately, during every step and throughout every phase of the total sales presentation) want his product so much that he would do almost anything, within reason, to purchase it.

The sales professional, if he wants to be considered a master closer, (or top producer) has to cut right into the very emotions and feelings of the customer. He has to examine what he finds, form a professional game plan ("closing attack") and then go in for the "close," the kill.

Remember, the closer's opponent is the customer and it's the closer's job to get a sale. The closer has to use all of his gut feelings, imagination and knowledge to accomplish that job. (Excluding lying and fraud, of course.) If the closer used anything less, he would get fewer sales than he should; if he gets fewer sales than his true potential allows, he would be less than a master closer.

"Closing Points"
(Pre-"Going in for the Kill" notes to keep in mind)

1. A good old rule: The closer should never listen to or pay much attention to a customer's first "No," or negative answer (response) to his buying question ("Give it a try?"), until the customer gives his fifth negative answer. This is because a customer will usually throw out stupid, silly and unimportant objections when first asked to buy the product. These negative "No, I won't buy" responses don't really mean much because they are just weak excuses on the customer's part, so he won't look like an easy sale to the closer. (Note: Bless his heart, even the customer who really and truly wants the product has to put up some form of buying resistance, just to make himself feel better.)

2. After the "close" and the contract is signed the closer should say to the customer, "Mr. Customer, remember I'm your man, if you ever need anything — anything at all. You call me first and I'll take care of it personally." (This not only makes the customer feel better and reassured, but if the closer ever has any problem with the customer he will hear the news first and have the best chance to solve any complaints before other nosey sales office staff or management get involved and blow everything out of proportion, as they usually do.)

3. The closer should never settle for less than all he can possibly achieve in his sales career. If a closer doesn't want to be a top closer then he should get out of the profession. Mediocre closers are just idiot salesmen or sales clerks — nothing more.

4. "When all is lost, ask for the order one more time." You never know what may happen and they just might say yes, if your level of charm, humor and warmth appeals to that reluctant, borderline customer.

5. The closer can always give the customer some intelligent "thought and emotion attacks" when the customer is reluctant and there seems to be no headway being made during the "closing procedure." "Attacks" such as these will at least get the customer moving in one direction or the other. For example: "Mr. Customer, at least do it for the love and future of your family," or "Mr. Customer, you don't build your future on dreams, you build it on actions, your actions."

6. The closer should try to put himself, pyschologically, in the customer's situation and then try to solve his problem from this angle.

7. The closer is only fooling himself if he thinks he has a deal when he has nothing on paper, or doesn't have a check. Customers do frequently tell little white lies, you will soon find out.

8. The closer has to remember that when "closing," money will be the major objection, 98 percent of the time. Customers will never tell the closer the true reason until it has been finally dragged out. But if the closer has done his job well and the customer still won't buy, then money is nearly always the reason.

9. When "closing" (asking for the order) the closer should lower his voice and "kind of" whisper, giving the "main event" an air of seriousness and almost reverence. Customers love to hear secrets or quiet statements and a closer's whisper of "Give it a try?" will often do the trick. The customer will have to listen closely to hear what the closer is saying and this is what was wanted in the first place.

10. The closer has to keep in mind that his total sales presentation — **all three phases — is over and finished only when he says it is,** *not* when the customer says or thinks it is.

11. If a customer really believes in something, then the best thing a **closer can do is to add a supportive idea or suggestion to it,** and then steer that belief toward a "close." The closer can, if he does it properly, put the customer's dream (his belief) into a compatible relationship with the product, thus producing a sale. For example: "Mr. Customer, that home you always wanted for your family could literally be yours very easily because we have our own financing and there will be no problem whatsoever in granting you a loan." (Note: The closer should never shatter a customer's dream or he's dead.)

12. When the customer tells the closer, after everything (the total sales **presentation) has been completed,** that he wants to look at all of the product information on paper, or see a brochure to take home with him, then the closer had better start his sales presentation all over with this customer, because he's not sold and is simply looking for a way out. (FACT.)

13. If the customer makes any kind of silly, low ball offer or tries to **pull off a bluff** (for example: The customer offers $10,000 for a $25,000 piece of property) the closer should go right ahead, if he feels all else is lost, and ask the customer for his check, telling him he will present it to management and see if they'll accept it. This may shock the customer into giving the closer the real excuse as to why he won't buy (the customer will usually start panicking and thinking up a lot of fantastic excuses for not being able to buy — which is good because it gives the closer objections to overcome so he can get the sale.) Or, the closer could get the sale by taking the low ball offer to the sales office, and when the deal is obviously turned down, go back to the bluffing customer without his check and tell him that management will negotiate. (Note: Don't let the customer see the check or he will probably grab it and tear it up. Checks have a terrible tendency to remind customers what just happened.) Then go in for the kill again, explaining why the property is really worth $25,000 and not the $10,000 the customer gave the closer. If the closer keeps working on this customer he will probably get the sale because the customer is already partly there with his verbal commitment as well as some of his money.

14. To totally "close" a customer the closer has to explain and justify the price of his product. The reason for this is that the customer, in his own mind, has to know that all of his labor, time, sweat and inconvenience was really worth purchasing the product. Sam said, "The price of the product has to be justified to the buyer so he believes it equals the trouble of making the money to buy it."

15. The closer, when he has "closed" a customer who doesn't really have much money should take the minimum amount necessary to get the sale financed or approved. The closer should never take all of his customer's bank account, because if he does then the customer will eventually resent him and might possibly cancel later thinking that all the closer really wanted was his money. If the closer leaves this buyer a little pocket money or throws in something extra, not only will the customer appreciate it but he will be a super customer later on down the road because the closer understood his problem, helped him out, and was also his friend.

16. If the closer loses the sale, whether it's his fault or not, then he shouldn't "burn" or anger his customer; he should make sure that he (in his "closing" attempt) has planted at least a seed of a thought about buying. If customers leave the sales office grinning or laughing to each other then the closer can rest assured that they were probably not serious about buying in the first place or never really took his product seriously. But if the closer plants a seed of a buying idea in the customer's head then when this "lost sale customer" is some day in the future interested, he will possibly come back to you to do his buying. Never underestimate the value of a good impression. It usually will translate into referrals.

17. The old saying, "Whenever the seller asks the customer to buy the product he should immediately *shut up,* **not say another word and wait for the customer to answer him (talk first)," is correct.**
When the closer asks for the order and then is silent, that silence puts pressure on the customer. The customer will feel this "silent pressure" building. Then when he answers, he breaks the silence and talks first. (Note: "Whoever talks first loses" is also true because the person, closer or customer, that does speak first has "broken" first or has given in. This is a subconscious reaction in the back of either party's mind. This reaction works in the same manner that arm wrestling does. Someone is going to have to give in (lose) and that is basically what happens when the first person talks — he loses, he broke that deadly silence first, he couldn't take it.)
The closer will not only know the customer feels the pressure but he will hear what the customer has to say, whether it's an objection, statement or whatever, and be able to respond and deal with it. The closer just has to

keep quiet and let the pressure mount up, even if it takes many minutes for the customer to answer. The wait will be worth it. (Note: If the closer has determined that the customer cannot on his own initiative say the first word, then the closer should quietly and calmly say to the customer, "Mr. Customer, give it a try?" If the closer asks for the order again it is not really breaking the silence, rather it puts even more pressure on the customer. The closer should then *shut up* and wait again for the customer to talk. The closer should never make a habit of talking first, but in some delicate situations, this little prodding may be exactly what's needed to get the customer to answer.)

18. After the closer has completed the total sales presentation and tried to "close" the customer as many times as he thought was necessary and still failed to get the sale but, the customer still hasn't left the sales office or is just standing around, then the chances are very good that he probably has some unanswered or unexplained questions on his mind. He's still interested in the product. The closer should give him a few minutes by himself and then go up to him and politely try to sell him again, by asking if there was anything additional he wanted to know or could be helped with. This usually makes the customer feel the closer truly cares (by showing that extra willingness to accomodate him), plus it gives the closer another shot at getting a sale.

19. If the closer is selling a product that has a legal cancellation clause attached to it — for instance, a three business days right to cancel the contract, after the purchase — then the closer had better not use that cancellation clause as a benefit to sell the product. The reason is that the customer may sign the contract just to get away from the closer and then go home and cancel. The closer who sells based on this cancellation feature will have more cancellations than anyone can imagine. (FACT.) When a closer sells he had better lock the sale in as best he can at the time the contract is signed and sealed. That way his cancellation percentage will be very low.

20. The closer always has to be in control of himself and his customer. He must demonstrate a sincere belief in his product and know what he is talking about. He has to give the customer a feeling of confidence at all times. The closer must think to himself that he is the only person in the world who is going to put the customer together with the product so he had better secure that potential sale with professionalism and nothing less.

1. Going In For The Kill

(The closer asks the customer to buy his product)

Sam said it was time to learn how the master closer asks the customer for the order. He said that if I put everything I had learned so far together with what I was about to learn, then there wasn't a customer alive I couldn't sell (close). Since my first sales talks with Sam, this was the lesson I had really been waiting for.

NOTE I — SETTING THE STAGE — At this point in the overall sales presentation, the closer and the customer are both sitting down at the closing table. They have already gone through a summary of: "the pre-closing questions," the pre-demonstration pitch, and the sales presentation. Now the time is right for the closer to ask the customer to buy his product. It should be kept in mind that the customer knows enough product information at this point to make a buying decision when asked.

NOTE II — It also has to be understood that the customer might or might not know the price of the product at this time. If he does know the product's price, he found out during the other phases of the sales presentation, and can make a buying decision by being shown some of the financial arrangements that are open to him, if financing is necessary. For example: The customer can't pay cash for the product, so he has to put down a partial payment and then finance the balance. The closer shows the customer the paperwork and then the closer asks for the order. He goes in for the kill.

Now, on the other hand, let's say the customer doesn't know the price of the product or any of the financial arrangements. The closer has been holding that information until the end, to use as a "closing" tool. If that is the case then the closer will simply tell the customer the amount of money involved and the details about buying and then he'll go in for the kill (ask for the order).

Both of these sales situations — knowing the price early and not knowing the price until the "closing process" — can be treated in about the same manner. What's important is that the closer must ask for the order at some point and get a response out of the customer; then overcome that response if it is negative. If the customer says no, the closer must maneuver until he can again ask the customer to buy the product or "give it a try." Persistence pays off — that is the bottom line.

It should also be remembered that a sale can be made anywhere or at anytime during the total sales presentation.

Sam said the formula for "asking for the order" was so simple that many closers not only overlook it, but often make it more difficult than it really is when trying to sell a customer.

The Formula For "Asking For the Order"

The formula for "asking for the order" is:

FEELINGS or EMOTIONS + TIMING = THE RIGHT OPPORTUNITY.

(That special, precise moment when the closer asks the customer to buy and the customer is ready.)

A. FEELINGS or EMOTIONS — They are made up from the customer's deepest and most personal thoughts and dreams. For instance, when the customer asks himself exactly what the closer's product can do for him and how he will benefit from owning it, he is in a world all by himself. The customer is thinking about his family and how they will use the product. He is daydreaming about how he will look owning the product. He is analyzing the product and all of its possibilities and how they will be advantageous to him. The customer is in a serious and realistic mood at this point and wants to think about the product positively and creatively. (Note: This is how the customer should be thinking if the closer has executed his sales presentation properly. If the closer hasn't given an organized and positive sales presentation up to this point, he can still get the sale, but it will be a little more difficult.)

B. TIMING — This subject has been explained earlier in the chapter, but Sam said it wouldn't hurt to take a quick look, just once more, so the closer doesn't forget. Timing is when the closer recognizes that special unintentional expression of contentment and satisfaction on the customer's face. The customer subconsciously radiates this physical expression not only through his eyes (they kind of sparkle) but the edges of his mouth will start to show a faint "satisfied smile." It can't be helped, it's normal, it's the same expression a person has when he knows the answer to a question about to be asked. It's that kind of exciting expression of anticipation customers always try to conceal. The closer, if he is alert and paying attention to the customer, can't miss it. Timing is knowing that special moment when the customer is waiting for the closer to ask him to buy the product because the customer feels he's ready to buy. He likes what he has seen and he wants it (the product). The customer will have a facial expression that says, "I understood what you told me about the product, Mr. Closer. Now what do we do?"

C. THE RIGHT OPPORTUNITY — This is when the closer thinks the customer's FEELINGS or EMOTIONS are right and the TIMING is right. Then, at that second, the closer asks the customer to buy the product. For the closer this is just like jumping off a high diving board for the first time, in the sense that he always feels butterflies, some excitement deep down inside, when he finally asks for the order. It doesn't matter if the closer is an old pro or a new man, that feeling will be there — guaranteed. (Note: If that feeling of excitement is not there the closer ought to get out of the selling business because he's had it. Excitement and enthusiasm are the backbones of any master closer and a master closer cannot function without them.)

Sam told me that right before the closer asks the customer to buy his product (give it a try) he has to mentally go over a "last minute check list" to make sure he hasn't forgotten anything and everything is in proper order. By doing this exercise the closer is far more likely to receive a positive response from the customer than a negative one.

CHECK — Intimidation, if the closer has to use it, then he should be prepared to use it. For example: "Mr. Customer, you've seen all the advantages of my product, and you know they're sound and good; I mean a one-eyed baboon can see that. Why don't you give it a try?"

CHECK — When the closer asks the customer to buy the product (giving it a try) he should make it sound like a "simple, friendly, concerned question," a question asked with some gentleness and sincerity, not a buying question that makes everything look like a gigantic, monstrous deal. This will only scare the customer. The closer's buying question should pierce (hit) the customer like a quiet and subtle arrow, not a loud and frightening cannon. For example: The closer should say: "Mr. Customer, if the monthly payments fit into your budget — and I know that they do — why not give it a try?" The closer should not say, "Mr. Customer, if you can afford it, buy it now."

CHECK — No matter how many objections the customer gives, when the closer answers them satisfactorily, he has to ask the customer to buy the product again (one more time). The closer has to answer every *real* objection one hundred percent to the customer's complete satisfaction and understanding. (Note: Some objections don't have to be answered by the closer. These objections are just silly statements the customer nervously makes and doesn't think about when he says them. All the closer has to do is look at the customer, with the facial expression of "Now, you know the answer to that," and keep right on "closing," paying no more attention to that meaningless objection.)

CHECK — If the customer, after he gives an objection and it is answered by the closer, still has another objection, he is simply not yet sold on the product. (FACT.) The closer has to find the real reason why the customer won't buy and overcome that reason (objection) before the sale can be made. Sometimes the closer has to go through ten to fifteen objections before he finally finds out what the *real* bottom-line objection is. But when that real objection is finally conquered and the closer gets the sale, then all the valuable time spent by the closer to find out what the real objection was will have been worth it.

CHECK — The closer has to understand he is going to have to stick with the customer, staying right in there until he "closes" him. He has to learn that tenacity is his middle name if he ever wants to be a master closer. It's not easy and sometimes it sure isn't fun, but a closer should never give up if he thinks the customer could possibly buy the product.

CHECK — The closer should know that when he senses the opportunity to "close" then he should "close." When the chance to "close" arrives the closer should drop everything he's doing and take it, ask for the order on the spot.

CHECK — The closer has to remember to never overreact to anything the customer says in response to his buying question. The closer shouldn't get angry, upset or too excited, but always show control and be calm. It doesn't matter if the customer's response is positive or negative. For example (Negative): The closer says, "Mr. Customer, why don't you give it a try?" and the customer says, "Are you kidding? Do you think I would really buy this stuff?" Or (Positive): The customer says, "I don't think I'll take one, I'll take four." The closer has to use "emotional restraint" most of the time when he is closing. It makes the customer feel more comfortable in his buying decision and in his relationship with the closer. (Note: Sometimes it's good for the closer to get very emotional and excited when he is "closing," if it's used to make a point and the customer is responding to that point. For example: The customer says that the product costs too much, and in response the closer says, "Mr. Customer, when was the last time you looked at real estate? Do you realize how much it goes up every year? Would you sell your house now, for exactly the same price you bought it for twenty years ago? Now, you tell me what you'd do. I don't think that you are really aware of what's going on in today's explosive real estate market. I'm telling you the straight truth about this property, so you'd better listen!")

CHECK — The closer has to make it easy for the customer to buy the product. In other words the closer has to make the customer think if he buys "it's no big deal," it's not the end of the world, or possible bankruptcy. The customer has to feel calm and reassured in his buying decision. This "customer calmness" can be accomplished by the closer through his positive statements and his warm relationship with the customer. The closer's overall concern and attentiveness toward the customer will pay off when it becomes time for the customer to make his buying decision. (FACT.) (Reminder: The closer's and customer's relationship begins when they first meet and gradually develops throughout the entire sales presentation.)

CHECK — The closer should never put off or procrastinate his buying question or "asking for the order" question. That will only drag the sales presentation out and make it boring and confusing for the customer. The closer should take the first good opportunity he sees and act on it. The sooner he hears the customer's objection and overcomes it, the sooner he can get the sale. The closer should act (ask for the order) on his first impulse that the time is right; that first impulse is usually correct. (FACT.)
(Note: This is not a contradiction to the "old pro's" saying of "ask 'em early," because that saying didn't have a thing to do with timing [the right opportunity]. This "check-reminder" has everything to do with timing, because the closer is asking for the order when he feels the time is exactly right and not just asking for the order to get some kind of objection out of the customer. There is a big difference.)

CHECK — The closer has to keep in mind that the customer of today is a lot smarter and more consumer-oriented than he was ten or twenty years ago. The customer of today knows everything about his rights and responsibilities. But there is one thing about a customer that will never change, and that is he wants, and will always want, to be better off, have more, and be more successful than the next guy. The customer really loves himself. (FACT.) So it doesn't matter how much today's customer knows about this or that in the sales industry, just as long as the closer works on his ego and gets the buyer motivated. The closer will not only make a friend, but get a sale, every time. (FACT.)

Asking For the Order

Sam told me there are *three* distinct "degree-of-interest levels" that customers fall into when they are about to be asked to buy the product. The "first-degree customer" is the easiest one for the closer to handle. The customer is "hot" — he's ready to be asked to buy the product.

The "second-degree customer" is the one who knows all about the product, but still needs that last-minute bit of product information, that little extra positive statement from the closer, before he's ready to be asked to purchase what you are selling.

And then there is the "third-degree customer." He's the toughest of all three. He is the customer who understands the product and acknowledges all of its benefits, but still needs some time to be left alone so that he can decipher and digest all of the information the closer has told him before he is ready to be asked to buy the product.

Sam said the closer has to handle each one of the three "degree-of-interest level" customers differently. The closer must eventually get all three "degree customers" in the right frame of mind (open, responsive, and receptive), just before they are asked to buy the product. (Note: It should be understood that the "first-degree customer" is already in the right frame of mind to be asked to buy, but the "second" and "third-degree customers" still need some extra programming before they are ready. Now when the closer accomplishes this additional programming exercise, getting the "second" and "third-degree customers" in the right frame of mind, he will be able to deal with all three customers in exactly the same manner, asking them the bottom line question of, "Will you give my product a try?" at the appropriate time.

A. The First-Degree Customer:

This customer is either already sold on the product or is just about sold on it. He is ready for the closer to ask him to buy. This customer might have one or two little objections before he buys the product, but these objections won't be any real problem for the closer. This customer is ready to be "closed" now.

B. The Second-Degree Customer:

This customer has been alert and attentive during the total sales presentation; he knows what the advantages of the product are and he understands the total product concept. This customer is seriously thinking about the pros and cons of purchasing — he's still open- minded. But this customer is also not quite ready to be asked to buy the product. The closer can tell this by the customer's facial expression. For example: The customer has a "Well, I don't really know" look about him or he has a "questioning or confused look" in his eyes. (Note: These facial expressions or concerned looks can be easily recognized by the closer if he just pays attention. It's practically impossible to misread these expressions.)

The closer can also tell that this customer isn't ready to be asked to buy yet by the way he is acting (standoffish and aloof). This customer is not as enthused or as excited as other interested customers normally would be at this point in the sales presentation. This customer either needs a little more last minute product information, extra guidance or some positive "thought statements" from the closer before he will be ready to be asked to buy. The rationale for these last minute "mini- conversations" is to make the customer feel a little more involved in the product, and to make him feel more comfortable and secure with the closer. This not only gives the customer the added strength and courage he needs to comfortably deal with the closer's buying question of "Give it a try?", but also makes the atmosphere easier for the closer to ask for the order. (Note: The "mini-conversation" is that something extra the closer does or says right before he asks the customer to buy the product.)

MINI-CONVERSATIONS:

When the closer sees the customer isn't quite ready to be asked to buy, when he knows deep in his heart that if he did ask the customer to buy, the only answer he would receive would be a flat "No," the closer should take one more minute before asking for the order to give this customer some positive and informative statements (through a "mini-conversation"). The "mini-conversation" has to be deliberately designed to bring the customer and the seller to a more understanding point before they discuss the closer's buying question of "give it a try?" The idea is to get the buyer thinking with a more open mind.

The best way to explain these "mini-conversations" that go with the buying question is to give a few examples.

1. "Mr. Customer, this product is an investment. It's just like a train: the longer you stay on it (or with it), the further you go. You can jump off anytime you want to — that's your decision — but first you have to get started, you've got to get on board. So why don't you "give my product a try?" (Note: The closer should then shut up and patiently wait for the customer's response.)

2. "Mr. Customer, you know the best thing to do before you say, "I'll take it," is to look at my product as though it were a new pair of shoes. What you need to do is try it on for awhile, walk around, and see how it fits. Then, if it doesn't fit right or if it feels uncomfortable, you can always liquidate your investment and get out. It's that simple. The worst thing that could happen to you while you are testing the product is that it makes you a little bit of money. So why don't you give it a try?" (Note: The closer should then shut up and wait for the customer's response.)

3. "Mr. Customer, you know you can either go first class or second class. It's all up to you. What you really want for your family is your decision. All that I can do is give you this opportunity. So why don't you give it a try?" (Note: The closer should then shut up and wait for the customer's response.)

4. "Mr. Customer, when people buy my product, most don't pay cash. What they do is put a little bit of money down and pay so much a month. By paying in installments, if they ever decide to sell the product, they wouldn't have that much of their own money tied up in it. Later on, if they wanted to keep the product, they could just go ahead and pay the installments. It's just like going swimming in a big lake: You don't stand on a cliff and decide to jump right in because the lake might be too shallow or there might be a tree stump or something in the water that could hurt you when you jump. What you do is go down to the edge of the lake first and gradually wade in and see exactly how deep and safe it is; then if you want to go up to the cliff and dive in you can, knowing the water is safe. When you buy my product it's the same thing — just put a little bit of money in it and watch it grow. Mr. Customer, give it a try?" (Note: The closer should then shut up and wait for the customer's response.)

5. "Mr. Customer, let me ask you something. Since you know all about the product and its benefits and advantages, plus now that you have all the facts because you've seen the product yourself — you wouldn't let anyone else who hasn't seen the product as you have shake your opinion of the product, would you?" When the customer answers "No," and in 99 percent of the cases he will, the closer should continue with his usual buying question, the good old "give it a try?" (Note: The closer should then shut up and wait for the customer's response.)

6. "Mr. Customer, let me tell you something, just man to man. If I were in the same financial situation that you told me earlier you are in, and if I had the same opportunity to buy this product, knowing in fact that it wouldn't do anything but help me, then there's nothing in the world that would stop me from buying, and that's the truth. So why don't you give it a try?" (Note: The closer should then shut up and wait for the customer's response.)

7. "Mr. Customer, did you know that you're just like everyone else who comes into this sales office? People come in here with no intention whatsoever of buying my product. But do you know what happens? After they've seen the product, understand and know the facts about the product, find out who is behind my company and what we've accomplished in the past, almost every person makes an honest and sincere business decision to buy. That's a fact. It's that simple, you're not alone. So why don't you give it a try?" (Note: The closer should then shut up and wait for the customer's response.)

8. "Mr. Customer, if you feel I've been using some pressure on you during this sales presentation or that I might seem to be too pushy or excited about my product, well, you're right. I have been, and the reason is because my product is that good. If it weren't that good, believe me I wouldn't be making a nuisance of myself. I've got a family that wants to be proud of their Dad too. All I want you to do is exactly what I did, plus what three thousand other people did, and that is give it a try." (Note: The closer then should shut up and wait for the customer's response.)

9. "Mr. Customer, I'm sure that you want more for your children than you had for yourself when you were growing up, and I know that you want them to have a solid financial footing — a chance, a good start in life. You know, you can give them the very things you've dreamed of and help them, the way someday they'll help their kids, if you get involved in this investment. So why don't you give it a try?" (Note: The closer should then shut up and wait for the customer's response.)

10. "Mr. Customer, remember earlier you told me your son was going to be an architect. You know, if you got him to help you build your vacation home on that property we were looking at, not only would he appreciate it, but it would help build the father-son bond that perhaps, because of his schooling and your business commitments, could be even closer that it is now. You only get one shot at life, Mr. Customer, and a man's family should be close (pause for three seconds). So why don't you give it a try?" (Note: The closer should then shut up and wait for the customer's response.)

C. The Third-Degree Customer:

This customer is the hardest one of the three "degree-of-interest- level customers" to handle. The reason is because this customer could very easily go either way (sale or no sale). He could get up from the closing table and walk out of the sales office or he could sit there all day and act as though he's not interested in the product at all, and then buy at the last minute. This customer knows and understands the product and has been basically attentive, but he hasn't shown very much emotion or any real excitement during the sales presentation. He is reserved and tends to make the closer feel somewhat awkward.

This customer needs some time alone so he can get his thoughts together before the closer asks him to buy the product. The best thing the closer can do to not only keep control of the situation but to get this customer in the right frame of mind for the buying question, is the following: When the closer is sitting at the closing table with this type of customer, and knows that this customer might at any minute say, "Well, I've seen enough of the product, I'll get back to you."

(Note: The closer can also recognize this "I'll get back to you" attitude not only by the disinterested air about him, but also by his lack of questions about the product and his unwillingness to have direct eye contact with the closer.)

This customer generally won't pay attention and can be easily distracted. The closer should just get up from the closing table (while the customer is still sitting and before he has had a chance to say "I'll be back,") and say to the customer, "Mr. Customer, why don't you think about and discuss the product, come up with some questions for me and I'll be back in a minute, I've got to check on something." (Note: Many customers want to leave before they have been asked to buy the product. This reaction is normal for them because they don't want to be hassled with pressure from the closer.)

After making this statement, the closer should immediately walk away before the customer has a chance to stop him and before he can give some stupid reason for not staying seated or for not staying in the sales office. (Note: Customers tend to feel obligated to remain seated in the sales office at the closing table until the closer returns and lets them go, "cuts them loose," or says good-bye. This works to the closer's advantage because the customer loses the chance to escape after the sales demonstration was completed and is still in the sales office surrounded by all of the product's promotions and sales material.

When the closer is away from the closing table he should keep an eye on the customer and watch his actions. If the customer is starting to talk seriously about the product, there is a good chance he's interested in buying.

The closer should be alert for clues by paying close attention to the customer at all times.

When the closer feels he has been away from the customer long enough (about five to ten minutes, depending on the customer and the situation) he should go back to the closing table, sit down and say, "Any questions?" (Note: Again the closer has to shut up and wait for the customer to speak first.) The customer will usually respond with an objection, and that is exactly what the closer wanted in the first place.

The closer should never go back to the closing table and say, "Well, what do you think?", because the potential buyers will most likely say, "Well, we talked about it while you were gone and we're going to pass on it this time," or the customers will say, "We'll let you know later on, thank you for your time." The closer left himself wide open for this type of response because the question "Well, what do you think?" means exactly the same as, "Are you going to buy the product or not, Mr. Customer?" The closer programmed and forced the customer to automatically and easily say "No." The customer didn't have any maneuvering room. The question didn't give him a way out, so he has to say "No," if he's not totally sold at that point. But a response like, "Any questions?" leaves the customer some room to talk and think; it doesn't offend the customer because it sounds like a noncommittal question that can be simply answered.

After the closer has asked, "Any questions?" and receives an answer or objection, he can proceed to ask the customer to buy his product. (Note: The closer, by walking away from the seated "third- degree customer" and giving him time alone to think — and then by coming back and asking for "Any questions?" has actually programmed the "third-degree customer" into the same receptive frame of mind that the "first" and "second-degree customers" have.) The closer can now ask the "third-degree customer" to "give his product a try," in the same manner that he asked the first and second-degree customers.

Sam said that once you understand how to put all three "degree-of-interest-level customers" into the right frame of mind to be asked to buy the product, you can continue to the next step which is to ask the customer for the order.

Money Information:

The closer can either tell his customer the price of the product at some point during the total sales presentation (when he thinks the time is strategically right), or the closer can wait to tell the customer the product's price at the end of the sales presentation (when he asks the customer to "give his product a try").

If the closer tells the customer the price of the product during the sales presentation, he has to summarize and repeat the price and financial arrangements to the customer again at the end of the presentation, right before asking for the order, to make sure the customer knows exactly how much money the closer is talking about. There cannot by any misunderstanding of the money matter or the sale could very easily be lost.

No matter when the closer tells his customer the price of the product, when he (the closer) is discussing the financial arrangements with the customer he'd better do it smoothly, calmly, comfortably and simply. The reason is this: At this late point in the sales presentation the closer can't afford to upset or frighten the customer, or the sale could be in jeopardy. For example: If the closer makes the financing look complicated and too technical for the customer to understand, the customer will simply put up his protective shield and not pay attention to another word the closer has to say. The closer has to make the price and the finances of the product look as uncomplicated and elementary for the customer as possible so the customer can make a simple and comfortable buying decision when asked to purchase the product.

The best way to show how the closer explains the finances and then asks the customer to buy is through an example. (Note: This example takes place at the end of the sales presentation, with the closer and customer sitting down at the closing table.) "Mr. Customer, that piece of property we were looking at costs .... thousand dollars. Now my company will do all of the financing itself. We'll take .... percent down payment or .... dollars, and then we will finance the rest at .... percent interest for .... years. That would make the monthly payments exactly .... Let me ask you this: Would these monthly payments fit into your budget?" The closer should then shut up and wait for the customer's answer. (Note: The closer should always ask the customer if the monthly payments are comfortable for him first, before he inquires about the down payment, simply because the monthly payments don't represent nearly as much money to the customer as the down payment, thus making it easier for the customer to answer "Yes" to a question that is directed toward the lesser amount of money. In other words, from the customer's point of view, the smaller amount of money is the same as a smaller obligation, and a smaller obligation is easier to take on than a large one. So the "monthly payment question" is easier for the customer to answer.)

If he's even half-way sold on the product, the customer will nearly always say, "Well, the monthly payments aren't any problem." The closer should then immediately say, "What about the down payment?" If the customer says, "I could handle that," then the closer had better say, "Then give it a try," and wait for an objection or answer. But if the customer says, "Now, the down payment — that would be a problem," the closer should say,

"Don't worry about that, I can take care of the down payment. We don't have to have it all right now, we can work with you on that. But just let me ask you this: If I could make the finances fit into your budget, would you then give it a try?" The closer should again shut up and wait for the customer's response. By using this approach, the closer can get a response and/or commitment out of the customer every time. Then the closer can continue on and go in for the kill ("close").

The closer should always remember when talking about financing, to ask the customer if he can handle the monthly payments first, then the down payment. If the closer asks the customer if he can handle the down payment before talking about the monthly payments, the customer (if he thinks he cannot make the down payment) will automatically put up his defensive guard and think or say "No" to the closer, thus creating a big objection right on the first round of the "customer close." So now the closer has not only received a negative answer from the customer by asking about the down payment first, but he also didn't get any kind of commitment as he would have if he had asked the customer about the monthly payments first. The closer must get the customer committed on an easy point first, and then and only then go in and "close."

Pen Techniques:

The writing pen is not only the closer's right arm, but it's the ever-present "hypnotic closing instrument." The closer has to get the customer accustomed to seeing the pen. (Customers tend to think the closer's pen is their enemy; it's against them because if they pick it up or touch it, they're that much closer to signing a contract with it. Customers think that if the pen wasn't there, a contract couldn't be signed and they'd be safe. That's why they're scared of the closer's pen.)

The closer also has to get the pen into the customer's hand so when it becomes time for the customer to write his name on the order (contract, working paper, etc.) he can.

The closer can best get the pen into the customer's hand by using these three methods. First, the closer can, when he wants the customer to have the pen, gently lay it down on the closing table in front of the customer with the writing end pointing away from the customer; or, the closer can calmly hand the pen to the customer, with the writing end pointing down and away from the customer; or (the trickiest way), is for the closer to purposely drop the pen on the floor near the customer. The customer will think it was an accident and automatically pick it up for the closer. Bingo, the pen is in the customer's hand. The closer should keep right on talking and never take back or ask for the pen again — let the customer keep it.

(Note: When the closer gets ready to ask the customer to buy the product, he'd better be prepared to write the order. The closer should have his pen and working paper or any other sales material he needs at hand, because if he doesn't, and the customer says that he'll buy the product now, the closer will have to take extra and valuable time away from the customer to look for his sales material. That wasted time could be all the time necessary for the customer to cool off and change his mind. The sale could be dead, plus the customer will think to himself, "Now if the closer is that disorganized about his paperwork, how in the world can he possibly be organized and dependable for me?" This thought alone could kill a sale. The closer has to be fully prepared to start writing up an order when he starts asking the customer to "give it a try.")

The closer can at times use his pen to hypnotize the customer to some degree. This hypnosis can be accomplished if the closer uses his pen not only for writing but as a pointer throughout the total sales presentation. By using it as a pointer, the customer gets accustomed to seeing the pen all the time and will start to subconsciously follow the pen and focus on it when the closer is using it to point out facts, figures and product information. The customer will be watching the writing instrument as it turns, swirls and moves continually around, thus making the customer's mind and eyes adjust to the pen's movements and positions during the presentation. This constant motion can have an hypnotic effect on customers, and the closer can use that effect to steer them more easily toward the "close."

Suggestions For Setting The Closing Scene:

When the closer asks the customer to buy the product ("give it a try") there should be dead silence, movement should stop, and there must be total concentration on the closer's part. The closer should have both feet flat on the floor. He should have his chair pulled up to the closing table with both hands on the table. The closer should lean slightly toward the customer, look him seriously and positively straight in the eye, without blinking once, while all the time thinking, "I love this customer, I know he's going to buy the product." (Note: If this mental exercise sounds silly to the closer, he should try it first before criticizing it, because it works wonders. FACT), and with a controlled and soft voice say, "Mr. Customer, you know everything about the product that I can tell you. This is the best opportunity you are ever going to have to buy this product at this price, and that's a fact. All I want you and your family to do is give my product a try, just that and nothing more — give it a try?" then, of course, the closer should shut up and wait for the customer to reply. When he does hear the customer's reply the closer should immediately go in and "close."

The closer should, right after he has asked the customer to buy the product, look directly and continually into the customer's eyes without blinking or looking away even once, and say over and over to himself, (smoothly and calmly) "Buy it ... buy it ... buy it ... buy it ...."

(Note: Positive thought *can* "psyche you up" to be more persuasive and aggressive, making positive things happen.) The closer should say this to himself repeatedly while he is waiting for the customer to answer him, all the time looking straight into the customer's eyes.

This type of determined self-psyching exercise works. The reason it works is this: the customer will actually feel the closer's intense eye contact, and that contact will put real pressure on the customer to act or talk whether it's in the form of an objection or another question. The "eye contact pressure" will not only make the customer feel uneasy, but obligated to say or do something. This unnaturally lengthy eye contact will also convey a sense of positive anticipation and a feeling of positive security to the customer. The customer will recognize this determination which will most likely be interpreted as sincerity and will further inspire the customer to give the closer a positive (Yes) answer to his buying question.

When the closer finally asks the customer to "give it a try" it should be so quiet that a pin could be heard when dropped. The closer shouldn't make a sound, he shouldn't clear his throat, tap his foot, move his hand — the closer shouldn't do *anything* until the customer moves and says something first. The closer has to have total and complete control at this time. (Note: Nothing should break the concentration between the closer and the customer.) The closer should realize this concentrated silence is only going to be broken when the customer looks away, coughs, or says something. Once the closer hears the customer's response he should immediately acknowledge it and then overcome and conquer it — "close."

How The Closer Handles and Completely Conquers The Customer's Objections

Sam said that at this point in the overall sales presentation, the closer has to be highly sensitive and alert to everything the customer says and does. He said this was usually the final meeting between the closer and customer and one of the two opponents had to lose. The closer has to use all of the information he has learned about the customer at this time and has to utilize all of his "closing" knowledge to win the final battle (get the sale). The closer has to use the customer's emotions and every little advantage he can think of to overcome objections and persuade the customer to buy the product. The customer will try to outwit, lie and dodge the closer's attempt to get the sale, but it's the "master closer's" responsibility to get the job done and "close." The customer will be a tough and worthy opponent for the closer, but the closer is the professional. He should usually win.

Before reviewing these techniques on how the closer handles customers' objections and then conquers them, there are six important "closing" facts that must be reviewed. These closing facts will show how the closer deals with the customer's objections, and specifically handles them. They will show what a closer must know about customer's objections if he expects to "close" every customer he talks to.

CLOSING FACT 1: The closer has to pin down the customer with the customer's own ammunition when it becomes time to "close." In other words, the closer has to trap the customer with his own words. The customer has been revealing information about himself throughout the sales presentation (stories about his family, his business and his personal interests) and the closer shouldn't have forgotten a thing. When the time to close has arrived, the closer should, if necessary, bring up an earlier mentioned family fact or design a story around the customer's personal interest that will "spear" this customer right through one of his emotional weak points.

CLOSING FACT 2: The closer has to realize that when the customer says "No" to a buying question, it only means that he is not *yet* sold on the product. He still has questions. It's true that the lack of money could be the real factor delaying the sale, but if it's not, there is no reason the closer shouldn't be able to sell the customer. The closer should never take "No" as the final answer, unless he is convinced in his heart that he is just wasting time while other prospective customers could be in his "closing clutches."

(Note: A "No" answer usually means that the customer doesn't believe the closer's pitch.)

CLOSING FACT 3: When the customer is asking a simple and obviously silly question, the closer, instead of getting frustrated with the customer, should turn around and ask the customer (nicely) what he would do or how he would answer that question. By gently and humorously suggesting the customer answer his own ridiculous question, the customer will either get his act together and start listening to your presentation or at least he will develop a little more respect for the closer, realizing you are capable of verbally defending yourself and your product.

In addition, this technique allows the closer not only to maintain control, but also gives him an opportunity to flatter the customer and say to him after he answers his own question, "Mr. Customer, that is exactly what we are going to do," or "Mr. Customer, my company feels exactly the same way."

CLOSING FACT 4: The closer must remember that more often than not he is the one who has to make the buying decision for the customer. The closer has to take the lead and proceed with any final paperwork. If the customer doesn't stop him, then the closer has a sale.

CLOSING FACT 5: The closer should recognize that when the customer says he has to "think about it," he is simply not sold on the product yet. The closer should realize that the excuse "I have to think about it," is not a true objection which the closer must overcome, but rather just a knee-jerk reaction on the customer's part that doesn't mean anything in particular. The closer needs a solid objection he can wrestle with and conquer. The "think about it" excuse isn't that kind of objection.

CLOSING FACT 6: The closer, if he feels he has to, should use the power of embarrassment to get the customer "closed." If the customer feels embarrassed badly enough, he will do almost anything to get out of that situation, including signing a contract.

To embarrass the customer the closer can use his family as leverage against him, as well as intimidation. For example: "Mr. Customer, do you mean to tell me, right here in front of your own children, that you don't make enough money to put some aside for their future education? What in the world are you working for anyway? You can't go from pay check to pay check, always worrying about tomorrow — that's not fair for you or your family. At least with my product you will have a solid investment, something saved for the future. That's what you should be striving for, so why don't you look at things realistically and consider giving my product a try?"

The Three Customer Responses

The "I'm Sold" Customer
The "I'm Nearly Sold" Customer
The "I'm Not Sold" Customer

Sam told me that when the closer asks the customer to give his product a try, there are only three basic responses the customer could give.

First Response: The first response is to answer the closer's buying question with a positive "I'm sold on the product" answer. For example, the customer will say, "All right, I'll take it" or "I'll give it a try," or "Well, I like it — you've got yourself a deal." This type of customer is sold on the product and says he'll purchase it when the closer asks him to buy the very first time.

Second Response: The second kind of response the customer could give would be a slightly objecting "I'm nearly sold" reply. For example: The customer will say "I'm not sure, that sounds like a lot of money you're asking for the product. I just don't know. I like the product, but I still have some looking around to do first," or "I'll tell you what: Let me sleep on it and I'll let you know later." This kind of customer will put up some good objections, but he can be "closed" without too much difficulty.

Third Response: The third kind of response the customer could give would be a negative "I'm not sold" reply. For example: The buyer will tell the closer "No, I don't think so, I'm going to pass on it. I don't want it, you are just wasting your time," or "It's not for me. No, I don't need it." This customer will not only put up strong objections, but in reality he is simply not yet sold on the product in his own mind. This customer's response is the hardest to conquer and "close." The closer has his work cut out for him when it comes to overcoming this kind of negative response.

To see how the master closer deals with each of these three customer responses and eventually "closes" all of them, Sam and I studied each response separately.

When the Customer Says, "I'm Sold"

When the closer asks his customer to "give his product a try" for the first time, the customers will usually look at each other and one of them will say something like, "I think it's a pretty good deal, do you want to give it a try?" When the other customer team member agrees, the closer has a sale.

(Note: This type of customer will have a couple of last minute questions or one or two light objections, but he is already mostly sold on the product. The questions or objections won't mean much and can easily be conquered by the closer. All the closer has to do is keep a positive attitude and answer the customer, then start writing the sale up.)

The customer could also simply say, "I like it — I'll take it." When the closer gets this kind of positive response from the customer, the closer should above all keep his professional composure and not act too excited or overjoyed.

STEP ONE: If the closer does show too much enthusiasm when the customer says he will buy the product, such overreaction could very easily scare the customer and possibly kill the sale. The customer might think to himself, "Gosh, if the closer is this thrilled that I'm buying his product then maybe I'm the only person in a long time that has bought. It could be I'm the only sucker around. There might be something wrong with this product that I don't know about. I think I'd better reconsider before I sign anything." The closer has to realize that showing too much excitement and overreacting when the customer says he will buy, is just as dangerous to a sale as a closer who gives a dull and unenthusiastic sales presentation.

STEP TWO: Immediately after the closer hears the customer say he will buy the product he should look the customer straight in the eye, and with a genuinely happy "Thank you" smile on his face, give the customer a firm and warm handshake. (Note: If the closer is working with a husband and wife customer team, it is perfectly acceptable for the closer to shake the woman's hand also. This little maneuver helps make the wife feel more involved in the buying decision.) The closer has to again remember not to get carried away with excitement when he shakes hands, but to stay cool and calm. When the closer is shaking hands (congratulating the customer for making the right decision to buy) with the customer, he should say something like "Welcome aboard," "Welcome to the club," "Congratulations, we're glad to have you," or a simple "Thank you."

(Note: The reason the closer has to immediately shake the customer's hand after he says he will buy is because that handshake will act as a "locking in" measure for the closer. In other words, the customer will suddenly feel both personally and morally obligated to buy because of the bonding handshake. The handshake usually has as much power as the physical act of having the customer sign his name on the contract. The customer, by shaking the closer's hand right after saying he will purchase the product, will be far less tempted to back off, cool off or change his mind during the "delicate time" it takes the closer to do the final paperwork.)

STEP THREE: The closer has to stop talking about the product and start writing up the order. After he shakes the customer's hand the closer has to change subjects (as tactfully as possible) and get away from talking about the product anymore. The closer should try to distract the customer away from thinking about the product by asking about the customer's job, his home town, his hobbies, anything, as long as it's not about the product.

If in the middle of this distraction the closer has to answer a customer's question, he should do it quickly and simply, then go right back to asking the customer questions about his personal life, or whatever. The closer has to do the best he can to keep the customer's mind away from the purchase so he won't start getting cold feet. When the closer answers a customer's question he should think first and make sure the question isn't one that is a trick or trap and get himself "boxed in." For example: The customer will sometimes try to trap the closer by asking a question the closer has already answered, just to make sure he gives the same answer.

The reason for the change of subject (from the product to something else) is to get the customer's thoughts away from the sales transaction. This will prevent the customer from being tempted to second-guess his buying decision. Another rationale for not talking about the product is so the closer won't accidentally bring up a point the customer didn't happen to previously think about, or something the customer doesn't like about the product. By continuing to talk about the product the closer could easily create unwanted, unnecessary problems, thus possibly killing an otherwise successful sale, even after the customer has said he will buy. For example: The closer could say, "Congratulations, Mr. Customer, welcome aboard. Do you know that the property you got is only one block away from a brand new grade school?" The customer might say, "School? I didn't know there was a school so close. I don't like kids running up and down the sidewalk screaming and hollering all the time. I like peace and quiet. If a school is nearby then that property is not for me." The closer has to be on his toes especially at this time in the closing sequence, to be sure the customer is happy, relaxed, calm and comfortable, so the working papers can be filled out and the contract signed in a smooth and uncomplicated manner.

STEP FOUR: The fourth thing the closer has to do is calmly and in a professional manner start filling out the working paper (order slip, sales slip, contract, agreement, etc.). This is a very delicate and sometimes frustrating time, not only for the closer but also for the customer because the paperwork process is usually a very routine and dull exercise, compared to the overall sales presentation and the "close." The closer has to make all of the paperwork and check writing process as painless and quick as possible.

There shouldn't be a noticeable change of pace in the closer's timing from his sales presentation into his "check writing" and working paper stage. The reason for this is, if the closer does switch from a crisp, enthusiastic and sharp presentation to a slow and boring paper shuffling process, the change of pace will tend to make the overall sales presentation seem disorganized and confusing to the customer. And the confusion could very possibly kill a sale.

The closer must make the paper work as simple and understandable as possible for the customer. If the closer is asking the customer questions — for instance his full name, how he spells it, or his correct home address and so forth — he should transform the "question-asking process" into a casual conversation. For example: The closer could say, "Mr. Customer, now you said earlier that you lived on North Palm Avenue. Isn't that close to a new hospital that's being built?" or "Mr. Customer, you have the same middle name that my dad has, you know that isn't a very common name. Is it an old family name?" This kind of "casual conversation" on the closer's part (while the closer is actually filling out the order sheet) will have a definite calming effect on the customer and tend to make the period of time it takes to fill out all of the paperwork go by faster. It will also make the customer feel more comfortable and relaxed with the closer. The customer and closer are now sharing personal stories and getting better acquainted, allowing the two opponents to relax a little, because the buying decision has been made (the pressure is off) and the closer and customer can talk as friends rather than opponents.

STEP FIVE: Getting The Customer To Sign The Contract: When the time is ripe for the customer to sign the contract, the closer should sit down "comfortably close" to the customer (creating a friendly, warm mood) and hold the contract himself so everyone involved in the sale can easily read and see it. (Note: When the closer holds the contract, he is still maintaining his control over the customer. At this point in the sales presentation, that control is very important because the closer doesn't have the customer's signature on the contract yet. The closer has to realize that the "closing process" isn't quite over until all the papers and contracts are signed, sealed and delivered.)

Then the closer should go over the contract in a simple, precise manner, and using his pen as a pointer, identify only the important facts in the contract. The closer should not attempt to read or explain every single word in the contract, because not only will the customer usually not understand the contract's language but the customer will tend to get bored and frustrated. (Note: The customer will be thinking to himself, "Boy, is this contract signing going to take all day?") The closer has to make the "contract reviewing process" seem uncomplicated and easy to follow.

The best way for the closer to put customers at ease so they won't think of the contract signing as a "life or death" experience, is to speak confidently, and calmly. The closer should talk in a more gentle voice while explaining the contract, to make the customer as comfortable as possible.

If the closer is nervous or excited (which is normal) and his hand is trembling, he should rest his hand on the table while holding the contract. The table will serve to stop the shaking so the closer won't be getting the customer nervous too.

When the closer has gone over the contract with the customer and the customer understands it or seems to, then the closer should take his pen and *first,* before the customer signs, write in his own name on the contract, while simultaneously saying, "Mr. Customer, now my name goes right here." After the closer has signed his name he should immediately without pausing for a breath turn the contract over to the customer and say, "Mr. Customer, I need your name there next to mine."

There is an "old pro's saying" that advises closers to never ask for the customer's signature (his John Hancock or John Henry), but instead say something like "Mr. Customer, I need your initials right here," or "Mr. Customer, will you approve this," or "Mr. Customer, I need your okay right here." This "old pro's saying" is generally on target, especially when it states not to use the John Hancock or John Henry method of asking for the customer's signature.

It has to be understood that when the closer says to the customer, "I need your name right here with mine," and when the closer signs his name first, these two maneuvers make the closer and customer more of a team. This can and does strengthen the total closer-customer relationship. By signing the contract first, the closer has shown the customer there is nothing to be afraid of, plus it makes the customer feel he is not alone while making his buying decision.

But the closer should, if he senses the customer is very sophisticated and sharp, ask the customer for his signature in a forthright manner such as: "Mr. Customer, I need your signature right here," or "Mr. Customer, I need your name right here." When the closer uses this upfront approach, the customer knows the closer is serious and the time to make the buying decision has arrived. The intelligent customer, if the closer asks him politely, won't be offended when he hears the word "name" or "signature." Sophisticated customers shouldn't be underestimated as they won't be appreciative of sales closer's subtle tricks. When a closer asks for their "initials" or "approval" that kind of "asking" often sounds to them like it came right out of a rookie sales book.

STEP SIX: Getting The Customer's Check: After and *only* after the paperwork is filled out (the preliminary working papers and not the final contract), the closer should ask the customer, in a very normal, casual way, "Mr. Customer, just make the check out to our company." The closer doesn't have to see the customer's check book, all he has to do is make a simple, encouraging, positive statement while fiddling with the paperwork, a pen or something else on the closing table. This casual attitude will make the customer feel the closer doesn't just want his money.

The customer will immediately feel unease if asked for the check right after saying he will buy the product. The closer has to first fill out the working papers and (if it's possible) have the customer sign or initial them before he asks the customer to sign the final contract. The reason for this delay is that the customer will subconsciously feel, even though the order sheet is not the real contract, that by signing the order sheet, he has actually signed the contract. Then when the time comes for the real contract to be reviewed and signed, the customer will be less likely to back out of the agreement and will not be as reluctant to sign his name again (this time where it counts).

When the customer has signed the order sheet and the closer casually asks for the customer's check and gets it in his hands, he has to tactfully hide the check within seconds. The old saying, "Out of sight, out of mind," is quite relevant in this situation. If the closer doesn't move the customer's check (discreetly putting it under some paperwork or in his pocket) the customer would be sitting there at the closing table just after making a difficult buying decision, looking at his own personal check on the table. With this kind of "check exposure" it is sometimes very tempting for the customer to change his mind. The customer might have last second "buyer's fear" and negative thoughts about the product could prevail, causing him to impulsively cancel the sale. Then, boom — an otherwise "done deal" is killed. If the check is hidden and out of sight this can't happen. The closer has to handle the hidden check trick with discreet and tactful professionalism. Above all, the closer has to act like the check is not a big deal, but just an ordinary, everyday business transaction that the closer is genuinely thankful for.

If the closer has a customer who wants to physically hold the contract and read every word of it for himself, the closer should let him. Most customers can't understand a contract and they are usually just trying to act the role of an intelligent buyer, either for the closer's benefit or for some other person in the customer's party. The closer, after he has handed the contract to the customer, should keep right on talking to one of the other members in the customer's team about his home town, his hobbies or any other kind of light conversation. This talking will tend to interrupt and distract the customer who is doing the contract reading; it won't take much time for the customer to get frustrated and ask the closer where to sign the contract.

This little trick works 99 percent of the time because the customer usually won't understand much of what he is reading and the closer's constant polite and tactful conversation will irritate the customer's concentration so much that he will think to himself, "Why the heck should I waste any more time trying to read this, I'd better just sign it already and get out of here." The net effect is the customer will be satisfied because he at least looked over the whole contract for a few minutes. In addition, he didn't lose face in front of the closer, his family or his friends.

Sam wrapped up this part of my lesson by explaining how closers have to keep in mind that the "I'm sold" customer is the easiest of the three customer responses to sell. This customer has been positively programmed all the way through the total sales presentation by the closer, so when it becomes time for the closer to ask this customer to give the product a try, the customer will generally do just that and buy the product.

Sam said the "I'm nearly sold" customer wasn't anything like the "I'm sold" customer. He warned me that closers have to start earning their keep with this type of customer.

When The Customer Says, "I'm Nearly Sold"

This customer isn't quite sold on the product, *yet*. He needs more convincing, more persuasion, from the closer before he will be ready to buy. This customer isn't negative in his thinking toward the product, but he certainly isn't positive. The closer has given this customer a good, solid, professional sales presentation up to this point, but when asked to buy the product he is hesitant and puts up objections left and right. (Note: The closer should remember the main reason customers don't buy when they basically want to and really like the product, is lack of money.)

The closer has done his job so far; all he has to do is apply some salesmanship to "close" this customer. The closer has already found the right opportunity to ask this customer to give his product a try and now the customer is just sitting at the closing table and making statements like, "I don't know if I'll ever use your product," or "I have to think about it." The closer can "close" this wishy-washy customer if he pursues him tenaciously, while logically, emotionally and convincingly pointing out to him how he can have his cake and eat it too (own the product for the least amount of money). This customer will eventually buy if he genuinely comes to feel satisfied that the product is advantageous for him and his family, and that he can afford to purchase it. (Note: This customer usually doesn't have the guts to make a buying decision on his own. He needs a push from the closer's persuasive presentation to direct him toward the sale and help him make up his undecided mind.) All the closer has to do is convince this customer that he can make a sound buying decision (with a little help from the closer).

To convince this type of customer that the product is good for him the closer has to repeat (summarize) some of the product facts not only to make sure that the customer understands them but to make sure the customer didn't miss any important product information during the earlier part of the sales presentation. Sometimes it is this missed information that sways the customer to buy. The closer has to also work on this customer's ego by building him up so he will have the strength and self-confidence to make a positive buying decision. This customer wants to be better off than he is presently and wants more for his family. The closer just has to describe his product or service in a way that makes the customer see how, by owning it, he can achieve his goals in life a little sooner and a little better than if he didn't own it. The closer has to emphasize emotional "closing" techniques when dealing with this kind of customer. He must also be persistent and at times politely forceful to maximize sales results.

To show how the closer "closes" the "I'm nearly sold" customer, it's a good idea to look at some closer vs. customer conversations and statements.

(Note: The closer, after he conquers an objection, should again ask the customer for the order, and again shut up and wait for the customer to give an answer.)

Sam said the best way to show how a closer "closes" this type of customer is to look at some of the closer's responses to the customer's objections. The following responses will give the reader an idea of how to handle this type of customer and "close" him.

SETTING THE STAGE: The closer has asked this customer to give his product a try and now, with both opponents (closer and customer) sitting at the closing table, the customer is throwing out objections and telling the closer why he won't buy. The customer then looks at the closer sheepishly as he listens to the closer overcoming his objections and asking him to give the product a try. Feeling the closer's pressure of "dead silence," the customer usually answers with a statement similar to this: "Mr. Closer, I don't really know. I'm just not sure it would be in my best interest to own your product at this time." This is the moment for the closer to go to work on really "closing" him.

The Closer's Responses

(With the customer's family present, if possible)

1. "Mr. Customer, you've seen my product and you know it is good, plus you know that you can afford it if you want it. Now let's be honest with ourselves. You've spent all your life working for your family's future, and I mean working hard; it shows — you're a good provider. But don't you think it's time to give yourself the things you've always wanted? What are you living for if you can't enjoy life? You work to make money, don't you? So why not invest your money to make more money (or to spend less money); plus, you can enjoy my product at the same time. Doesn't that make a lot of sense? Why don't you give it a try?"

2. "Mr. Customer, right now you have the opportunity to purchase my product at the lowest price possible due to our close-out sale. You'll never have a chance like this again, and that's a fact. All I want you to do is save some of your money and give my product a try. I know you will like it — how about giving it a try?"

3. "Mr. Customer, did you know there are only four ways a person can really make serious money? The first way is to earn it, work for it, and you know in today's economy that is practically impossible. The second way is to inherit it from a rich relative, and how many time does that happen? The third way to make money is to steal it, but sooner or later you'll get caught and have to go to jail and that sure wouldn't be worth it. And then there is the fourth and final way to make money, and that is to wisely invest in something. Mr. Customer, believe it or not, my product is just that kind of solid investment, and that's a fact. You know it and I know it, so why don't you give it a try?"

4. "Mr. Customer, if you don't want to buy the product for yourself, at least get it for your wife and children. They depend on you for their future, their lives are literally in your hands, just as my family depends on me. Why don't you give it a try, at least for them?"

5. "Mr. Customer, talking to you man to man, you know there are times in every man's life he has to make a decision about his future and his goals. He has to take up the challenge himself. Mr. Customer, don't — like so many people who fail — run away from the opportunity to have something important and to accomplish something important by making a simple decision. This product is exactly what you need and deep down you know it, so why don't you give it a try?"

The "I'm nearly sold" customer can be sold if the closer uses emotional and hard-hitting responses on him, over and over again, continually conquering every objection. After every single customer objection is overcome, the closer has to ask the customer to give his product a try. Then he must shut up and wait for the customer's response. This customer, if he has the money and understands the benefits of the product, usually is not good at taking emotional pressure from the closer. This customer will eventually back down and surrender — he will purchase the product. If this customer doesn't think he has the financial ability to buy the product, then the closer, by using pressure plus emotions, can find this true and factual objection and go from there to try to get the sale by saying something like (in a soft and sincere voice) "Mr. Customer, what we are really talking about here is money, isn't it? Let me ask you this: Do the monthly payments fit into your budget?" If the customer answers in the affirmative, the closer should keep "closing" as explained earlier. But if the customer says, "No, I can't afford the monthly payments," the closer can do one of two things: Either let the customer go, or try to "close" him harder from another angle — a new game plan. Perhaps it will require lowering the monthly payments by stretching the loan period, providing the financing, or lowering the price. The closer can "close" any customer if he gets him emotionally and sincerely involved enough in the product. (Note: It can't be stated enough that the only reason a customer won't buy a product, if he is really sold on it, is because of lack of money.)

Note: After the closer has "closed" and gotten this "I'm nearly sold" customer to say he will buy the product, the closer should go through the same "follow-up-steps" that were described in the "I'm sold" customer's illustration.

When The Customer Says "I'm Not Sold"

This customer is the hardest of the three types of customers to "close." This potential buyer either isn't sold on the product, or isn't sold on the closer. Consequently, this customer tells the closer he's not interested and won't buy the product. The closer has to realize that this customer, like all others, has to be properly programmed to buy the product from the very first phase of the total sales presentation. If a customer is not sold during the overall sales presentation it is the closer's responsibility to put on the pressure at the closing table and use all his tricks, traps and ammunition to get that sale ("close").

The closer must not only use reverse psychology, but intimidation and plenty of positive and determined psychological force. This "I'm not sold" customer will put up a grand and resourceful argument with the closer. The ensuing battle of wits can go on for thirty minutes or five hours. It all depends on which opponent gives up first and loses by being overcome by the other's arguments.

(NOTE: The closer must always remember that if a product isn't beneficial to the customer he shouldn't in any way try to pressure the customer into buying it. In the long run it doesn't pay off to sell people things they don't need. The extra sale will never equal the lost business from all those dissatisfied customers and the bad reputation they will spread about you and your products.)

When this type of "I'm not sold" customer says he isn't sold on the product that usually means one of four basic things: The customer doesn't like the product; he doesn't believe the closer; he doesn't have the money to buy the product; or there is some unknown problem, objection or condition that only the customer knows about that keeps him from purchasing. The closer always has to discover the real objection and then go in for a serious "closing" effort. The closer can discover this information by asking questions, picking up on subtle comments the customer has made during the sales presentation, and by listening to the customer's children and friends. Much information can be gained by reading between the lines. If the closer does all these things, he can put together an accurate overall picture of the customer and use everything he's got to go in for the "close."

This customer can be closed if the closer knows his product inside out and if the closer has the guts and self-confidence to stand up to his customer and fight for what he believes in (his product). The closer has to show enthusiasm and always maintain a positive attitude. The closer can't let this type of customer get him down and make him feel intimidated or ashamed of his product. The closer has to demonstrate some class, be polite and not get nervous or lose control during this confrontation with the customer. Most importantly, this customer will consider purchasing, no matter how tough he is, if the closer shows genuine interest and respect for him. It doesn't matter how hardened this customer is, he cannot continue to reject the closer's kindness and true sincerity, over too long a period of time. The customer will start to "melt" and let his defensive shield down. (NOTE: A customer like this usually isn't accustomed to someone being nice to him, so when the closer keeps acting polite and sincere, it tends to put this potential buyer off balance.) When the closer senses this "relaxing of the defenses" on the part of the customer, he can tactfully and vigorously go in for the kill (close). Slowly the customer will give in and buy the product, if you're good. But the closer has to be prepared for a hard and sometimes long and drawn-out fight.

To illustrate how the closer handles this kind of customer using emotions, reverse psychology, and intimidation, Sam said the best thing to do was to study examples of what the closer says to the customer.

For example: After the closer has asked a customer to give his product a try, the customer might say something like this, "Mr. Closer, I'm not really interested. I just came out here to see what you have and I can see it's not for me." The closer again goes to work, and part of that work is to "hit" the customer's "on-switch" to get him activated and start him thinking about the product in a positive manner.

(NOTE: The closer has to remember that when he listens to a customer objection, he first has to completely hear the customer out and then and only then give a serious and conquering response.)

When the closer is talking to a customer he has to look him straight in the eye and have a positive, confident expression on his face. There isn't a person anywhere in the world who hasn't at one time or another purchased a product from a closer. The closer has to always remember this and visualize himself getting the sale. He must truly believe it is worth the effort he put into selling the product, if he expects to convince the customer of the genuine and sincere enthusiasm he has for the product.

The Closer's Responses

(With the customer's family present, if possible)

1. "You know, Mr. Customer, some people are dreamers, some are lookers, and there are others who are doers. Mr. Customer, you and I might not be able to change the world, but I can guarantee that we can change ourselves and help our families. I have already bought this same product and my family is enjoying it right now. Why don't you do the same for your family and give my product a try?"

2. "Mr. Customer, let me ask you a very candid question. If I just turned around and gave you my product free, would you take it? Now tell me the truth." If the customer answers in the affirmative then the closer should realize that "money" (affordability) is the key to the solution. On the other hand, if the customer answers the closer's question with a negative response, for instance, "No, I still wouldn't take it," then the closer should look slightly surprised and ask, "Why?" The customer will either give the closer an answer that the closer can work with to "close," or the customer will start acting kind of silly, laughing nervously and not really answering the closer. The reason for this customer behavior is because the closer caught the customer off guard. The customer doesn't have a ready answer. The closer should again ask the customer, "Why?" until the customer finally answers. Then the closer can go ahead and proceed to "close" by overcoming the customer's objection, eventually asking him again to give the product a try.

3. "Mr. Customer, you and I won't live forever. Someday we are going to die. Tell me what is going to happen to your family five or ten years after you're gone. Mr. Customer, hindsight is twenty-twenty, but foresight is different. It only takes a little planning, a little thought, and the future will be secure and comfortable for you and your family. You will never find yourself looking backwards to the past, thinking about what you should have done. Why don't you give it a try?"

4. "Mr. Customer, you know the sad thing in my profession is that no matter how good a product I have or how much I explain all of the product's benefits, some people try to make the buying decision harder and more complicated than it really is. Please, Mr. Customer, don't make the same mistake. You can really benefit from this product. If you can afford it and if the payments fit into your budget, then give it a try."

5. "Mr. Customer, you get exactly what you pay for. If the product is of good quality — like my product — then that's exactly what you get for your money. Remember, it is up to you, Mr. Customer. You have to live with and put your confidence into the product that you buy. Doesn't it make sense to purchase quality? Why don't you give it a try?"

6. "Mr. Customer, do you want a guarantee? All right, I will give you one. I can guarantee you that my product will make you and save you money, if you can guarantee me that you will be around (alive) to collect it. I'll put that guarantee in writing if you like. (Note: The closer must deliver this statement in a joking, light manner, kidding the customer. Otherwise this can be taken as a rude remark.) Now, let's be realistic — why don't you give my product a try?"

The closer can "close" this customer if he just keeps after him and doesn't pay too much attention to his first few "No" responses to the closer's buying questions. Those objections usually don't mean much, so the closer shouldn't let them get him down. This customer is a *pushover* if he *likes the closer and believes him.* (NOTE: When the closer has to use a lot of pressure on this customer and finally "closes" him, the closer should then apologize to the customer in a friendly manner and say something like: "Mr. Customer, believe me, if my product wasn't as good as I've told you, I wouldn't have tried as hard to get you and your family involved. So I apologize if I said anything wrong. I'm happy to have you as a new owner and I know you will be an asset to our company." The reason the closer should apologize to the customer — that is, if he feels he needs to due to the use of excessive pressure — is because after the customer signs the contract and goes home he will start thinking about how he was treated and pressured and he could still very easily cancel the contract. The closer has to always protect his interest by making sure his sale stays closed. Sometimes a strategic apology can diffuse an anxious, wavering customer.

After the closer has "closed" the "I'm not sold" customer by repeatedly conquering and overcoming his objections, and by making this customer like him, the closer should use the very same "follow-up steps" described in the "I'm sold" customer's illustration. The closer should remember something Sam always told me, "You can attract more sales with honey than vinegar, no matter how troublesome the customer is." (Simple logic but very TRUE.)

Sam told me the closer has to keep in mind that when he's dealing with these three different kinds of customer responses, he has to stick to the basics, use different degrees of pressure, constantly "closing" throughout the entire sales presentation. If the closer can win the crucial confidence of the customer, bingo, he's got the sale.

Closing Tricks To Remember

A. When the customer says he will try it (buy the product), then no matter where the closer is located he should as quickly and calmly as possible get the customer to sign a working paper, an agreement, or anything that obligates and commits the customer (in writing). This way the typical slippery customer will be much less likely to back out of his verbal agreement to purchase the product.

B. When a customer leaves the sales office and the closer didn't "close" him, the closer should always give the "missed customer" some kind of brochure or literature. This way any new customer in the waiting room or on the lot, that the closer hasn't talked to yet will see this "customer" leave with some paperwork. This will create the impression for the other customers that the previous "customer" bought. The observing customers will automatically feel a little more interested and friendly (knowing someone else just bought a few seconds ago) toward the closer's product.

C. The closer should always be carrying several crisp one-hundred dollar bills. This will allow the closer, when he is explaining money or investments to a customer during the sales presentation, to take out the hundred dollar bills and use some showmanship to better illustrate just how much money he is talking about. This "flashing the money" trick will get the attention of the customer and will bring home the closer's point. The closer can dramatically show the customer exactly how much money he would either save or lose (depending on the sales pitch) by not buying the product immediately.

D. The closer can make the following nonchalant statement just about any place in the sale presentation and it will get the customer thinking: "Mr. Customer, some folks will buy this product and some won't and the only real difference between who buys it and who doesn't is money. But that's a private matter and everyone knows their own personal financial business better than anyone else, right? The customer will automatically, without thinking say, "Right." Now the closer has planted a "thought seed" for the customer to consider. He should now continue closing the customer, focusing on other positive aspects of the product. Once the closer gets the customer to start agreeing with him about the product, the sale is around the corner. Since the closer already tricked the customer into agreeing with him on the subject of finances, the next area of agreement will be that much easier to find.

E. If a closer needs help in "closing" a difficult customer he shouldn't be so foolish as not to ask another closer for help. With the persuasive power of two closers, a sale can often be made that would otherwise be lost.

Wrapping Up The Sale
(The closer "buttons-up" the customer)

Sam told me it was time to see how the closer finishes up a sale (buttons it up). He explained that a closer has to treat the customer with just as much respect, courtesy and enthusiasm *after* the sale is made as he did when he first met the customer. The customer needs all the attention and reassurance the closer can provide after the sale, so he (the customer) won't get cold feet and start feeling as though he made a bad decision by purchasing the product. The closer's responsibility when buttoning up a sale is to keep the customer not only happy, but relaxed and confident, making him believe he has made an intelligent and productive decision for himself and his family.

Sam suggested it would be a good idea for me to remember three "Button-Up" examples that demonstrate how the closer wraps up the "closing process" with the new owner of the product.

A. The closer has to remember that after he has sold (closed) the customer he has to bring the customer back down to earth. After buying something, everyone is a little excited and enthused. This calming down of the customer can be accomplished by changing the subject (away from the product) and having a simple enjoyable conversation with the customer. This parting, friendly conversation will be the last memory the customer has of you so it is important that it be a positive one. This will insure a high likelihood of future business and referrals.

B. When the closer "closes" the customer and the contract is signed and the pleasant parting conversation has been exhausted, it is time for the closer to say "goodbye" to the customer not only with a simple "Thank you" but with a "double handshake." The special emphasis on the handshake will insure that the customer feels even more appreciated. (Note: The "double handshake" is when the closer takes both of his hands and shakes the one hand of the new customer welcoming him "aboard" or "to the club." This type of appreciation on the closer's part will make the customer feel more welcome.)

C. If at all possible, the closer should walk the customer to his car after he has sold him. The extra time and effort it takes to accompany the customer will make him feel that the closer didn't just want to make the sale and then get rid of him. The customer will feel the closer appreciates his business more if he takes that extra few minutes to see him to his car and safely on his way home.

The Master Closer's Deadly Rules of Closing

M 1. MAKE THE CUSTOMER LIKE YOU
A 2. ASK THE CUSTOMER QUESTIONS ABOUT HIMSELF
S 3. STAY CLOSE TO THE CUSTOMER (Create A Bond)
T 4. TELL THE CUSTOMER A SECRET ABOUT THE PRODUCT
(Make him think he knows something special that others don't know).
E 5. EARN THE CUSTOMER'S RESPECT BY SHOWING
R 6. REFUSE TO ACCEPT "NO"

C 7. CARE ABOUT THE CUSTOMER'S NEEDS
L 8. LISTEN TO THE CUSTOMER
O 9. OBSERVE EVERYTHING ABOUT THE CUSTOMER
S 10. SHOW THE CUSTOMER YOU CARE AND APPRECIATE HIM
E 11. EMOTIONS ARE THE KEY TO "CLOSING"
R 12. REMEMBER TO THANK THE CUSTOMER FOR THE SALE

Important "Closing Notes" to Remember

1. The closer has to be acutely aware of how the customer answers his buying questions. For instance, the customer could say he's not interested in the product either seriously or jokingly. The closer has to pay attention so he will know the customer's true attitudes when he responds to the closer's questions and comments. If the closer doesn't analyze the customer's answers and attitudes correctly he could easily misjudge the situation, and this could lead to a missed sale.

2. The closer should never, never beg the customer for a sale. Not only will the closer fail to get the sale (because the customer won't respect that type of desperate sales approach), but the customer will probably never ever come back and will definately tell others of his bad experience.

3. The closer should remember that when he thinks he has lost the sale, if his negative attitude is detected by the customer, then in most cases he has. The trick is to always think positively, no matter what.

4. A closer can know all of the tricks and "closes" in the world and still miss a sale. If the closer doesn't "close" continually throughout the sales presentation and keep every sales step in its respective order, building up to the "closing question," then the customer will become confused and disoriented, and the sale will often be lost.

5. The closer has to develop a degree of tolerance for the customer's problems and views if he ever expects to become a "master closer."

6. The closer has to learn that if he disagrees with the customer he shouldn't be disagreeable. He must be a master diplomat to succeed.

7. The closer has to remember to always take the time to listen to the customer, because sooner or later they will tell everything about themselves.

8. The closer's brilliant sales presentation means nothing unless he gets the customer's signature on a contract and a check.

9. If the closer honors the customer with sincerity and genuine appreciation, the customer will usually buy the closer's product.

10. If a closer acts as if the customer's mediocre job is important and responsible, and shows a sincere interest in whatever else he has to say, the customer will be like putty in the closer's hand.

Sam said this finished my lesson on "closing." He told me a closer, above all other things, has to love his profession and his customers first, if he wants to be the best. There is no other way. You can't fake loving sales and enjoying your customers. They'll catch you most of the time.

THE TWENTY-FIVE GREATEST "CLOSES" ON EARTH

Chapter Ten

THE TWENTY-FIVE GREATEST
"CLOSES" ON EARTH

The Book Close

DESCRIPTION: This "close" is especially designed for this book. The closer can use this "close" with any customer, anytime, and get positive results. This "close" is intended to embarrass and control the customer, and it does just that.

How the Book Close is Used

The customer tells the closer, "I'm going to have to talk to my brother in Chicago before I buy this product, because he's in the same kind of business you are, Mr. Closer." The closer should calmly take out this book, *The Art of Closing Any Deal*, and say to the customer, "Mr. Customer, let me show you something that you've never heard of or seen before. This book that I'm holding tells me in Chapter 3 exactly what kind of attitude people like yourself, in your type of business, have. Then in Chapter 10, page 213, this book tells me exactly the objection you just stated and shows me how to answer your objection in three different ways. (It's ok to make up the chapters and page numbers for spontaneous effect). Again, from this book I can tell how you planned all along, from the first time we met, to think of and develop an objection. Mr. Customer, just think, there is a book written all about you, what you're thinking and what you're going to say. Now let's be realistic: that excuse about your brother isn't important. We're really talking about finances, aren't we?" When the customer says "Yes," the closer should work the money matter (the real objection) out and then ask the customer to give his product or service a try.

(NOTE: When the closer uses this "close" he has to make the customer's objection look ridiculous to the customer himself, and then find out what the true objection is so he can "close" again.)

The Power of Suggestion Close

DESCRIPTION: This "close" will work if the closer plants the seeds of "imagination and suggestion" in the customer's mind early in the sales presentation. By doing this the closer can actually get the customer to "close" himself by using these positive thoughts. The customer will actually think at the end of the sales presentation that these "closer-planted ideas" were his own from the start.

How the Power of Suggestion Close is Used

When the closer is with his customer during the early stages of the sales presentation he should deliberately drop little hints and make positive suggestions concerning the customer and the product. For instance, the closer could say, "Mr. Customer, do you know that by putting my product in your home, you will have the most beautiful home on your whole block?" or "Mr. Customer, did you realize that by starting an investment plan now with my company, your children's education will be paid for when it's time for them to go to college?" or "Mr. Customer, by buying my product at this time in the off-season you will save a lot more money."

After making these suggestive statements the closer has to give the customer plenty of time, so these thoughts will sink in and take hold in the customer's subconscious. When the closer thinks the timing is right (during the last stages of the sales presentation) for him to ask the customer for the order, the closer should say:

(1) "Mr. Customer, remember you wanted to have the best looking house on your block, something your family could really be proud of? Then why don't you give my product a try?" or,

(2) "Mr. Customer, remember you wanted your children to have a good education and you didn't want to worry about that financial burden when they reach college age? Then why don't you give my company a try?" or,

(3) "Mr. Customer, remember you wanted to get the best buy for your money on my product? This is absolutely the best time to buy. Why don't you give my product a try?"

In this "close" the closer, by planting suggestions early in the sales presentation, has actually activated the customer's mind early in the presentation. During the rest of the presentation the customer has been thinking about these "closer-planted suggestions." When the closer finally asks for the order and brings up these suggestions again, the customer, because of the time span and all of the sales activity during the sales presentation, will actually believe these ideas were originally his. The customer will usually forget that the closer suggested them first. So the closer can go ahead and "close" with his customer's full and enthusiastic cooperation.

The Sharp Angle Close

DESCRIPTION: In this "close" the closer throws the customer's objection right back at him and makes him eat his own words.

How the Sharp Angle Close is Used

The customer says something like this to the closer:

1. "Mr. Closer, I want to see the lake from my property and I can't from this piece of real estate." The closer should immediately respond with, "Mr. Customer, if I show you some property for the same price where you could see the lake, would you give it a try?"

2. "Mr. Closer, I don't like the color combinations on that car -- I like royal blue." The closer should say, "Mr. Customer, if I can get that same automobile in royal blue, would you take it?"

3. "Mr. Closer, I don't have enough money for the down payment right now." The closer should say, "Mr. Customer, would you give it a try if I made arrangements so you could comfortably handle the down payment?"

4. "Mr. Closer, I think your product is overpriced -- I'm not going to pay that much money for it." The closer should say, "Mr. Customer, if I can talk to my boss and get the product's price down to where you think it's fair, would you try it?"

The Demonstration Close

DESCRIPTION: This "close" is to be used by the closer only after he has demonstrated his product to the customer. The demonstration "close" speaks for itself, and does its own "closing." All the closer has to do is set this close up properly, then follow it through and Bingo! The closer automatically has a sale.

How the Demonstration Close is Used

The first thing the closer has to do is set the customer up for this "close." For example: "Mr. Customer, if I could show you the prettiest view of a lake you could ever hope to find, and the price was right, would you buy it?" The customer, knowing the odds are with him, will say "Yes" or "Probably." All the closer has to do now is show the customer the view or property (and it had better be beautiful), make sure it fits into the customer's budget, assume the customer is buying and start writing up the details of the contract. If the customer stops the closer from writing, the customer will most likely give the closer a real objection. All the closer has to do is overcome that objection by saying, "Mr. Customer, remember you said you'd buy the property if it was exactly like I described?" The closer should again start writing up the contract in a positive and self-assured way.

Here are three more examples of how this "close" works:

(1) "Mr. Customer, if I proved to you beyond a shadow of a doubt that my product would make you more money than any investment you now have, would you give my company a try?"

(2) "Mr. Customer, would you give my company five dollars a day every day for a year if at the end of that period of time, my company gives you back all your original money *plus* one thousand dollars? Would you do that if I could prove it to you?"

(3) "Mr. Customer, if I could show you that this automobile has the best ride in the world and was more economical than you might have thought, would you buy it?"

(NOTE: The closer had better be able to back up his statements if he wants this "close" to work.)

The Three Devil Close

DESCRIPTION: This "close" is great for the older, reserved customer, and especially good for very religious customers. The three devil "close" actually tells the customer to go to hell when he says he has to think about buying the product. The good thing about this "close" is that the customer won't realize what the closer has just said to him until it's too late to do anything about it. This "close" will absolutely destroy the "I have to think about it" customer.

How the Three Devil Close is Used

When the customer tells the closer he has to think about it, the closer should look directly at the customer and say "Mr. Customer, have you ever heard the story about the three devils?" When the customer says "No," the closer should continue. "Well, Mr. Satan was down in hell one day, and he was trying to figure out how to get all the people on earth down there with him and away from heaven. Along comes a devil who walks up to Mr. Satan and says, 'I know how to get fifty percent of all the people on earth down here with us.' So Mr. Satan says, 'How are you going to do that?' The devil answers, 'I'll dress up as a mortal and go up to the earth and tell everyone there is no God, no devil, no heaven, no hell, no good nor any evil, and they can do whatever they want -- wild women, booze, gambling -- anything at all. And I promise I'll get fifty percent of the people on earth down to hell.'

"Mr. Satan said he liked that idea. Suddenly a second devil walks up and tells them both *he* can get seventy-five percent of all the people on earth down to hell. Mr. Satan and the first devil asked the second devil how he would do that. The second devil said, 'I'll go up to earth dressed as a mortal also, but I'll tell all the people there is a heaven, there is a hell, there is a God, and there is a devil, so they'd better go to church every Sunday morning and evening, plus on Wednesday nights. But during the rest of the week they can do anything they want to do -- no limit. This way the people will rationalize their wild conduct during the week, because they'd still be going to church. This logic is sure to pull the wool over their eyes and in the end get seventy-five percent of the people down here to hell.'

"Mr. Satan really liked that idea. He thought that plan was the one to go with, when a third devil walks up and tells them they are all wrong. This third devil says he could get *everyone* on earth down to hell, one hundred percent of the people. Mr. Satan looked shocked and asked the third devil how he would do it. The third devil said he too would dress up as a mortal and go up to earth, but he would tell all the people there was a God, there was a devil, there was a heaven and there was a hell there was good and there was evil and if everybody didn't follow the straight and narrow, the teachings of the Bible and accept the Lord, then they would automatically go straight to hell. But before they had to accept these things, the third devil was going to give the people on earth *all the time in the world to think about this special offer.*"

When the closer has finished with this confusing devil story he should look straight at the customer and in a soft and serious voice, say, "Now let's be realistic, why don't you give my product a try without giving yourself *all the time in the world to think about this special offer?*"

(NOTE: After the customer hears the devil story he will usually laugh a little, thinking it's cute. When the closer asks for the order the customer will get serious again, but he will be much looser and easier to close on. The story really doesn't make that much sense so don't waste time trying to figure it out. All I can tell you is, it does work.)

The Ben Franklin Close

DESCRIPTION: This "close" uses logic to get the closer's point across to the customer. It is a good "close" to use on a customer who is a thinker or who is reserved and overly cautious when buying a product.

How the Ben Franklin Close is Used

"Mr. Customer, in America everybody has always regarded Ben Franklin as a pretty smart fellow. When Ben Franklin had a problem to solve or something important to figure out and make a decision on, he would take a piece of paper and draw a line down the middle of it. On the left side of the paper he would write the word "Yes" and on the right half he would write the word "No." In the "Yes" column Ben would make a list of all the positive and beneficial factors that would favor his decision to pursue or purchase something. And in the "No" column he would list all of the reasons for not doing or not buying something. When Ben was finished with this "Yes" and "No" process, he could simply look at the list and his decision would already be made for him. He would either have more yesses or more no's. It was that simple. Mr. Customer, why don't we try that and see what happens, it sure can't hurt?"

(NOTE: The closer should hand the customer a sheet of paper and a pen and have the customer fill out the "Yes" and "No" column. The closer should tactfully assist the customer on the "Yes" side by giving out suggestions, but on the "No" side keep quiet and not say a thing. The "Yes" side will always, with the closer's help, win. When this process is finished the closer should look the customer straight in the eye and ask him to give the product a try.)

The Kids vs. Parents Close

DESCRIPTION: In this "close" the closer uses the excitement and innocence of the customer's children against the customer himself. This close is powerful -- in fact it could backfire and kill a sale, but if the closer handles it with tact and with class the customer won't get too upset and he will wind up purchasing the product.

How the Kids vs. Parents Close is Used

When the closer first meets the customer and his family (providing the customer has children), the closer should try to have a small live pet available for the kids to play with while the closer makes his first pre-pitch introduction. (Note: The small pet could be anything from a hamster to a puppy dog to a shetland pony. It doesn't really matter that much, just as long as the customer's kids like the animal and have fun playing with it.) When the closer shows the customer his product, he can go back to he subject of small pets and say to the customer's kids, "Did you kids like that little dog you were playing with?" The kids will automatically say "Yes." Then the closer should say, "If that little dog was yours what would you name him?" The kids will say something like, "We'd name him Cookie." The closer should immediately say (in front of the whole family) "Well, I'll tell you what, if your dad buys my product then Cookie is your very own dog, free!" Then the closer should say to the customer and his family, "Why don't you all talk about it for a few minutes," and then walk away, not letting the customer stop him.

This is where the fun begins, because the customer's kids will go wild with excitement and beg dear old dad to buy the product. The closer doesn't have to do a thing except stay away from the customer long enough for the customer's kids to have time to break down their dad's resistance. The customer won't appreciate the closer using this trick on him, but there is a very good chance the customer will buy. When the closer comes back to the customer all he has to do is give a sincere smile and ask the customer how he spells his name for the contract.

The Summary Close

DESCRIPTION: This "close" should be used by the closer when he has a customer who either says he has to think about buying the product, or seems confused and unable to make a buying decision. (NOTE: When a customer says he has to think about buying, he is simply not sold on the product yet. The closer not only has to work a little harder on this type of customer to "close" him, but the closer has to translate the statement of "I have to think about it" into a real and conquerable objection.

How the Summary Close is Used

When the customer tells the closer he has to think about it, the closer should calmly and sincerely say, "Mr. Customer, just for my own information, exactly what is it about my product that you wanted to think about? Is it my company's reputation?" If the customer says "No," the closer should immediately continue without pausing and say, "Is it the size of the property (or the product)?" If again the customer says "No," the closer should keep right on talking and say, "Is it the down payment?"

The closer shouldn't stop asking the customer what he wants to think about until the customer finally says, "Yes, that's what I have to think about, it's the _____." Now the closer has a solid objection he can work with and successfully conquer.

(Note: When the closer is asking the customer these questions, he'd better not go too slowly in his delivery or pause. That would give the customer time to think and automatically say something like, "I just have to think about the whole thing." And if the customer says this, then the closer is in serious trouble and better shift gears into another one of the closes.)

The Intimidation Close

DESCRIPTION: This "close" is designed to embarrass and pressure the customer into buying the service or product. The closer can be very effective with the following "closing statements" if he executes them properly. (Note: This kind of "close" has to be used on the customer subtly and tactfully for full effect; if the closer mishandles this "closing procedure" he could kill a sale.)

How the Intimidation Close is Used

The closer can use these "closing statements" to gently and effectively intimidate the customer:

1. "Mr. Customer, I'll bet you that when you and your wife first got married you would have bought two of my products for her, wouldn't you? Well, don't you love her at least half as much now? Won't you consider taking one?"

2. "Mr. Customer, I don't think you need a shirt that expensive. Can I show you something at a lower price?"

3. "Mr. Customer, I don't want to bother my boss with an offer unless it's serious and since you're so young, you may not have the financial capability to purchase this product. Why don't you make an offer when you're serious."

4. "Mr. Customer, my product only costs a few dollars a day to own. Why, your kids could pick up pop bottles and make that much money."

5. "Mr. Customer, I'll tell you what: If, as you say, you can make more money on another investment or product than you can with mine, then here, you can take my check for three thousand dollars and invest it for me. Who do I make the check out to?"

NOTE: The closer should just keep throwing out these "closing statements" until the customer really reacts. The closer should then focus on a particular objection or problem he has flushed out and go in for the kill by trying to overcome it.

The Negative Close

DESCRIPTION: This "close" has a lot of power and effect if the closer knows how to use it properly. The closer can turn even the toughest customer into a weak pup if he uses this "close" in the right manner. If used correctly, this "close" will get the closer more sales than he ever thought possible, and, at the same time, the "tough customer" will never know what happened to him.

How the Negative Close is Used

When the closer has a customer who thinks he knows everything or thinks he is too good to talk to the closer or to purchase the product, the perfect solution from the closer's trick bag is the "negative close." It works in this fashion: When he is with this type of customer, the closer has to act nonchalant, professional, polite, and really uninterested in selling him anything. The closer has to act as if he couldn't care less if this customer purchases the product or not. He can also tactfully let this customer know that he has sold two or three of his products already that day. (It doesn't matter if the closer hasn't sold anything, just as long as this customer really thinks he has.)

This kind of attitude on the closer's part will automatically spark the curiosity of this type of customer every time. The reason is simple: If the closer acts as though this customer can't afford to buy the product, or is not qualified to buy it, or it won't make a big difference to the closer's company if this customer buys or not — then this customer will tend to buy the product just to prove the closer wrong and to show the closer he is important and should be treated with more respect. For example: The closer should say the following to this kind of customer, "Mr. Customer, my product (or service) doesn't appeal to everyone, if you know what I mean." (At this point the customer really doesn't know what the closer is talking about; the closer has started to arouse his interest.) "Our company is highly specialized and only handles certain clients. I'm sure you know we have a reputation for being very selective in our products (or services) and our customers. Now I'm sure that you have good intentions in checking us out, but I hope you understand that you have to qualify first. You know, in this industry you run into some pretty strange people, those with champagne taste on a beer budget. You know what I mean?"

The closer should then wait until sometime later in his sales presentation and say, "Mr. Customer, do you know whether or not you could qualify for one of our products in the event you were interested? I'll tell you what, before we continue why don't we fill out a simple credit application to see how you look on paper. That way I won't be wasting your time and you won't be wasting mine." When the customer starts to justify his qualifications and show the closer his buying capabilities, the closer should continue to stay somewhat nonchalant and start warming up slowly to this customer, getting prepared to carry on with an ordinary but somewhat reserved "close."

The Alternate Choice Close

DESCRIPTION: This closing technique was a series of questions to maneuver the customer into a position where he has two or three choices to make. This "close" will not only take the customer's mind off one single and scary buying decision, but when the customer answers these carefully devised "closing questions," no matter what choice he makes, he's about to buy the product. In answering the questions, he's made a purchasing decision. Then all the closer has to do is start writing up the order.

How the Alternate Choice Close is Used

The closer should ask the customer several questions similar to these:

1. "Mr. Customer, you've already been approved. Do you want to use your own financing or do you want to use ours?"

2. "Mr. Customer, which one of these two colors would you prefer on this particular model?"

3. "Mr. Customer, which piece of property do you like the best, the one overlooking the golf course or the one overlooking the lake?"

4. "Mr. Customer, do you write your name using your full middle name or do you just use an initial?"

5. "Mr. Customer, how many do you want: two or all three?"

Once the customer responds to this line of questioning, the closer must gently turn the answers into a sale.

The Contest Close

DESCRIPTION: This is used when the closer wants the customer to feel he is getting a very special deal or a real break when purchasing the product. This "close" makes the customer think he has lucked out and happens to be in the right place at the right time.

How the Contest Close is Used

Near the end of the sales presentation, at the closer's own discretion, the closer should tell the customer something like this: "Mr. Customer, you might not believe what I'm going to tell you because it sounds like a sales pitch. There's something I haven't told you, because when we first met it didn't make that much difference. But now things have changed a little, and I have to tell you. Every year my company runs a sales contest for its closers. Well, we're at the tail end of that contest right now; the winner gets not only a large cash bonus, but he gets to take his family for a free two-week vacation in Hawaii. I have been leading all the other closers in the company for the whole contest, but just about an hour ago my top rival sold three of these products (or services). Now he's ahead of me, only in dollar volume — that's how the company chooses the winner. Now, I want you to listen to me very closely. This contest ends in one hour, and that's a fact. I can beat that other guy if I have one more sale. And believe me, it means a lot to me, not only to win but to be able to give my family a super vacation. In fact, it will be the first real vacation we've had in over three years. Here's what I can do if you just keep it to yourself so I don't get into any trouble. My product (or service) costs us X number of dollars -- my company won't take anything less, and that's the way it is. If you buy from us, you won't have to pay anything near the asking price. I have a big bonus coming, so I can let you have the product for five hundred dollars less than anyone else can possibly sell it for. I'll make up part of that five-hundred-dollar difference out of my bonus money. So not only do you get the product for five hundred dollars below our bottom-line price, but I still get the rest of my bonus money plus the Hawaii vacation. My company will assume that I sold the product for exactly what they wanted in the first place. So, we can both help each other if you give it a try?"

(NOTE: The first thing the closer has to do is offer the product (or service) at the high end of the price range that you generally use. This will allow you maneuvering room to close the final deal for something near your usual price, giving the customer the perception he is getting a terrific, unbeatable, bargain price. Secondly, the closer has to convince the customer to believe him. This "close" works on the larceny factor in the customer's heart, and it usually works wonders.)

The Airplane Close

DESCRIPTION: This "close" is intended to gently and logically show the customer how ridiculous his objection is when the customer says, "Well, I don't know for sure, a buying decision like this is hard to make," The closer can usually use this "close" with great success on older customers, and those who tend to get scared when buying a product (or service), always wondering if they made the right decision.

How the Airplane Close is Used

When the closer has a customer who can't make up his mind, the closer can make a simple and thought-provoking statement like this: "Mr. Customer, you told me that you liked my product but it was hard for you to make a decision. Well, that's normal, so don't feel bad. You know when you make a decision you're always going to wonder a little if it was the right one or not. In fact, it's just like getting on an airplane to, let's say, New York or Los Angeles. Did you know that every day, of all the planes that take off, fly, and land, three percent crash (You can make up a percentage that sounds good to you). Now I'm talking about all the planes in every country of the world. Three percent do not make it, and that's a fact. So tell me, are you going to get on that airplane without even knowing the captain and crew and fly to New York or Los Angeles? Of course you're going to make the decision to get on board, even though three percent of you may be scared. Mr. Customer, buying this product (or service) is the same thing. You might be a little uneasy about buying at first, but don't worry about it -- get on board and you will thank me a year from now. So why don't you give it a try?"

The Order Sheet and Assumption Close

DESCRIPTION: These two "closes" are first cousins. The first "close" (the order sheet) works with paper, the second "close" (the assumption) works with a handshake, but both closes are used in the same basic way to "close" the customer.

How the Order Sheet and Assumption Close is Used

The Order Sheet Close: When the closer has overcome the customer's basic objections, the closer should say something like this, "Mr. Customer, now let me show you what it [finances and facts] looks like on paper." Then the closer should take out an order sheet and ask the customer, "Mr. Customer, what exactly is your full name?" If the customer doesn't stop the closer from writing down information then the customer has almost automatically bought -- he's "closed." But if the customer does try to stop the closer from writing, he will nearly always bring out his real and final objections. The closer should conquer the objection, as he is well trained to do, and then continue to write down information on the order sheet, acting as though it were the normal procedure. When the entire order sheet is filled out the closer should sign it first and then calmly hand it over to the customer and say, "Mr. Customer, I just need your name right here with mine and then we can have this approved." The closer's casual attitude of assuming the customer was going to buy all along will only help convince the customer that it is perfectly OK for him to sign the order sheet. (Note: The closer should also take notes on the actual order sheet or contract, if possible, during the sales presentation. This way the customer will become accustomed to seeing this otherwise unsettling paper. When it finally becomes time for him to sign, the customer won't be as surprised and scared by the sight of the order sheet or contract.)

The Assumption Close: When the closer has conquered all of the customer's objections and the closer knows the customer is ready to be asked to buy the product (or service), the closer should confidently say, "Mr. Customer, why don't you give us a try?" (The closer's arm should be outstretched, waiting to shake hands and congratulate the customer.) In most cases the customer will automatically shake the closer's hand (having the same effect as an unsaid yet affirmative buying answer.) This sudden and impulsive response on the customer's part will make him feel somewhat committed; the closer, acting as if there is nothing more to be said and the deal is done, should immediately start writing up the order sheet. (NOTE: The Assumption Close requires you to act as if you know that you are going to "close" the customer the minute you first meet him.)

The Referral Close

DESCRIPTION: This "close" is designed to be used by the closer on a customer who can't afford the down payment, monthly payments, or the product itself. This "close" works wonders if the customer believes the closer.

How the Referral Close is Used

When the closer sees he has the customer sold but the customer doesn't have enough money to buy the product, the closer should say something like this: "Mr. Customer, my company has found through the years that the best form of advertising is the simple method of 'word of mouth.' Good recommendations from a satisfied customer to a prospective future customer is our goal. My company is willing to take advantage of this form of advertising through our newly created referral program, which has been very successful for us. This is how it works: If you bring a prospective customer into our sales office who buys, my company will make your monthly payment for you. The same process works for the down payment. If you start bringing in new customers, we can also arrange to take care of the down payment. This way my company gets new customers, and you get our product (or service) without any expense to you at all. I'm sure you know enough people to at least get you started with our referral program."

The closer should immediately hand this customer a "referral sheet," or a piece of paper and a pen and say, "Now, who would be the very first person you would recommend?" If the customer doesn't initially go for the idea the closer should repeat the referral program to him, showing its advantages and then asking him to give his company a try.

"The Change Places Close"

DESCRIPTION: This is a good "close" to use after the closer has already gently tried everything else he can think of, but doesn't really want to use a lot of pressure to get the sale. This type of close is easy-going and doesn't offend the customer at all.

How the Change Places Close is Used

When the customer won't budge and the closer has built up a good rapport with him and doesn't want to get rough, the closer can sincerely say something like this: "Mr. Customer, let me ask you to briefly put yourself in my shoes. What if you had a fantastic product and you knew that it was priced right, and you also knew the product would be beneficial to your customer and his family, but your customer won't buy the product and really won't even give a reason why he won't buy? Now, Mr. Customer, let me ask you what would you do?" (NOTE: In most cases the customer will tell the closer the real hidden objection for not purchasing. Then the closer can start "closing" all over again trying to overcome the newly discovered objection. This "close" is a good one for discovering customers' real reasons for not making the buying decision.)

After the closer says this, he should wait to hear what the customer says. If the customer gets kind of embarrassed and says, "I don't know," the closer can assume it's a financial problem he's dealing with and firmly ask the customer, "We're really talking about money, aren't we?" When the customer says "Yes," the closer can continue to overcome the problem and "close" again.

"The Multiple Unit Close"

DESCRIPTION: This "close" is designed to embarrass or shame the customer into purchasing the product. The closer has to program the customer throughout the entire sales presentation for this "close" if it is to be used effectively at the end of the "closing process."

How the Multiple Unit Close Is Used

When the closer is describing his product to the customer, he should make the customer think that the only way someone could buy the product would be in groups, sets, or a package of four. For instance: The closer is selling real estate lots, so he makes the customer believe that the only way to purchase any real estate from him is to buy four lots. When it becomes time for the closer to ask the customer for the order he simply says, "The price of this group (unit of four lots) is X amount of money. Why don't you give it a try?"

If the customer still thinks he can't afford the property, the closer should excuse himself, get away for a few minutes, then return and say, "Mr. Customer, I've talked to my boss and in very special cases like yours, where I know you are interested in owning the property, our company will — if you keep it confidential — let you purchase a quarter of the package [one lot]. Surely, Mr. Customer, you can afford one-quarter of a unit for yourself and your family, so why don't you give it a try?"

When the closer uses this "close" he will more often than not sell two or three items instead of just one. This "close" often makes the customer feel intimidated and embarrassed. He doesn't want it to seem that he can't at least afford to buy one-quarter of what is being sold.

"The Think About It Close"

DESCRIPTION: This "close" makes fun of the customer who has to "think about" buying the product.

How the Think About It Close Works

When the customer tells the closer he has to "think about it" after the closer has asked him to give it a try, the closer should look surprisingly happy and with some excitement say, "Mr. Customer, that's perfect, you'll fit right into our company's Think-About-It program. What our company has done is develop a program for people like yourself, who have to think about the product. The program works like this: You, Mr. Customer, go ahead and place a down payment and then hold on to my product (or service) for twelve months. Every month, all you have to do is just send in that small monthly investment. Now during this twelve-month period my company wants you to be in touch with us as many times as you wish to see how everything is developing. Then, at the end of the twelve months, if you don't like the product (or service) we will help you sell it. That way, you not only can make a little money — more than you would have if you had put your money in a bank — but you had a whole year to think about whether you like what you've bought. You can have your cake and eat it too."

The closer should then proceed to write up the sale. If the customer stops the closer and says, "Wait, hold on, I have to think about that," then the closer can look right at the customer and ask, "Mr. Customer, you mean to sit there and tell me that you have to think about the Think-About-It program?" The closer should then wear a frustrated look on his face and resume confidently writing up the sale.

(NOTE: In most cases the customer will feel like an idiot and sheepishly go ahead with the purchase.)

"The Lost Sale Close"

DESCRIPTION: This "close" should be the very last "close" that the closer uses on his customer. When the closer delivers this close he must look sincere and defeated, as though the customer has won and the closer has lost the negotiation.

How the Lost Sale Close is Used

The closer should sheepishly say something like this to the customer: "Mr. Customer, I was wondering if you would help me with something before you leave. I know you're not going to buy anything, but would you tell me confidentially and personally why you really don't like my product. You see, this is how I make my living and support my family. I'd be grateful if you could, just between the two of us, tell me the reason. Then, when I am dealing with another customer I won't make the same mistake. I might be able to answer the other customer's questions better than I did yours."

When the customer gives the closer the real reason for not buying, thinking he is off the hook, the closer can immediately act surprised and say, "Mr. Customer, no wonder you didn't buy. It's my fault for not explaining that product (or service) to you properly. Here, let me quickly tell you how it really works." At this point the closer can proceed to go in for the kill.

The Safety Deposit Box Close

DESCRIPTION: This "close" is nothing but raw power and force. It not only works, but it is so strong that the customer will definitely become activated. (WARNING: When the closer uses this "close" he had better be prepared in case the customer becomes violent). This "close" should be used when everything else fails, including even the "lost sale close."

How the Safety Deposit Box Close is Used

When the closer has used everything in the book to try to "close" the customer, and the customer by this time has said he won't buy the product (or service) a hundred times, the closer should take out a work sheet or order form, right in front of the customer and his whole family (it helps if the customer has kids) and say something like this: "Mr. Customer, this is an order sheet with all of the facts and figures about the product, with today's date on it. I want you, right in front of your family to go ahead and sign it for me." The customer will get angry and say something like, "No, I told you I'm not signing anything today!" The closer should sternly continue, "Mr. Customer, I want you to sign this order sheet right now, right here in front of your family, and I'll tell you something else, I don't even want a copy of it. All I want you to do is sign it and then fold it up and take it home with you. And when you get home I want you to put that order sheet in your safety deposit box or a safe place along with your valuable papers, such as your will, your insurance policies, the deed to your home, whatever. Because one day we all have to pass on, and when it's your turn, your wife and kids are going to be going through all of your personal papers and they are going to discover this order sheet dated on this day. Then your wife and kids will look at it and see how you could have bought our product (or service) years ago for practically nothing, with a little money down and a small monthly payment. Your wife and kids are going to actually see how close you came to leaving them better off. So Mr. Customer, please sign that order sheet and take it with you."

If the customer won't sign, the closer should say, "Mr. Customer, what can you lose by signing it? What's wrong, are you afraid that your family is going to learn about your mistakes or see how close they were to being a lot better off?"

If the customer still won't sign, the closer should look at the customer's children and say, "Kids, why don't you ask your dad why he won't sign a piece of paper that I don't even want?"

This close will always get results. The customer will either sign the order sheet, making the closer a sale, or he will break down and give the closer the real objection, which is usually lack of money. Otherwise, he will get angry and turn his rage on the closer for his impudence. Either way this "close" creates real excitement.

"The Paper Fold Close"

DESCRIPTION: This is a great close, in fact it's an old insurance close that works miracles. The purpose of this close is to show the customer, through in a very simple example, how by not buying the product "today," the customer will forget all that he has learned from the closer, thus missing the opportunity to make an intelligent buying decision. This close will never fail to get the attention of the customer. The closer should practice this close several times before trying it on a customer, because if it is presented awkwardly or in an unsmooth manner the closer will wind up looking exactly like a rookie salesman on his very first cold call. (FACT)

How "The Paper Fold Close" Is Used

When the closer and the customer are both sitting down at the closing table, after the closer has given his full sales presentation, if the customer still can't be moved from the preference that he is going to have to go home and think about it, then it is the perfect time for the closer to use this close.

First: the closer picks up the work sheet from the closing table which has all the products information written down on it, such as prices, financing, percentages, quotes, etc., and holds it up in front of his customer. Then the closer says and uses the following closing technique simultaneously and continuously without stopping. "Mr. Customer, on this piece of paper there is written down all of the information you will really need to know about my product, but here is exactly what is going to happen if you leave this office without making a buying decision. Let's say after you get home you decide to call me back about the product, by then you will have forgotten one-half of all the things we talked about."

(NOTE: At this very point the closer folds the work sheet in half to demonstrate how the customer, by waiting a certain time period, has forgotten one-half of the sales information talked about earlier in the closer's sales office.)

"Or you, Mr. Customer, might wait until the next morning to call me about the product, and by that time you will only remember one-fourth of what we had talked about."

(NOTE: At this very instant the closer should again fold the half-folded work sheet into another half so it is now one-fourth the size of the original paper he started with.)

"But, Mr. Customer, let's say you wait until two days from now and then call me back. By then you will only remember one-sixteenth of the things we discussed."

(NOTE: At this time the closer again folds the work sheet into another half, so it is now one-sixteenth the size of the original work sheet.)

"And then again Mr. Customer, you just might wait two and a half days to call me, and by that time you'll only remember one-thirty-second of what we talked about."

(NOTE: Again the closer folds the work sheet to represent one-thirty-second of the whole piece of paper.)

"Now let me ask you a serious question, Mr. Customer, are you going to make a buying decision on only one-thirty-second of what you know,"

(NOTE: At this point the closer holds up the work sheet folded down to the one-thirty-second of the original total work sheet.)

"Or are you, Mr. Customer, going to make a business decision based on one hundred percent of the information in front of you." (NOTE: As the closer makes this last statement, he simultaneously starts to unfold the work sheet to get it back to the size of the original sheet of paper. This simple act demonstrates right in front of the customer how, the more he puts off his buying decision, the less he will remember about the features and benefits of the product, thus the less will be his chances of making an informed decision about buying the product.)

The closer has to practice this close time and time again to get it smooth, but once this close is mastered, the rewards to the closer in terms of future sales are phenomenal. (FACT)

"The Closer Comparison Close"

DESCRIPTION: This close is exactly like the Ben Franklin close except the closer compares himself, personally, to his customer sitting in front of him. This is not only a factual close, but an emotional one as well. The closer has to keep in constant eye contact with his customer all the way through this close, so the closer can see if his customer is paying attention and getting the point. This close works wonders if the closer is slow, deliberate, and sincere when applying it.

How To Use "The Closer Comparison Close"

Again, when all seems lost for the closer, he should take out a piece of blank paper and draw a vertical line down the middle of it then on the top of the left hand side he should write the name of his customer, always using the customer's first name, as the closer wants this to be a personal experience. Then on the top of the right hand size of the page the closer should write his own first name. After the closer has both names on the page, divided by a single vertical line, he should then slowly and methodically start writing down, one after the other, all of the good things that he assumes his customer has acquired or created in his lifetime such as:

(1) Family
(2) A home
(3) Two cars
(4) An art collection
(5) A motorcycle, etc.

Then, on the other half of the page the closer should write down all the things that he has acquired in his lifetime, naming each of them, just as he did his customer's, one after the other. So far, so good. But here comes the close. When the closer is filling out his side of the page, (always after the customer's list is made out first,) he should list all of the extra, good, and beneficial things he has received or that have resulted because he personally owns the product being sold. This way the customer can actually see for himself what he has missed by not owning the closer's product.

The closer must be sure to only write down very real and serious points on his side of the list, or his customer will just laugh at him. The closer has to convincingly show the customer just how better off he would have been if he had purchased the closer's product (or service) at the same time the closer himself bought his. When the list has been completed, the closer should turn the paper toward the customer so he can examine it more closely, and then be quiet, letting the customer see the great difference between his list of benefits or achievements, compared to the closer's longer list. The closer must convincingly demonstrate that the only real difference between them was simply that the customer didn't have the advantage of previously owning the closer's product (or service.)

When the customer looks up from the paper, back toward the closer, the closer should put out his hand in a congratulatory manner and say to his customer, "Now, give my product a try." The customer will automatically shake hands. The closer has sold his product.

"The Closer's Check Close"

DESCRIPTION: This close is designed to do one thing and one thing only. It gets a customer who won't make a decision to act now (make a move), which will hopefully be an immediate buying decision. Whether that decision turns out to be "yes" or "no" concerning the product or service is not a function of this close. This close will definitely make your customer react, then it's up to the closer to direct that action toward a positive, "yes," buying decision.

How To Use "The Closer's Check Close"

(NOTE) To use this close, the closer has to have a new or nearly new personal checkbook with his home or business address on the checks, plus a phone number (IMPORTANT). The checkbook being used as a prop in this close can not be an old beat-up one, it should be crisp and new looking.

All right now, here we go. At the closing table, when all seems lost for the closer because the customer has said no a hundred times and won't sign or make any kind of positive buying move, the closer should stop talking, look the customer "sincerely" straight in the eye, and reach for his own personal checkbook. Then, without saying a word, the closer should add up the total amount of money that the customer would have spent on the product (or service) in a full year plus any interest or finance charges. Then the closer should write a check payable to the customer for that full amount. (NOTE: Try to involve the customer by asking him what the interest rates are these days. Then, calculate your interest costs based on his information.)

Now, when dating the check the closer should post-date it exactly one year. After the check has been made out in full the closer should present it to the customer sitting across the table from him and simply say, "Mr. Customer, in one year from today, if my product or service hasn't done exactly what I said it would do, if my product hasn't lived up to your own expectations, then you just take my check to your bank and deposit it. I am authorized to do this. It will be good." After the closer has made that statement with all sincerity, he should shut up and wait for the customer's response because believe you me, there will be one. The closer should just keep looking at the customer with a serious business expression on his face until the customer says something. Now the customer has nothing to lose and he knows it. Not only can he have the product or service for a year, but if things don't work out, he can get all his money back plus better interest than he would have received from his own hometown bank. What in the world is the customer going to do? He has to make some kind of decision and response.

That is exactly what the closer wanted him to do in the very first place. The closer's main objective with this "pressure close" was to get the customer off the fence and force him to make a move one way or the other. Then, after the customer says something, no matter what it is, the closer can take that response and overcome any objections, or maneuver the customer into a more advantageous situation where the closer can benefit by setting up another closing trap.

This close works. It will get the customer to act, but the closer has to remember one very important procedure that takes place at the end of this close and that is to get the check back in his pocket. This is how it's done. After the customer has said yes, he'll give the product or service a try, the closer has got to place the post-dated check that was laying on the table underneath the order form or work sheet when he is filling it out, keeping it out of the customer's sight, allowing it to get lost in the paper shuffling. The closer should never again bring up the subject of his check, but proceed to ask the customer all the order taking questions that have to be filled out and put on the work sheet. The customer will, in most cases, forget about the check and get further involved in his purchase. If by any chance the customer does bring up the question "Where is the check?" after the contract has been signed and the product purchased, the closer should look at the customer with a humble prankster grin and simply say, "Mr. Customer, that business about my check was just an illustrative way for me to get you to consider this product seriously. I knew you would benefit from what we are offering, but you just needed a little push. My check isn't the reason you are buying our product. You are buying it because you know it is a good purchase, and I thank you and do appreciate your business." Then the closer should just carry on with his routine follow-up questions or comments.

"The Acts Are Facts Close"

DESCRIPTION: This close is sound, logical, and simple. It demonstrates to the customer, through common sense, how it would be advantageous to own the closer's product or service. The closer has to remember when using this close to slow down and be deliberate in his delivery. If he rushes through this close with excitement and too much enthusiasm, it will lose its power.

(NOTE: This close is a mixture of facts and emotions. The closer has to convincingly use them both.)

How To Use The "Acts Are Facts Close"

The closer has his customer sitting down at the closing table, after a full sales presentation, and the customer still won't make a decision, or move from his decision of not buying "today." The closer should put away his presentation materials, his "pitch book" and any extra papers that happen to be littering the closing table, and simply place both hands, folded, on the table. Without a pen, or any other threatening sales paraphanalia, say to the customer, "Mr. Customer, before I shake your hand and let you go home, allow me to explain something. I have not only told you what my product will do for you but I have actually shown you what it will do with written information — which by the way if incorrect would be fraud and since you have it all in front of you on paper we'd be in big trouble. I have also actually demonstrated to you how my product works. You have witnessed that for your very own self. In addition, you have physically examined our product, you have touched it, and experienced it. All these things are facts, are they not? (Wait for the obligatory "yes" response.) Well let me ask you Mr. Customer, if you were me what else could I possibly do to show you the advantage of owning my product? What kind of advice could you give me to help me convince you that my product is good for you? Could you please answer that for me?

(Note: At this point the closer should shut up and let the customer talk. If the customer does give an answer, then he will also be giving the closer another objection, something that the closer can get his teeth into and overcome, but if the customer remains quiet and unresponsive then the closer should continue with the following line of thought.)

"Mr. Customer, if you had a product, and you knew that it was good for me, and if you had demonstrated it to me with all of the sincerity and professionalism you could muster, and I still wouldn't buy the product, wouldn't you think that there was something I'm not telling you, something that prevents me from purchasing? (Wait for the obligatory "yes" response.) "Of course you would, and in most cases the reason is simply money. Well, we, Mr. Customer, realize that a person's finances are his own personal business, and in many cases finances are the real reason someone won't buy. So we have set up a special financial arrangement that can be custom tailored to your own personal financial situation. Now, let me show you how easily it all works.

(Note: At this point the customer should start to see that the closer isn't out to take advantage of him, but rather, to work with him, and it's at this point that the customer starts to melt and explains to the closer that the reason he doesn't buy is really because of money. Once this is out in the open the closer can continue along his regular game plan, and finish closing the deal.)

This close is a soft and slow one — and it is sure to work because it slowly melts down the customer's resistance, with understanding, good will and friendship. The closer should practice this close, put it in his own words and personality, and be very sincere when delivering it. This close may sound very general, but it delivers. It's a people to people close, with no real tricks, but it will make any closer who uses it with feeling, more sales than he or she has ever seen before. (FACT).

"The Write Objection Close"

DESCRIPTION: This close is an easy one to use. It makes the customer see for himself how silly and ridiculous his own excuses are for not buying the closer's product. In fact, this close is so simple and direct it really works wonders, but it has to be executed by the closer with sincerity, and genuine feeling, or the customer will know exactly what is taking place and just walk away from the closer, leaving him with a blank look on his face, not to mention a blank order form.

How To Use "The Write Objection Close"

When the closer is with his customer at the closing table and the presentation has gotten to the point where all of the closer's sales information is in writing on the order form or work sheet, but the customer still says, "No, I'm not buying today because I have to talk to my father, etc., etc.", then this is how you must use this special close. The closer should say to his customer, "Mr. Customer, I understand completely, you can't make a buying decision, without talking to your father, who by the way is back home in Chicago (or wherever), right? (Wait for the obligatory "yes".) Well, no problem, but just help me out if you will. Our company likes to know why some folks don't buy our product and others do. So I would be grateful if you could, just for our own records, write down your reason for not purchasing my product right here on the work sheet where it says remarks, and please sign it. We really do appreciate your comments. This helps us to become a better and more service oriented company."

Now that the customer thinks that he is off the hook, that he is free to leave the sales office and the pressure is off, he will, in most cases, start to write down his reason for not buying today on the work sheet you have handed him. When the closer uses this close with conviction, the customers never do finish writing all of their excuses. What happens is this, about halfway through the paragraph or sentence explaining why he can't buy today, the customer will start to see how silly, and shallow his excuse looks to everyone around him, including his own family. Plus the customer knows that after he has written down his "trumped-up" excuse for all the world to see, he will have to further embarrass himself because he agreed to formally sign it. This is the time when the customer's objection starts to fall to pieces. The customer will at this point, often put down the pen, and look up from the table to the closer, and meekly say "Now, just what kind of money are we talking about anyway?" or, "How did you say I could finance this product?"

This is all the closer wanted to hear in the first place. This kind of a response from the customer was the entire purpose of the close. After the customer makes his statement, then the closer can finally make the move toward getting the customer to agree to buy the product. (Note: One great advantage this close has over all the other closes is that it gets the pen into the customer's hand, and also gets the customer used to writing on the order sheet, which he will have to do at some point when he signs for your product or service).

Remember: This simple close that maneuvers the customer into writing his made-up excuse, with his own hand, in front of his own family, works. It will create sales all day long, just as long as the closer uses it in a very sincere manner when explaining to customers why he needs their objections written down.

Chapter Eleven

FIFTEEN CUSTOMER OBJECTIONS
AND
FORTY-FIVE CLOSER RESPONSES

Chapter Eleven

Fifteen Customer Objections
And
Forty-Five Closer Responses

The Customer's Objection: "I'll Be Back"

CLOSER'S RESPONSE:

1. "Great, Mr. Customer. I trust you — I know you'll be back tomorrow. Why don't you take my watch with you and bring it back when you return. Here, go ahead and take it; I know you will give it back tomorrow."

(Note: This maneuver really puts the customer on the spot and embarrasses him because he's just been trapped and he knows it. The closer should then keep prodding to find out what the real objection is and "close" it. No one will want to take your watch so don't worry.)

2. "Since you're that interested, let's go ahead and fill out an order sheet and take a "hold check" for the product. That way, when you come back we can take care of the paperwork a lot easier."

3. "You don't have to come back to sign the papers or anything. I'm going to be in your neighborhood tomorrow, so I'll just drop by. How's that for good service?"

The Customer's Objection:
"I Have to Talk to My Dad (Son, Uncle, etc.) First"

CLOSER'S RESPONSE:

1. "When are you going to see your dad — in a week or so? All right, I'll tell you what I'm going to do. I'll take off work for a week and go see my dad. Then, while you are asking your dad if you can buy my product, I'll ask my dad if I can sell it." You must not be sarcastic when saying this. It is meant to be a light joke and you have to deliver it as a joke. Laugh afterwards and tell the customer you were just joking.

2. "Let me ask you this, and tell me the truth — does your dad ask for your advice before he buys something?"

259

3. "Why are you going to talk to someone — you have all the information and facts concerning the product right here in front of you. Whoever you want to talk to sure doesn't, because he's not here. What could you possibly ask him about the product that you don't already know, unless it's a question related to finances?"

The Customer's Objection:
"We Never Buy on the Spur of the Moment"

CLOSER'S RESPONSE:

1. "We don't want you to buy immediately, and we don't want cash; all we want you to do is try our product (or service) for a while. Put a little down payment on it and we'll structure some comfortable monthly payments. Then during that time, come back to visit and watch the progress my company is making. If you're not satisfied you are always able to resell our product (or service)."

2. "If you just walked into this sales office and said you wanted to buy the product, *that* would be on the spur of the moment. But you've seen how our product works, all its advantages and benefits, plus you have all the facts needed to make an intelligent buying decision. So, seriously, why don't you give it a try?"

3. "Well, I know you like my product, so why don't I give you time to think about it. I'll tell you what I'll do so you won't lose any money. I'll go ahead and date the contract and all of the working papers for today's date. That way you can get the product at today's sale price, but you'll have a few days to think about it."

The Customer's Objection:
"I Just Can't Make a Decision Now"

CLOSER'S RESPONSE:

1. "Do you mean to tell me that you are fifty-five years old and you doubt your ability to make an intelligent and correct business decision?"

2. "You don't have to think too long if something you are considering will make money for you, do you? All right, that's exactly what we're talking about with this product (or service.)"

3. "Mr. Customer, a decision is like playing football — you can't make a touchdown by sitting on the bench. You have to get out on the field and participate. You know that you now have enough facts and information about my product to make a buying decision. All I want you to do is give it a try."

The Customer's Objection:
"I'm Just Looking Around, Just Shopping"

CLOSER'S RESPONSE:

1. "Since you're doing that, why don't you go ahead and buy (or invest) here, since you now know the potential of our company. Then look around and see if you can find anything better. If you do find a better buy (or investment), we can liquidate your purchase (or investment) in thirty to forty days and you not only would have made a little more money to invest in your new-found product (or service or investment), but you would be enjoying the benefits of my product (or service or investment) while you were looking. If you don't find a better product (or service or investment), then you're already secure with our company at today's special price.

2. "There are lookers and there are doers. Lookers always pass life by, just dreaming about things and never really having them. It is the doers who have money; they have a portfolio, something solid to build on. Don't ever fool yourself."

3. "Everyone has to look around. But when you have an opportunity like this, where you can see the potential and advantages of my product (or service or investment) and you now know that our product (or service or investment) is superior to all others, isn't that what you have been looking for in the first place? When you find what you want, don't overlook it and pass it by. Why not give it a try?"

The Customer's Objection:
"I Can Make More Money or Do Better Someplace Else"

CLOSER'S RESPONSE:

1. "I'll tell you what. Let's go to a phone in the sales office and you let me talk to those people who make more money (or have done better in price) on this type of an investment (or product or service). Who knows, I might want to get a job with the company your friends are dealing with." This usually embarrasses the customer into taking your pitch more seriously, especially when he doesn't reveal where this better deal is.

2. "Why don't you come on over to my house sometime this week and talk to some of my friends about these better investments (or products or service). I'll go ahead and set up the meeting because I just might want to invest (or purchase) myself. When can you make it?"

3. "Then what are you doing looking at my product in the first place?"

The Customer's Objection:
"I'm Too Old to Buy"

CLOSER'S RESPONSE:

1. "No, you're not. You're only as old as you think you are. Why, this product (or service) would put a little pizaz in your life. Besides, our company needs people like you. Why don't you give my product (or service) a chance?

2. "You're not too old to think about your wife's care and comfort or your grandchildren, so why don't you buy the product (or service) for them — you know they would enjoy it."

3. "You know, life goes on. And you now have the time to enjoy the product (or service) and all its benefits. So do something good for yourself and your family and give us a try."

The Customer's Objection:

"We Can't Buy Because We Have Other Obligations at Home: Sickness, the Farm, Kids in School, etc.

CLOSER'S RESPONSE:

1. "Those obligations come first, you're absolutely right. But now, this is an opportunity that just doesn't present itself every day — that's a fact and you know it. If we could work out the payments with you so that they're compatible with your present obligations and don't interfere, would you then give it a try?"

2. "What are you going to have tomorrow, new problems? What did you have yesterday, old problems? You're always going to have problems and obligations — everyone does. You just have to start building a future for your family sometime, and now is the perfect time to get started. Not yesterday or tomorrow, but now while you can, while you have the chance right before you."

3. "You know you don't have a monopoly on problems and obligations; we all have them. But some people are better off than others because they started with a plan and followed it through. They knew they would have problems, but they were willing to work around them and deal with them.

That is the only difference between people with money and folks who don't have as much money as they really need. All you have to do is plan and carry that plan through. You'll find that your problems aren't as bad as you thought. So why don't you start planning for a change and give my product (or service) a try?"

The Customer's Objection:
"I've Already Bought Someplace Else"

CLOSER'S RESPONSE:

1. "Then go ahead and buy here too, you know the potential. Don't make the mistake of putting all your eggs into one basket. Diversify yourself and do business with us."

2. "Then write the people you bought from and tell them you're not satisfied with their product and want your money back. You will then be free to buy our product (or service), knowing that you saved money and purchased a better product (or service)."

3. "Then what you should do, knowing my product's potential and liking it, is to purchase one of my products for another member of your family, someone who would really appreciate it."

The Customer's Objection:
"I Have to Think About It"

CLOSER'S RESPONSE:

1. "Let me ask you this: If you owned this product and you wanted me to sell it for you, and a customer came up to me and said, 'I have to think about it,' would you want me to let him go, or would you want me to show him what he's missing by not buying the product?

2. "The only thing you have to really think about is money, isn't it? Well, you know your finances better than I do, so why don't you sit here and have some coffee and see how your finances look. I'll be back in a minute."

3. "I don't blame you; this is a major purchase. I've got to make a phone call, so why don't you think about it while all the product information is still fresh in your mind, and I'm here to answer any of your questions. Now that makes sense, doesn't it?"

The Customer's Objection:
"Your Product Costs Too Much"

CLOSER'S RESPONSE:

1. "Compared to what? The product (or service) you now have or some other one that doesn't have as many benefits as this one? Tell me, what are you comparing my product's price to?"

2. "You can go first class or second class; that's your decision. But you get exactly what you pay for. You have to remember that my product (or service) is the top of the line. If it doesn't fit into your future plans then I don't think you need it."

3. "If my product (or service) is too expensive, as you see it, what do you think it will cost a year from now? Why don't you try it before it gets even more expensive; and I can assure you that it will. Believe me, if you can't afford my product (or service) now, you sure won't be able to afford it later."

(NOTE: The closer can very easily turn this objection around and say to the customer, "Well, what do you think my product (or service) should be worth?" If the customer answers, the closer should write it up and submit it for consideration to his boss. A lot of sales have been made that way.)

The Customer's Objection:
"Why Is This Product for Me? Why Should I Buy?"

CLOSER'S RESPONSE:

1. "Because no one in this world is adverse to making or saving money and you can see the potential of my product (or service) right here before your eyes. If you know it will help you in your financial future you should buy from us. But if you really think we can't help you, then by all means don't. Someone will be glad you didn't!

2. "Why wouldn't this product be for you? Please answer me that."

3. "This product is for you because it benefits you. The product provides protection for your hard-earned money in today's economy. And besides, this product wouldn't be near the success it is if it weren't for people like you who understood the product's potential. You need the product, more than it needs you. Why do you think we've sold so many?"

The Customer's Objection:
"I Can't Afford It"

CLOSER'S RESPONSE:

1. "I know what you mean. If someone asked me for that kind of money, I'd say I couldn't afford it either. In fact, I was in the same boat as you are now, not long ago. Let me explain to you how I handled that situation."

(NOTE: The closer should then show the customer how the product, service or some similar investment made money for him. The customer can relate to this approach, and the closer has created a common bond with the customer, thus making the "close" that much easier.)

2. "What do you mean, you can't afford it? Can you really afford not to? Do you realize how much the price of everything is going to rise in the future? If you can't afford to buy my product (or service) now — something that you really want — then you better get a new job that pays more."

3. "Do you mean to tell me that you can't put aside X amount of money each month? Did you realize you were in that bad of a financial situation before we started discussing finances? Here, let me show you how you can afford my product more easily than you thought."

The Customer's Objection:
"We Can't Buy, We Just Got Married"

CLOSER'S RESPONSE:

1. "Well, could you think of a better wedding present for each of you to give the other?"

2. "You can start to build your future together as man and wife right now, in your very first joint investment. This investment will be a starting point for your future family and for times to come."

3. "You have, believe it or not, an opportunity that very few newlyweds enjoy. By buying this product (or service) now you can share a feeling of accomplishment for years to come. You'd be surprised how many people say they are going to start an investment when they first get married, but don't because they say they don't have the money. You know, there is the expense of setting up a new household. Then they say they are going to invest when they have their first baby, but don't because of the hospital costs and doctor bills. Then they say they will invest when the kids leave home, but don't because they now have to pay for the kid's college. Then they say they will invest when the kids are out of school, but don't because by that time they're trying to save for some type of retirement. And so they retire together years later without any money because they never started an investment for the future. It's a sad story, but it's very common. You people have the chance to direct your lives away from that kind of ending right now. So why don't you give my company a try?"

The Customer's Objection:
"I Have to Talk to My Lawyer or Money Manager"

CLOSER'S RESPONSE:

1. "That's a good idea. Let's get him on the phone right now and you can explain to him how good everything is about this product (or service). Then ask him if he thinks it's a good investment. Now what do you think he is going to say? I'll tell you what he'll say. He'll say, 'How should I know if it's a good deal or not? I'm not there to see it. You are. How can I tell you about the product? And he will be right to tell you that. "Well, what are your impressions about the product?"

2. "Does your lawyer call you when he's going to buy something that's in your line of business?"

3. "All your lawyer can really do is say, 'Don't sign anything.' That way he's protected. Even if he knew it was a good investment, he wouldn't dare tell you to go ahead and purchase something he hasn't seen himself. If he thinks his decision has any risk whatsoever, he'll be overprotective in his comments every time. And what kind of sound advice is that? Anyone can be negative because there's no risk if you advise your clients to do nothing."

Conclusion

THE ART OF CLOSING ANY DEAL

The first of September finally arrived and my summer job at Green Vista Estates was coming to an end. I would be going back to school, but I wasn't as excited about it as I guess I should have been. Green Vista Estates was a total success. I never saw anything grow and develop more in three short months in my entire life. I asked "Big Bill" if I could have my same job back next year and he said he had better things planned for me, so I guessed that meant I had some kind of a job.

I think the reason I felt kind of sad about having to go back to school was the fact that I wouldn't be seeing Sam anymore. That morning Sam walked up to me and told me my lessons on "closing" were over. He said if I stayed with Green Vista Estates and practiced what he had taught me, there was no way on earth I couldn't become a top master closer.

Sam said he wouldn't be coming back next summer because he had completed his job here, whatever that meant. He said I had been a good student who deserved more than just to see what the inscription on the inside of his gold ring said. He gave me the ring. When he handed it to me he had tears in his eyes and told me to always wear it.

I forgot about the inscription and just stood there watching as Sam turned around to walk toward the guard house. He look at me and said, "I'll be seeing you, but not here and not for several years."

"But how will we keep in touch? I don't have your address," I said in a voice gone raspy.

"I will be following your career, my boy. The world will be following you as a master closer and, soon enough, as a master sales manager. That's when I'll come back. We'll do some serious talking then, son."

Sam was halfway across the parking lot when I called out, "You are talking about a lot of maybe's and a lot of years from now."

Sam turned and spoke in a voice that carried all the way to me, all the way to my soul it seemed. "You believe? You believe in me? You believe in yourself?"

I nodded each time. He waved and was soon out of sight.

I felt like crying because my old friend was going to leave me just like that. I put the ring in my pocket and started to run after Sam, wanting to thank him for everything I had learned, and tell him how much I cared about him. I ran right up to Sam's guard house and jerked open the door to say, "Sam, what are you doing, giving me your ring?"

When I looked inside the guard house it was empty. I looked outside, but Sam was gone.

Later that night I drove back to my folk's home, trying to figure out how my life had seemed to change so much in one summer. I felt in my pocket and there was Sam's gold ring. I pulled off the highway into a rest area and just stared at his old, worn-out ring. Then it dawned on me to see if there really was any inscription in the ring. I opened the glove compartment to get some light and there, inside the gold ring, was a real inscription. Sam told me if any person wanted to be a master closer all he had to do was follow the rule of the ring's inscription. The ring's inscription simply read *Sum Tertius* — "I Am Third."

From listening to Sam I know what it meant: Put God first in your life, the other fellow second, and yourself always third. If a closer kept that kind of attitude, there is no way he could fail. "I Am Third," that sounded just like Sam. Sometimes he was rough, but he always had a heart of gold.

Well, that is what happened to me seventeen years ago when I was going to school and working at Green Vista Estates in the summer. I kept working there, always wearing that ring, and never mentioned Sam again to anyone. Today I'm a highly successful entrepreuner. All thanks to my mysterious friend? But the story doesn't end there.

I knew I had met a friend who gave me his ring and taught me some very valuable lessons about life and "closing" sales. I cherished the memory of Sam Johnson, and knew he'd return as he promised. And I now know that there is a "Sam Johnson" living in every master closer's heart.

I know I've made Sam proud of me, and I know you'll want to hear about our next encounter. In my follow up book, *More of the Art of Closing Any Deal: How To Be A "Master-Closer" And "Master Sales Manager,"* my remarkable friend told me all there is to know about Sales Management. It is my special privilege to have lived both books, and to be able to pass them on to you.

The End